Carl M b

The Size of Nations

The Size of Nations

Alberto Alesina and
Enrico Spolaore

The MIT Press
Cambridge, Massachusetts
London, England

This book was set in Palatino by Interactive Composition Corporation (in LATEX) and was printed and bound in the United States of America.

Library of Congress Cataloging-in-Publication Data

Alesina, Alberto.
   The size of nations / Alberto Alesina and Enrico Spolaore.
      p. cm.
   Includes bibliographical references and index.
   ISBN 0-262-01204-9 (hc. : alk. paper)
   1. States, Size of. I. Spolaore, Enrico. II. Title.

JC364.A39 2003
320.1–dc21
                                                          2003051201
10 9 8 7 6 5 4 3 2 1

to Susan
to Deborah and Edoardo

Contents

Acknowledgments

Our greatest debt is to Romain Wacziarg who coauthored with us several papers that form the foundations of chapter 10 and part of chapter 12. His expertise on the empirical work was essential. An earlier collaboration of Alesina with Ignazio Angeloni and Ludger Schuknecht also underlies parts of chapter 12, and we are grateful to them for helping us understand the issues confronting the European Union.

Andrei Shleifer read a very early draft and gave us challenging comments that led us to do more and better; so we thank him for the prod. Conversations with Robert Barro and Herschel Grossman were continually insightful. We are also indebted to a long list of colleagues, students, and coauthors for useful discussions and comments. While we are grateful to all of them, we can only name a few: Daron Acemoglu, Jim Alt, Robert Bates, Reza Baqir, Bill Easterly, Jeff Frieden, Oded Galor, Phillip Garner, Ed Glaeser, Vern Henderson, Caroline Hoxby, Eliana La Ferrara, Peter Howitt, Paolo Mauro, Roberto Perotti, Herakles Polemarchakis, Jaume Ventura, and David Weil. The students of economics 2410g at Harvard University suffered through an early version and their written comments were very useful. The students of economics 125 and economics 221 at Brown University provided invaluable feedback on a subsequent but still quite preliminary draft. With great patience and endurance Gerry Adler read the entire manuscript word by word through the eyes of a "non–social scientist." His comments on our writing helped us avoid jargon and use more accessible language. Participants in seminars and conferences gave us further comments and suggestions. Although we cannot acknowledge everyone individually, we are very grateful to all.

Five anonymous referees provided very useful comments. In some cases some comments opposed those of others, so we could not satisfy them all. On the points of agreement among the referees, we tried our best.

Alexander Wagner, Prianka Malhotra, and Matt Parker read early drafts and helped us with the exposition. Gustavo Suarez provided excellent research assistance for chapter 10. Daniel Mejia splendidly assisted in the research in the critical last stages of production. Shelley Weiner was exceptional at typing the manuscript; she cheerfully and efficiently went through an endless number of revisions. One of the authors (whose name starts with A) is one of the remanent of a bygone era when people did their writing by hand. Dana Andrus of The MIT Press edited the manuscript with exceptional skill.

Both authors are grateful to the National Science Foundation for a series of grants thorough the National Bureau of Economic Research. Alesina is also grateful to the Weatherhead Center for International Affairs at Harvard University for a sponsored leave that allowed him to work on this book.

1   Introduction

1.1   The Main Questions

Nations come in all sizes.[1] China, the largest country in the world, has
1.2 billion inhabitants. Tuvalu, the smallest country with a seat at the
United Nations, has less than 11,000 people. In recent years the number
of independent nations has increased dramatically. The breakup of colonial empires, the collapse of the Soviet Union, and numerous secessions
all over the world have led to the creation of many new sovereign states
over the past few decades. In 1945 there were 74 independent countries.
Today there are 193.[2] As a result many of today's countries are quite
small. More than half are smaller in size than Massachusetts, which has
about six million inhabitants. Even when no new countries are formed,
regional separatism, ethnic conflict, and various centrifugal forces are
in motion. Often regionalism and separatism take relatively peaceful
manifestations, as in the case of Quebec or Catalonia. In other cases, as
in the Basque region or in the Balkans, separatism has led to violence.

While in most parts of the world we observe a tendency toward separatism, Germany and Yemen have reunified, and the European Union
is evolving from a free trade area to some form of political integration.
Interestingly the process of European integration has not eliminated
the pressures for more decentralization within many of the European
Union's member countries, such as Belgium, Britain, France, Italy, Spain,
and the United Kingdom.

These events raise two questions: What determines the size of nations
and how does their size change over time? Does a country's size matter
for economic success?

Philosophers, historians, and political scientists have devoted much
effort to the study of the formation of sovereign states, their optimal
size, and the evolution of size over time. Plato even calculated the opti-

mal size of a polity down to the precise number of households, namely 5,040 heads of family.[3] The formation and breakup of states has always been at the core of historical analysis.[4] By contrast, economists have generally taken the size of countries as "exogenous"—that is, not to be explained.[5] In fact, while international economics is, by definition, about economic exchanges across national borders, borders themselves are treated as part of the geographical landscape, like coasts or mountains. However, national borders are not a natural phenomenon; they are human-made institutions and they can be studied with the same tools of political-economic analysis that have been profitably applied to other areas of human activity. For example, in important work on the geographical determinants of income per capita, Jeffrey Sachs and co-authors have stressed the costs of being a landlocked country, such as Bolivia or Afghanistan.[6] But a county's being landlocked is as much an outcome of politics as of geography. Bolivia was not landlocked before it lost part of its territory to Chile in 1884, and Utah or Colorado would be landlocked countries if they were independent. Political borders, like many other institutions, are the outcome of choices and interactions by individuals and groups who pursue their goals under constraints. This book studies the formation and change of political borders with the tools of economics.

Our main concern in this book is with the number and size of sovereign states, which, as Tilly (1990) puts it, have been "the world's largest and most powerful organizations for more than five thousand years." However, the definition of a "state" is controversial. Some authors include ancient empires, medieval theocracies, and Greek and Italian city-states. Others restrict the definition to modern national states, characterized by recognized borders over a territory, a population, and a national, centralized government with the monopoly of the legal use of coercion.[7] While our focus will be on modern states, we will also consider other forms of territorial organization, such as autocratic empires, supranational organizations, and decentralized jurisdictions (regions, provinces).

Consistent with current English usage, we will use interchangeably "nation," "state," and "country," to mean "sovereign state"—and specifically to the sovereign "national state," which is the main political subdivision of the world. We are aware that some readers may object to using these terms interchangeably as "nation"—and to some extent, "country"—have additional distinct meanings.[8] For example, "nation" is often regarded as a group of people who share language, customs, and a "sense of homogeneity,"[9] or, more humorously, according to a well-known definition cited by Deutch (1969), as "a group of people united by a common error about their ancestry and a common dislike of their neighbors." In this sense a nation does not need to be an independent state. If it is, one usually talks about "nation-states"—another term with multiple meanings. We are not interested in "nations" as distinct from "nation-states." However, differences in individual preferences—which in the modern world tend to be connected to linguistic, ethnic, and cultural differences—will play an important role in our analysis of the formation and breakup of states.

1.2 The Basic Trade-Off

In this book we will argue that the sizes of national states (or countries) are due to trade-offs between the benefits of size and the costs of heterogeneity of preferences over public goods and policies provided by government.[10]

What are the benefits of large population size? First, the per capita costs of public goods are lower in large countries, where more taxpayers are available to pay for them. Think of defense, monetary and financial institutions, a judicial system, infrastructures for communication, police and crime prevention, public health, embassies, and national parks, just to name a few. While the costs of many publicly provided goods may increase proportionally with the population, often some aspects of these costs are independent of the number of users or taxpayers.[11] Thus the per capita costs of many public goods generally decline with the number of taxpayers.[12] Also large countries have means for more efficient forms of taxation, for example, income taxes relative to the less efficient custom taxes. This is because income taxes have larger bureaucratic setup costs relative to something like custom duties.[13]

Second, it is often argued that a large country (in terms of population or national product), all other things equal, can better protect itself from foreign aggressions by its greater military power. Defense is a public good, and the per capita cost of defense decreases with country size. Small countries can enter into military alliances, but, in general, size determines the extent of military power.[14]

Third, the size of a country affects the size of its economy. To the extent that larger economies and larger markets increase productivity, larger countries should be richer. However, the size of a country's "market," that is, the number of individuals and the amount of spending in an economy, depends on the openness of the country to trade.[15] A country integrated in the world economy has the world as its market. If the political borders did not limit economic transactions, the size of a country would be independent of its economic success. In reality, however, political borders do interfere with economic transactions, so the economic benefits of size depend on the openness of a country.

Fourth, large countries can provide regional "insurance." Take Texas, for example. Should Texas experience a recession that is more severe than the US average, it would receive fiscal transfers, on net, from the rest of the country. The reverse holds as well; if Texas does better than average it becomes a source of transfers to other US states. Now, if Texas were an independent state, it would have a more pronounced swings to its business cycle, since it would not receive help during recessions and would not subsidize other states in boom periods. The interregional transfers that operate through various channels of the fiscal code and of spending programs, are quite sizable in the United States.[16] The benefits of this insurance are particularly evident in times of natural calamities.

Fifth, large countries can build redistributive schemes from richer to poorer individuals and regions, thereby achieving distributions of after-tax income that would not be available were its regions acting independently. This is why poorer regions seek to form alliances with larger countries inclusive of richer regions, while the latter may prefer independence.[17]

If there were only benefits from size, then the tendency should be for the entire world to be organized in a single country. In principle, as countries become larger, administrative and congestion costs may defeat the benefits of size pointed out above. However, in practice, these costs vary for very large countries. Hence administrative and congestion costs alone do not determine the size distribution of countries as many of the 193 countries are quite small.

More important is the consideration that in larger countries there are more diverse preferences, cultures, and languages within the population. A country's heterogeneity of preferences increases as it become larger. Now, why should heterogeneity of preferences matter? Belonging to a country implies agreeing to a set of policies, be they redistributive schemes, public goods, or foreign trade. Heterogeneity implies that very diverse groups of individuals should be in agreement on these matters. Of course, certain policies can be delegated to localities, in order to allow for local preferences, but not every policy can be treated this way. With increased heterogeneity there are more individuals or regions that are less satisfied by the central government policies. Indeed, many violent domestic conflicts around the world associated with racial, religious, and linguistic heterogeneity have threatened the stability of national governments.[18]

Concerns about the political costs of large and heterogeneous communities go back a long way in the philosophical and political debate. There was, for example, the argument of Aristotle that a polity should be no larger than a size in which everybody knows personally everybody else. As he wrote in *The Politics*, "experience has shown that it is difficult, if not impossible, for a populous state to be run by good laws." As noted by Dahl and Tufte (1973), this Greek view of a small polity in which everybody knows each other often resurfaces in later philosophers, such as Montesquieu, who, in *The Spirit of the Laws*, wrote:

In a large republic, the common good is sacrificed to a thousand considerations. It is subordinated to various exceptions. It depends on accidents. In a small republic, the public good is more strongly felt, better known, and *closer to each citizen*.[19]

The founding fathers of the United States often mentioned Montesquieu's views when they worried about the "excessive" size of the new federation at the Constitutional Convention held in 1787.[20] As documented by Dahl and Tufte (1973, pp. 9–10), the Antifederalists "contended that a republic with such a large territory inhabited by such a heterogeneous population was an 'absurdity, and contrary to the whole experience of mankind.'" In response to such criticisms, in Federalist paper 10 Madison provided a famous counterargument. He objected that a large size, far from being a problem, was actually an advantage for a democracy. His point was that the larger a territory becomes in size, the greater will be its variety of parties and interests, and hence the smaller will be the chance that "a majority of the whole will have a common motive to invade the rights of other citizens; or if such a common motive exists, it will be more difficult for all who feel it to discover their own strength, and to act in unison with each other." In other words, according to Madison, in larger states rent-seeking groups who want to "invade the rights of other citizens" will have a harder time to overcome problems of collective action. Moreover, according to Madison, "the influence of factious leaders may kindle a flame within their particular States, but will be unable to spread a general conflagration through the other States." This part of Madison's argument can be viewed as a clever

application to the political sphere of the "insurance" argument we mentioned before, where the existence of "factious leaders" is analogous to
a natural calamity, such as a hurricane. If an individual lives in a small
independent state where power falls into the hands of a tyrannical and
factious leader, he is lost. In a large federation, made up of many heterogeneous states, factious leaders can at most take over a single state,
but the neighboring states, being under control of other groups, can
provide "insurance" against threats of takeover and keep the political
crisis confined to local boundaries. Madison's views contain some important truths, and should be entertained when studying the benefits
and costs relating to the optimal size of a polity. However, it is questionable whether such "insurance" benefits stemming from the existence of
many heterogeneous groups can be sufficient to offset the political and
economic *costs* associated with heterogeneity. As Dahl and Tufte (1973,
p. 11) note: "Whether the classical arguments were actually refuted by
American experience is . . . doubtful." The Civil War sheds some serious
doubts for the Madisonian defense of large size. Our hypothesis, which
is backed by extensive empirical evidence, is that, on balance, heterogeneity of preferences tends to bring about political and economic *costs*
that are traded off against the benefits of size. Think for a moment about
the extremes. Madison would have to agree that a fully homogeneous
country could work well, since there would be no need for conflict. In the
opposite extreme where widespread heterogeneity degenerates into an
internecine war, a civil society cannot function. The Madisonian argument can be restated in saying that sometimes, within intermediate levels of heterogeneity, augmenting certain types of heterogeneity may actually increase the quality of institutions. This is a point we will explore,
but we do not see it as undermining the basic fact that in general, homogeneous polities function more harmoniously in both large and small
countries.

Hence we arrive at a concept of "equilibrium" country size that results
from a trade-off between the benefits of size and the costs of preferences
of a heterogeneous population. How this trade-off is effected by the
many politicoeconomic variables is the main theme of this book.[21]

1.3   Optimal and Equilibrium Size: A Brief Methodological Detour

What do we mean by an equilibrium size of a country? As is usual in
economic analysis and political economy, we will use different concepts
of "equilibrium" in this book.

First, we will consider the optimal country size using standard economic tools of optimization under constraints. The optimal size of a national state is one that reaches the highest level of average welfare and that given certain constraints.

It is useful to contrast our discussion of optimality with that of Dahl and Tufte (1973). They discuss various trade-offs concerning the size of polities, and they conclude that since there are trade-offs, the optimal size of a country does not exist. In their words, "no single type or size of unit is optimal for achieving the twin goals of citizen effectiveness and system capacity." For us, this is a valuable insight insofar as it stresses the impossibility of achieving an absolute best in which two goals are perfectly attained at the same time. However, if we want to consider the extent to which a goal can be achieved (more or less effectiveness, more or less capacity), the presence of trade-offs between goals does not mean that the *optimal point* on the trade-off has not been or cannot be reached. Consider an individual who values both leisure and consumption, but must be employed to pay for these pleasures. He could maximize leisure by not working at all, but then he would obtain no consumption, since he would have no income with which to buy goods. Or he could maximize consumption by working twenty-four hours a day, but then he would get no leisure time. This does not mean that there is no optimal combination of leisure and labor. The individual could choose to work up to the point where the extra consumption earned by the last hour of work would give him the same utility as the last hour of leisure he would enjoy: that is for him an "optimal" point. Analogously, the optimal size of a country would be characterized by some optimal point between the benefits of size and the costs of heterogeneity. This is precisely our starting point.

Our purpose is not only normative but also positive. We do not want only to compute the optimal size in an ideal world where borders are as they "should be." We are interested in learning why in reality countries attain certain sizes. We argue that the trade-off matters and explain the observed configuration of borders. However, that does *not* mean necessarily that we should expect to observe an optimal size. On the contrary, although we talk about an optimal number of countries, we do not believe that every month, or year, or even decade, the world population computes the optimal number and shape of countries and rearranges borders accordingly. As we will argue, remappings of borders are effected by political and economic forces and so may show systematic deviations from any optimal configurations. Nevertheless, from a politicoeconomic viewpoint considerations of efficiency and economic trade-offs are useful for several reasons.

First, we could argue that over time various forces drive institutions (in our case political borders) toward efficiency.[22] For those readers who remain skeptical about this argument, it may be useful to regard country sizes as trade-offs in economic efficiency. We can take this perspective and compare historical evidence using predictions of models based on principles of economic efficiency. Even where an efficiency explanation might fail, we should be able to understand *why* it fails and to learn something about the politicoeconomic forces at play. An efficient configuration of borders, by definition, would maximize the "size of the pie." Hence, in principle, the population segment that would suffer loss if borders were drawn optimally would be compensated by the winners, and everyone would be better off with efficient borders.[23] Therefore, if an efficient allocation is not observed, one must understand *why* the "size of the pie" is not maximized to everyone's benefit. In fact, as we will argue in this book, compensation schemes will be difficult or impossible to implement through political institutions. More generally, there are systematic reasons that keep the sizes of countries away from their optimal levels, as we will see below.

We will contrast optimal solutions with two different concepts of equilibrium: (1) voting equilibria where borders are determined by democratic vote and (2) equilibrium border configurations determined by dictatorial Leviathans.[24] In a voting equilibrium, as we will see, ideally the borders are determined through majority voting (referenda). This concept was enacted in a few historical cases. However, where borders have not been determined by direct vote, a voting equilibrium might prove useful in assessing the consequences of democratically redrafting borders. That is, a voting equilibrium could conceivably approximate a situation where the borders reflect fairly reasonably the will of the people. The other concept of equilibrium (the Leviathan equilibrium) is based on a darker but realistic assumption that, for most of history, borders have been determined by rulers who attempted to maximize their net rents, broadly defined, with little regard for the will of majorities. This concept allows us to understand borders from a more realistic perspective, how they appear on maps.

Both voting and Leviathan equilibria reveal the critical role of political institutions in the determination of the size of nations. We will see how alternative democratic rules might lead to different configurations of borders. The contrasting configurations of countries in a world of dictators and democratic regimes allow us to observe some correlations. It should be clear that the optimal size of a country for a ruling dictator may not be that size that maximizes average citizens' welfare, but it may be the size that maximizes the ruler's wealth and welfare. Our concepts of optimality and equilibria serve as benchmarks for our analyses, and as a direction for further theoretical and empirical research.

There are two types of books. Those that provide a "definitive" word in a widely researched area, and those that open new areas and raise more questions than they have answers for. This book is intended to be of the second type. Our goal is to show how economic thinking can be used to study the evolution of country size. We are aware that often highly complicated events have led to specific configurations of borders and that the same borders may last for centuries. Changing borders is a costly activity, and border changes are relatively infrequent. More generally, the actual dynamics of border formation are complex, and they may include several interactions of variables and effects that are difficult or even impossible to capture in simplified equilibrium relationships. However, this does not preclude finding systematic forces behind the formation and transformation of countries. Borders matter and borders change. Repeatedly at critical junctures of history, the redrafting of borders has involved global politics. For instance, in the nineteenth century the combined movements of nationalism and liberalism fixed their sight on the building of nation-states and redrawing the map of Europe. The colonial empires more or less peacefully drew borders that distributed to them large portions of the world. After the First World War, the world leaders faced the task, in Versailles, of redesigning country borders in Europe, and as many have argued, they failed. After the Second World War the decolonization of empires left borders open to dispute. Many students of Africa believe that inefficient borders have contributed heavily to the economic failures of countries on that continent.[25] The collapse of the Soviet Union in the early 1990s led to a tremendous explosion of number and shape of nations in Eastern and Central Europe. The process of deep economic integration in Western Europe, accompanied by pressures for political decentralization, has called into question the role and function of national states. We hope that our analyses can shed some light on important issues related to these complicated events.

Finally, many readers may be struck by our fixation on keeping our models as simple as possible. We chose to extract only the most important elements of the real world in order to bring the points we want to make into focus. The benefit of keeping models as simple and general as possible was well understood by Vilfredo Pareto (1935, p. 323), who wrote:

Every now and then scientific theories of economics and sociology are challenged as disregarding certain particulars. That, instead, is a merit. One must
first obtain a general concept of the thing one is studying, disregarding details,
which for the moment are taken as perturbations.[26]

Simplicity is also valued by those who do not use formal models. For instance, Samuel Huntington (1993) wrote in a *Foreign Affairs* article:

[W]hen people think seriously, they think abstractly; they conjure up simplified
pictures of reality called concepts, theories, models, paradigms. Without such
intellectual construct there is, as William James said, only a "bloom buzzin."

Of course, we are aware that simplicity can lead to oversimplification. At the end of the day, the test of a simple model is its ability to provide useful insights for a complex reality. It will be up to the reader to judge whether we have come close to that goal.

1.4 Organization of the Book, and a Brief Synopsis

We have made every effort to write a book that can be read both by nontechnical people and by those inclined toward analytical formaliza-
tion. In every chapter we begin our arguments informally. Then, in the next sections, we provide the analytical formalization. These sections are identified by an asterisk (*). Readers who intend to avoid any equations could skip the technical sections and still follow the arguments of the chapters. Those nontechnical readers who are especially interested in the empirical discussion and in history, after reading this introduction, should gloss over the nontechnical parts of chapters 3, 5, and 6, and then read the three chapters entirely devoted to historical facts, chap-
ters 10 through 12. In what follows we provide a brief chapter by chapter description of the book.

Chapter 2 introduces the basic trade-off between the benefits, in terms of lower per capita taxes, in having large jurisdictions, and the costs of differences (i.e., heterogeneity) in preferences over the policies of a ju-
risdiction. To choose the best arrangement along this trade-off, we want large heterogeneous jurisdictions that provide public goods and policies for which benefits of size (i.e., economies of scale) are large; alternatively, small homogeneous jurisdictions should provide public goods and policies for which the heterogeneity of preferences is high and economies of scale are relatively low. So why does one need central governments

to provide a bundle of public goods and policies? In other words, why have countries? Why is the prevailing organization one in which individuals organize themselves around a single national government that provides most of the public goods and policies? An alternative, and potentially more efficient, organization, as we just mentioned, would be one in which various groups of individuals share certain public goods with some regions and other public goods with other regions. For example, California might share a currency with Mexico, and army with Oregon, and a supreme court with Nevada. Or, two adjacent cities share a school system, but not an army. The guiding principle would be that large jurisdictions would provide public goods for which benefits of scale are relatively large and heterogeneity costs low, and vice versa.

There are two problems with this organization. One is that overlapping jurisdictions create a large amount of transaction and communication costs, which, in fact, would naturally increase in the amount of overlap of several administrative bodies and in the distance between groups of individuals sharing the same policy/administration. The second problem is that it may be impossible for regions to share a public good if they do not also share some other goods, in particular, defense and monopoly of coercion. It is hard to imagine individuals sharing public goods, public property, and policies if they do not share the ultimate monopoly of coercion and the legal use of violence, which is what defines a "state." We can therefore think of a state as a political organization that concentrates in its government a relatively large and important number of policy functions, including defense and monopoly of coercion.[27]

Having established the rationale for a state, in that it provides a bundle of public goods and policies, with an eye on the trade-off between the benefits of scale and the costs of heterogeneity, we turn to how various politicoeconomic forces determine the equilibrium choice of country size along this trade-off. In chapter 3 we discuss the formation of democratic institutions within countries whose borders can be decided by majority vote, and also the formation of regions that are free to proclaim their independence. We examine, in particular, the difference between the evolution of optimal country size and the country that results from majority vote on its borders. The optimal size is the size that maximizes average welfare. In general, it is not certain whether a democratic equilibrium reproduces the optimal configuration of borders. The idea is that in a one-person, one-vote rule, everyone contributes equally to the decision on borders. However, individuals far away from the administrative center of the country (i.e., removed from the administrative center of government in preferences and location) could vote to break up a country because they do not experience the benefits of public goods as much as closer regions in preferences to government policy making. In particular, when individuals with the same income have to pay the same taxes no matter how "far" they are from the government—the number of countries in a voting equilibrium will be larger than the optimal. In other words, if borders are decided by vote, there could be many secessions and breakups, creating countries that are inefficiently small. Average welfare then might be increased if the individuals in distant regions that are opting to secede are compensated and this way induced not to break up the country.

In chapter 4 we carry this discussion forward into the direction of interregional transfers. We consider a region located far from the center of government whose preferences differ from those of public policy. As in chapter 3 we analyze the case where it may be in everyone's interest to compensate the distant region with favorable fiscal policy in order to avoid inefficient secession. We discuss the extent to which these transfer schemes are economically and politically feasible.

Chapter 5 considers a world of rent-maximizing governments (Leviathans). Since Leviathans are interested in extracting the largest possible rents form their populations, they prefer large country sizes in order to have more people to tax. An autocratic leviathan is unconstrained by its subjects' preferences. Large dictatorial empires like the Indian empire, the Ottoman empire, or the Soviet Union served precisely the purpose of providing the elites with rents and power. Only threats of insurrection keep the size of a dictatorial empire in check. Thus even dictators must guarantee some minimum welfare to some part of their citizenry. This strategy becomes difficult as empires increase in size and become more heterogeneous. The equilibrium country size then is reduced as government is induced to satisfy the needs of large fractions of their population; this way leviathans can become democratic. At the other extreme, where individuals are free to choose country borders, we will have small and somewhat homogeneous units. In this case the rulers do not extract rents but direct the policy preferences of relatively homogeneous populations. Thus democratization should lead to the creation of many new countries, which is precisely what we observed after the collapse of the Soviet Union.

Chapters 2 to 5 have emphasized the benefits of country size as economies of scale in the provision of public goods. In chapter 6 we consider the size of the economy. The size of the market for any country depends on the trade regime and on the state of international economic relations. Imagine for a moment a world of complete autarky in which all borders are closed. In this world the size of each country's market is determined—equivalent to—the country's size. Consider a world without international trade. Since the size of markets favors economic growth, large countries would have an advantage. At the opposite extreme is a world of completely open to trade in goods, factors of production, and financial instruments. In this world political borders do not delimit markets in any way, so the political size of a country has no relationship to the size of its markets. Small and large countries compete in the same marketplace: the world; political size is irrelevant for economic success. Now in the real world we are somewhere in between these two extremes. Autarkic systems have not prevailed, but political borders do matter for economic transactions. However, as globalization progresses, we can expect the world to move closer to free trade where the benefits of large country size fade away. Therefore economic integration should go hand in hand with political separatism.

Chapters 7 and 8 raise the question of international conflict. Chapter 7 presents the basic facts and a simple model, and chapter 8 extends the modeling in various dimensions. In these two chapters we analyze the choice of spending on defense and how the amount spent might affect the resolution of a conflict. Then we consider how different conflict types might affect country size, and vice versa. Next we look at the benefits of size with relation to external threats of aggression. In a peaceful world any regions considering separation may feel that they will be safe from aggression. But, as the number of seceding countries increases, many more borders must be defended by many more armies. This alone could raise the frequency worldwide of localized conflicts. In fact, while the end of the cold war created a more peaceful world by drastically reducing the possibility of a nuclear confrontation between the two superpowers, local military confrontations have not disappeared. One could even argue that, on average, local military conflicts have increased.

Chapter 9 addresses decentralization, or the subdivision of a nation's government into local jurisdictions. In this chapter we do not digress into the vast field of fiscal federalism but rather cite what literature is appropriate to our perspective on political border formation. We discuss how decentralization can, up to a point, substitute for secessions and how different political regimes might experience more or less decentralization. In particular, we show how centralized dictatorial regimes come into being.

Chapters 10 and 11 present empirical evidence for the various arguments developed in the preceding chapters. Chapter 10 introduces the statistical evidence for two important implications of our model. The first concerns the economies of scale argument. We find that the size of government is actually inversely related to country size, meaning that the ratio of government spending over gross domestic product (GDP) is larger in small countries. The second implication concerns the relationship between country size and economic success. We find that the benefit of size depends on the trade regime. Small countries can prosper with free trade, and large countries prosper in closed economies.

Chapter 11 presents a historical discussion on the evolution of states, starting from the Italian and Low Country city-states. We use the lens provided us by our theoretical analysis to discuss the evolution of national states in history. Building on the theory of chapter 6 and on the empirical evidence of chapter 10, we argue that economic integration and trade liberalization have accompanied and encouraged the rise of countries since 1945. Often one hears arguments about a so-called economically viable size for a country. Whatever that size is, it will be smaller as world markets become larger. This is precisely why so many very small countries can prosper in today's world of relatively free trade compared with other periods in history. To see this, imagine the difficulties a country the size of Singapore would face in the protectionist interwar period? In today's world of free trade relatively small ethnic regions can "afford" to stay small and homogeneous, whereas this would be too costly for them in a protectionist world. More generally, in chapter 11 we argue that our theoretical analysis helps illuminate several aspects of the evolution historically of country shape and size.

Chapter 12 deals with present-day European integration. The European Union is not a national state but a supranational union of countries. We can observe this institution with the same lenses that we have used so far. In terms of efficiency, the European Union can offer a set of public goods and policies for which the benefits of size cannot be handled efficiently within country borders. This prerogative would not apply to public goods and policies with low economies of scale and high heterogeneities of preferences. Consistent with our analyses in chapters 5 and 9, we find that in areas where excessive centralization occurs, there is a democratic deficit at the root of the problem. The EU example helps us address a more general issue on the need for, and limits of, supranational institutions in a world of highly integrated and sometimes very small countries.

Chapter 13 recapitulates our main argument that democratization, trade liberalization, and reduction of warfare are associated with the formation of small countries, whereas historically the collapse of free trade, dictatorships, and wars are associated with large countries. The chapter concludes with a number of open questions for future research.

2

Overlapping Jurisdictions and the State

2.1 Introduction

When many individuals share the same public goods and policies, they can take advantage of several benefits of size: economies of scale, larger markets, mutual insurance, protection against foreign aggression, and power and influence in international organizations. On the other hand, if a great many diverse individuals share the same public goods and policies, they face increasing costs of heterogeneity of preferences, since they have to agree with each other and share common policies. We will discuss the determinants and consequences of country size starting from this basic trade-off.

For some public goods and policies, the benefits of size are large and the costs of heterogeneity low; for others, the reverse is true. In addition geographical proximity facilitates sharing certain public goods, while for others distance may be insignificant. Suppose that for each public good and policy individuals organize themselves in jurisdictions of the size that maximizes welfare, given the trade-off between size and heterogeneity. This would lead to a complex web of overlapping jurisdictions in which some individuals would share some public goods and others would share different ones. Without transaction costs, economies of scope, and organizational costs, this would be the ideal type of political organization. In reality, however, these costs and economies of scope do exist and are large, and lead to political jurisdictions (national states) that concentrate a large fraction of the production of public goods and policy prerogatives.

While national governments assume the responsibility for several policy prerogatives, they do not have a monopoly on public policy. Subnational levels of government are important providers of public goods.

Decentralization within a country can in fact be seen as an intermediate step between a world of unconstrained overlapping jurisdictions, and one at the opposite extreme with only one jurisdiction that controls every policy and provides every public good. We return to these issues in chapter 9. In comparison, supernational organizations are institutions that provide the goods or policies that have economies of scale or externalities that cannot be internalized by national governments. Historically a country as a whole joins an international organization; we do not observe, say, California joining the United Nations but not the World Trade Organization (WTO), and Massachusetts, say, the North American Free Trade Agreement (NAFTA), but not the UN, and so on. Thus we have a "pyramid" in the organization of political jurisdictions. In chapter 12 we consider in some depth an important example of international organization, the European Union.

In effect, a national state could be said to emerge as an organization that optimizes the trade-off between size and heterogeneity in the provision of public goods and policies taking into account the transaction and organizational costs that would emerge from a maze of complex overlapping jurisdictions.

2.2 The Trade-off between Size and Heterogeneity

There are many advantages of size. In this chapter we focus on only one: the provision of public goods. We think of public goods in a broad sense. For instance, a monetary and financial system, tax collection and fiscal institutions, a legal and judicial system, infrastructures, communication systems, law and order, public libraries, national parks, and embassies. In most instances the provision of these public goods include fixed costs, that is, some fraction of the total costs of providing certain public goods is independent of the number of taxpayers who pay for it and use it; it follows that the per capita costs for the taxpayer decline as the number of taxpayers increases.

Different individuals have different views about how the polity should spend their tax money.[1] For a given total tax collection some citizens prefer a strong defense while others prefer better public schools. In addition individuals may disagree on the amount of public goods and the public policies that accompany them. For example, two citizens may agree on how much to spend on public education, but they may disagree on the curriculum. Policy preferences (ideology, if you wish) differentiate people.

Public goods have not only an ideological dimension but also a geographical one: being close to a public good (e.g., a school) minimizes travel costs. Also several public goods (communication system, bureaucracies, etc.) are often concentrated in one location, the capital, so being close to the capital has its advantages. This effect may vary depending on the extent of centralization of a country. For instance, in France which is a more centralized country than the United States, it is advantageous to live around Paris, whereas in the United States living around Washington makes no difference to most people. In Italy the decision concerning where to locate the main "hub" of the main national airline, either in Milan or Rome and, as a consequence, which airport to enlarge, had substantial implications for the distribution of travel costs in different parts of Italy. In Spain recent proposals on where to locate the first lines of fast trains generated much political discussion.

Therefore we can think of two dimensions of heterogeneity: geography (i.e., how distant an individual is from a public good) and ideology (i.e., how close public goods and policies are to the individual's preferences). In reality both of these dimensions are important. Suppose that the geographical distance did not matter: then a political jurisdiction would not be identified by proximity. That is, an Irish person who happened to agree with a Japanese person on school policies would set up a joint public school system. However, the transaction costs of such a system would be enormous. In fact jurisdictions are generally geographically compact; even though some government functions do not require geographical proximity, almost all countries are geographically connected.[2] From a modeling point of view, one could assume that there are administrative costs in having disjoint countries; if these costs are high enough, one would obtain a configuration of compact countries (i.e., not disjoint). However, this may not be the main, or the only, reason why countries are not disjoint.

There may be a second and more subtle reason why jurisdictions are geographically connected: individuals who are close together in space are also more alike in preferences, for three related reasons. One is sorting. Individuals with similar attitudes, ideology, preferences, income, religion, and race tend to live close to each other. The second is that hundreds of years of proximity generate more uniformity of beliefs and preferences. A common language is also something that evolves from geographical proximity, and it is an important determinant of "nationality." Third, the degree of heterogeneity may itself be influenced by explicit policy decisions. National governments naturally use policies that increase cultural homogeneity, either peacefully or by persuasion in democracies, and by more questionable means in dictatorships. Geography and preferences are likely to be correlated within countries as well. A vast literature applied to US localities has demonstrated both theoretically and empirically the occurrence of sorting by income, race, and ethnicity.[3] Since the characteristics by which individuals sort themselves are correlated to their preference for public policies, the geographic and ideological dimensions go hand in hand. For example, consider the issues involved in locating a public school in a US city. The black community of the inner city might want the school in their part of the city and to have a curriculum that emphasizes African-American culture. The Latino minority living in the same inner city area would like the public school moved closer to their neighborhood and to have bilingual-lingual (English and Spanish) education. The white community living in the suburbs may not want the public school in the inner city and also may not want bilingual education.

At this point we have acquired enough justification to make a very useful assumption: that geographical and ideological proximity are positively correlated. In the extreme case, we can think of positive correlation as a perfect correlation. This way we can model the world as a space where the distance between two points on a segment represents both an ideological and a geographical dimension. More specifically, to further simplify our formal analysis, we will model the world as a unidimensional space: a linear segment. For our results a perfect correlation is not necessary. What is crucial is a positive, even if not full, correlation. A referee for this book wrote that as a "liberal Democrat who lives in a largely Republican neighborhood because of better schools," he/she has "very little in common politically with his/her neighbors." While this example shows that the correlation between location and ideology in the real world is not perfect, it does point to the amazing degree of geographical/ideological sorting in the United States: by the referee's own admission, most of his/her neighbors (although not the referee himself/herself) do live in the same area *and* share very similar political preferences! Also the referee and his/her neighbors share the same preferences for good schools, and the willingness and means to pay for them.

The most problematic consequence of our assumption is that as we consider the number and shape of nations, we cannot easily capture the issue of ethnic, racial, religious, or cultural minorities located in the middle of a country. In the language of our model, these groups would be captured as surrounded by others with radically different preferences. Given our framework, individuals with "minority" preferences (i.e., with preferences that are far from the median preferences) must be located far from the middle of the jurisdiction. We will return to this issue later.

Let us consider how individuals might organize themselves in a political jurisdiction, as defined by borders that identify individuals who pay taxes for a specific public good that they, and only they, can then use. We assume that the policies followed by one jurisdiction do not affect any other jurisdiction. In the language of economics we say that there are no externalities—positive or negative—across these jurisdictions.[4]

Suppose that different public goods differ in the shape of the trade-off between size and heterogeneity. In this case, in order to maximize welfare, one would want to have small jurisdictions that supply public goods with low economies of scales and large heterogeneity costs, and vice versa. So, for instance, one would want large jurisdictions that share a currency, and much smaller ones that share a school system.

In theory, we have potentially a complex web of overlapping jurisdictions. To see this, say two individuals, i and j, live relatively close to each other geographically and share a small jurisdiction that offers a good with "low economies of scale and high heterogeneity costs," for example, a public school. At the same time, individuals i and j could belong to two different large jurisdictions that provide a good with high economies of scale and low heterogeneity costs, for example, a common currency. That is, these two individuals could share a school district but use a different currency. Of course, this is an absurd configuration of jurisdictions, as one would need a currency exchange office in the school in order to buy lunch.

In reality, we observe that small jurisdictions (school districts, municipalities) are not crossed by the borders of large ones (states, currency unions). That is, a large jurisdiction generally encloses smaller jurisdictions. Some rare exceptions may occur within subnational levels of government, but no exceptions occur across national borders. Citizens of two different countries do not share public goods offered at the subnational levels of the governments, such as municipalities and counties. Some functions of governments are distributed to local governments in a concentric fashion, and whole countries could belong to supranational organizations.

The concentric type of organization prevails because the alternative, overlapping jurisdictions, would imply excessive organizational costs. By contrast, a concentric system can internalize economies of scope in the production of public goods. Economies of scope imply that the total costs of two activities is lower if the same entity performs them, and they are widespread in the production of private goods. For example, McDonald's can produce both hamburgers and French fries at a lower average cost than what it would cost two separate firms to produce the same goods, because McDonald's provides the same food storage and preparation facilities for hamburgers and French fries. Multiproduct companies, such as Proctor and Gamble, can hire top graphic designers and marketing experts and spread their skills across the product lines, and so lower their average total costs of production. Analogous economies of scope exist in the public sector. For example, military forces can be used for external defense and to keep law and order within the domestic borders. Obviously the existence of economies of scope in two distinct public goods is not sufficient, per se, to justify their provision to be concentrated in a single government. The economies of scope must be large enough to offset the losses that centralization necessarily entails in terms of a reduction in governments' ability to satisfy heterogeneous preferences. Transaction costs work in the same direction. Sharing a local government but not a currency or an army would be extremely inefficient.

Musgrave (1971) describes a world free of transaction costs and economies of scope and organized in overlapping jurisdictions as follows: "a person residing in one location would be a member of various service clubs, aimed at providing him with different services. For some services he would join close neighbors only, while for others the neighborhood concept would be extended to involve a radius of 10, 100, or 1,000 miles. The system would be exceedingly complex." The same author (Musgrave 1998, p. 175) notes that in such a system "detailed mapping would thus call for a maze of service units, creating excessive costs of administration and surpassing administrative feasibility."[5] Frey and Eichenberger (1999) advocate, at least for Europe, the use of overlapping jurisdictions as the optimal organizational structure. However, they disregard any realistic discussion of the transactions costs and economies of scope of this structure, and they do not deal with the issue of indivisible goods like the monopoly of use of legitimate coercion.[6]

The bottom line is that we can think of a state as a political jurisdiction that monopolizes the provision of certain essential public goods, and policies (like defense) and takes prerogative on a host of other functions for reasons of economies of scope or transaction costs. Some functions are delegated to subnational level of governments, but the national borders fully enclose subnational jurisdictions, whose borders do not cross the national ones. Among the attributions of a central government, the monopoly of legitimate use of coercion plays a special role; to some extent it defines the very nature of a state, a view shared by Max Weber and more recent scholars like Riker and North.

*2.3 A Model of Specialized Jurisdictions

2.3.1 Overlapping Jurisdictions
For simplicity and given the justifications discussed above, we model the "world" as a linear segment of length normalized to 1.[7] Unidimensional spatial models have a long pedigree in economics and political economy, going back to Hotelling (1929). They have been used extensively by economists in economic geography, regional economics, and local public finance.[8] Obviously land is bidimensional. However, the increase in complexity by moving to two dimensions is very high, and the gains in terms of realism are relatively limited.[9] We will assume for simplicity that the distribution of individuals on the segment is uniform. In chapter 3 we will briefly consider a generalization of this assumption.

There are M public goods, indexed by $j = 1, \ldots, M$. Each public good is available in a continuum of types, and each type is identified by a point on the segment. If good j is located at $\frac{1}{4}$, or, equivalently, is of "type" $\frac{1}{4}$, it means that this good is at the midpoint of the first half of the segment.

A jurisdiction for the jth public good is defined by three points on the segment: for example, A, B, and C, with $A < B < C$. The middle point B indicates where the public good is located; the other two are the borders of the jurisdiction. In figure 2.1 we illustrate this as $A = 0$, $B = \frac{1}{4}$, and $C = \frac{1}{2}$: the jurisdiction includes the first half of the segment, and the type of the jth public good supplied by the jurisdiction is located right at the middle of the jurisdiction.

We define a jurisdiction that provides public good j as a j-level jurisdiction. A distribution of jurisdictions for the jth public good is the set of the three points that identifies separate jurisdictions. So, if there are two j-type jurisdictions, the size of each jurisdiction j is $\frac{1}{2}$.

An individual belongs to one and only one jurisdiction that provides the jth public good. The individual obtains utility from his consumption, which is equal to his income y minus taxes t_i, and a disutility

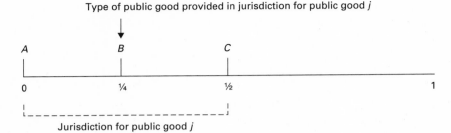

Figure 2.1
Example of a jurisdiction

because of his distance from the public good. We denote by l_{ji} the distance between the location of individual i and the location of the jth public good in his j-level jurisdiction. These costs are zero if the individual is located exactly where good j is. Formally we write

$$u_i = y - t_i + g - \sum_{j=1}^{M} a_j l_{ji}, \tag{2.1}$$

where a_j is a positive parameter that measures the marginal cost of distance from public good j. Total utility from all public goods is given by $g - \sum_{j=1}^{M} a_j l_{ji}$.[10]

Each jth public good's total cost c_j in a certain jurisdiction is given by

$$c_j = k_j + \gamma_j s, \tag{2.2}$$

where s is the size of the jurisdiction, k_j is a fixed cost that is independent of the jurisdiction's size, and γ_j is a positive parameter. Total taxes in a j-level jurisdiction with borders at A and C must equal c_j:

$$\int_A^C t_i \, di = c_j, \tag{2.3}$$

which obviously implies a balanced budget for each jurisdiction.

Therefore the sum of everybody's utilities is given by

$$\int_0^1 u_i \, di = y - \sum_{j=1}^{M} \left(k_j N_j + \sum_{x=1}^{N_j} \gamma_j s_{jx} + a_j \int_0^1 l_{ji} \, di \right), \tag{2.4}$$

where N_j is the number of j-level jurisdictions and s_{jx} is the size of a j-level jurisdiction x for $x = 1, 2, \ldots, N_j$. Consider the problem of a utilitarian social planner that intends to maximize the sum of individual utilities defined as above. The following proposition which we prove in the Appendix of this chapter characterizes the solution.

PROPOSITION 2.1   For every public good j, the social planner divides the world into N_j jurisdictions of equal size $s_j = 1/N_j$, and locates at the middle of each jurisdiction a public good j. N_j is the *integer* close to $\sqrt{a_j/4k_j}$.

Without loss of generality, assume that the public goods can be ordered as follows:

$$\frac{a_1}{k_1} < \cdots < \frac{a_j}{k_j} < \frac{a_{j+1}}{k_{j+1}} < \cdots < \frac{a_M}{k_M}. \tag{2.5}$$

From proposition 2.1 it follows that

$$N_1 < \cdots < N_j < N_{j+1} < \cdots < N_M. \tag{2.6}$$

The size of each jurisdiction is inversely related to the ratio a_j/k_j; that is, the size is decreasing with the marginal cost of distance and increasing with the economies of scale in the production of the public good. Thus the social planner chooses many small jurisdictions for the good with a high ratio of heterogeneity costs relative to economies of scale and a few large jurisdictions for the public goods with the opposite characteristics.

Next let us consider two public goods j' and j'', for which $N_{j'} = 2$ and $N_{j''} = 3$. The optimal configuration of jurisdictions is as given in figure 2.2: public good j' is provided by two separate jurisdictions of size $\frac{1}{2}$ each, with the first j'-jurisdiction providing a public good j' of type $\frac{1}{4}$ and the second j'-jurisdiction providing a public good j' of type $\frac{3}{4}$.

Good j'' is provided in three jurisdictions of size $\frac{1}{3}$ each, with the first j''-jurisdiction providing a public good j'' of type $\frac{1}{6}$, the second j''-jurisdiction providing a public good j' of type $\frac{1}{2}$, and the third j''-jurisdiction providing a public good j'' of type $\frac{5}{6}$. In this example it is worth noting that jurisdictions may well "overlap": there are individuals who belong to the same j'-jurisdiction (e.g., the first j'-jurisdiction) who obtain their j'' good from different j''-jurisdictions (e.g., some from the first j''-jurisdiction and some from the second j''-jurisdiction), and conversely, there are individuals who belong to the same j''-jurisdiction who obtain their j' good from different j'-jurisdictions.[11]

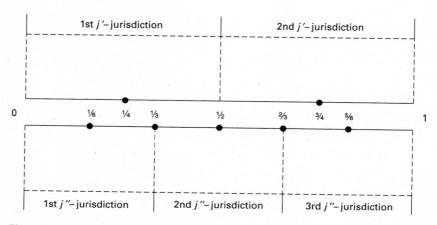

Figure 2.2
Overlapping jurisdictions

2.3.2 Economies of Scope and the State

The configuration of jurisdictions described above implies the "maze" of borders described by Musgrave (1971). One could provide all public goods at a lower cost, by centralizing the provision of public goods within the same "jurisdiction," but this solution may not be optimal. The lower costs from joint production may stem from multiple sources. For example, multiple overlapping jurisdictions may imply transactions costs between different policy makers with authority over overlapping groups of individuals if the provision of different public goods requires some form of coordination. Generally, one talks about *economies of scope* in the production of public goods whenever the total cost of producing the public goods decreases as a result of increasing the number of different goods produced.

Formally let us consider two public goods (good 1 and good 2). If provided by separate governments, the two goods cost, respectively, k_1 and k_2. However, if they are provided by a single government, their *aggregate* cost is

$$k_c < k_1 + k_2. \tag{2.7}$$

For simplicity, we will assume that $\gamma_c = \gamma_1 = \gamma_2 = 0$. The analysis can be easily extended to the case $0 < \gamma_c < \gamma_1 + \gamma_2$.

As we saw earlier, if the two goods are provided separately, average utility will be maximized by having good 1 supplied by N_1 governments, and good 2 supplied by N_2 governments, with $N_1 = \sqrt{a_1/4k_1}$ and

$N_2 = \sqrt{a_2/4k_2}$. To fix ideas, we will call this the "specialized" solution. By contrast, if both goods are provided by the same government, the average utility will be maximized by the formation of N_c jurisdictions, where $N_c = \sqrt{(a_1 + a_2)/4k_c}$.[12] We will call this the "centralized" solution. It is immediate to show that the following:

PROPOSITION 2.2 The centralized solution is more efficient than the specialized solution if and only if

$$\sqrt{k_c} < \frac{\sqrt{a_1}}{\sqrt{a_1 + a_2}} \sqrt{k_1} + \frac{\sqrt{a_2}}{\sqrt{a_1 + a_2}} \sqrt{k_2}. \tag{2.8}$$

The proof of this proposition is provided in the appendix to this chapter.

Thus we have centralized jurisdictions if the economies of scope are high enough to offset heterogeneity costs from centralization. A numerical example may help us illustrate our result. To simplify matters, suppose that the two public goods have the same aggregate costs when supplied by separate governments: $k_1 = k_2 = 1$. However, communities differ more in their preferences for types of good 2 than for types of good 1 : $a_1 = 16$, but $a_2 = 144$. In other words, public good 2 is more "local" than good 1, because the benefits from good 2 fall much more rapidly with distance from the government. Consequently, if the two public goods are provided by separate governments, good 2 is provided in smaller and, therefore, more homogeneous jurisdictions while good 1 is provided in larger and less homogeneous jurisdictions. It turns out that for these parameter values, separate provision of the two goods entails the formation of four equal-size jurisdictions for the supply of good 2, and two jurisdictions for good 1.

Suppose that the provision of both public goods can be achieved at a lower cost $k_c < 2$. Should such unified provision take place? According to proposition 2.2, this is possible only if $k_c < 8/5$. For example, if $k_c = 10/9$, utility is maximized by $N_c = \sqrt{(16 + 144)/4(10/9)} = 6$ jurisdictions, each having a unified government that provides both public good 1 and public good 2.

In this example the number of jurisdictions is equal to the optimal number of jurisdictions N_2, should good 2 be supplied separately. Of course, that is not a general result. In general, we have $N_c > N_2$ if k_c is low enough, and $N_c < N_2$ for a higher k_c.

We have illustrated thus the role of economies of scope for two public goods, and the analysis can be easily extended to a larger number of public goods. At the limit, where economies of scope are large enough across the *complete* spectrum of public goods, the joint production of all public goods would cost

$$k_c < \sum_{j=1}^{M} k_j. \tag{2.9}$$

Let $\bar{k}$ denote total costs of all public goods:

$$\bar{k} \equiv \sum_{j=1}^{M} k_j. \tag{2.10}$$

The higher $\bar{k}$ is, the more important *economies of scale* become in the provision of public goods. Now define ξ as

$$\xi \equiv \frac{k_c}{\bar{k}}, \tag{2.11}$$

where $0 < \xi < 1$. The parameter ξ measures the extent of the *economies of scope*. The higher ξ is, the *more* important economies of scope become in the provision of public goods. Let $\bar{a}$ be defined as

$$\bar{a} = \sum_{j=1}^{M} a_j. \tag{2.12}$$

Hence $\bar{a}$ measures total heterogeneity costs in the provision of different types of public goods.

A straightforward extension of proposition 2.2 is the following:[13]

PROPOSITION 2.3   An efficient configuration of jurisdiction is given by N_c jurisdictions, each providing all M goods to its citizens, if and only if the following holds:[14]

$$\sqrt{k_c} < \sum_{j=1}^{M} \frac{\sqrt{a_j k_j}}{\sqrt{\bar{a}}}. \tag{2.13}$$

The optimal number of jurisdictions is then given by

$$N_c = \sqrt{\frac{\bar{a}}{4\xi\bar{k}}}. \tag{2.14}$$

The implications of proposition 2.3 are intuitive. Larger heterogeneity costs ($\bar{a}$) imply more centralized jurisdictions. Higher economies of scale ($\bar{k}$) and higher economies of scope (ξ) lead to a smaller number of centralized jurisdictions. Under these conditions for parameter values, the ideal organization is to have a certain number of jurisdictions (call them countries) within which a government provides all public goods and policies.

We have emphasized here economies of scope as the force that leads toward the elimination of overlapping jurisdictions. However, other forces like organizational and transaction costs point in the same direction.[15]

2.4 Conclusion

The optimal size of a jurisdiction is the result of a trade-off between economies of scale in the production of goods, services, and policies provided by it, and the heterogeneity of the population. The optimal "point" in this trade-off is generally different for each good, service, or policy. This could lead to a complex "maze" of overlapping borders. However, this maze may be suboptimal in the presence of economies of scope. We derived conditions on the size of economies of scope such that a system of "centralized" jurisdictions would be the optimal solution. For high economies of scope, the world would be optimally organized in a number of nonoverlapping centralized jurisdictions, each providing its citizens all the necessary public goods and services.

We consider these centralized jurisdictions to be countries, whose central government provides all the public goods and prerogatives. In this case moving from multiple public goods to only one entails no loss of generality. In chapter 9 we will see that "concentric" decentralization can be considered an intermediate solution halfway between the maze of jurisdictions and the single centralized jurisdiction that does everything. In chapter 12, with specific reference to the European Union, we address the issue of transfer of prerogatives from the central government to multinational organizations.

2.5 Appendix: Derivations

Proof of Proposition 2.1
The sum of utilities to be maximized is given by

$$\int_0^1 u_i \, di = y - \gamma - \sum_{j=1}^M \left[k_j N_j + a_j \int_0^1 l_{ji} \right]. \tag{A2.1}$$

For public good j and for a given number of jurisdictions N_j, the sum of distances $\int_0^1 l_{ji}$ is minimized if the public good is located at the midpoint of each jurisdiction. Hence the sum of distances is given as $\int_0^1 l_{ji} = \sum_{x=1}^{N_j} s_{xj}^2/4$, where $\sum_{x=1}^{N_j} s_{xj} = 1$. The sum of squares is minimized by choosing jurisdictions of equal size, $s_j = 1/N_j$. Therefore the solution for each N_j is the positive integer that solves

$$\min_{N_j} k_j N_j + \frac{a_j}{4N_j}. \tag{A2.2}$$

The first-order condition for N_j (ignoring the constraint that N_j must be an integer) implies that

$$N_j^* = \sqrt{\frac{a_j}{4k_j}}. \tag{A2.3}$$

In general, the sum of utilities is maximized by a positive integer close to N_j^*.

Proof of Proposition 2.2
Proposition 2.1 implies that centralized jurisdictions are optimal if and only if the sum of utilities they provide is given by

$$u_c = y - k_c N_c - \frac{a_1 + a_2}{4N_c}. \tag{A2.4}$$

Abstracting from the integer constraint and substituting N_c with its optimal value $\sqrt{(a_1 + a_2)/4k_c}$, we have

$$u_c = y - \sqrt{k_c(a_1 + a_2)}. \tag{A2.5}$$

Analogously, with specialized jurisdictions total utility is given by

$$u_{12} = y - k_1 N_1 - k_2 N_2 - \frac{a_1}{4N_1} - \frac{a_2}{4N_2}, \tag{A2.6}$$

which becomes

$$u_{12} = y - \sqrt{k_1 a_1} - \sqrt{k_2 a_2} \tag{A2.7}$$

when we substitute N_1 and N_2 with their optimal solutions. Proposition 2.2 is obtained by comparing u_c and u_{12}.

3   Voting on Borders

3.1   Introduction

We argued that a "state" emerges from economies of scope and from the transaction costs associated with the maze of overlapping jurisdictions. Now we proceed under the assumption that a single central government provides all the public goods and assumes all policy prerogatives. Chapter 9 is devoted to a generalization in which the central government decentralizes some policies to localities. We begin by characterizing the number and shape of jurisdictions as if a benevolent world planner maximized the sum of individual utility. This is the "optimal" number of countries that achieves the highest level of total welfare given the trade-off between the benefits of size and the costs of heterogeneity.

The fact than an optimal configuration of borders exists, however, does not imply that it is automatically reached. The question we address in this chapter is whether or not in an uncoordinated equilibrium we obtain the same optimal number of countries. That is, will the optimal number of countries emerge from a system where individuals choose the organization of borders? The answer is "not necessarily." If borders can be redrawn by majority voting, and unilateral secessions are permissible, then, in general, there is no guarantee that a noncentrally planned equilibrium will produce the social optimum.

An important factor that affects the answer to this question is whether or not one allows for a system of side payments, or transfer schemes, among the citizens of each country. The intuition is the following. Suppose that the first best, that is, the optimal configuration of borders, maximizes total welfare but the distribution of welfare is uneven. By this we mean that some individuals are very well off and others not so well off. The disadvantaged individuals may want to change the configuration of borders. However, precisely because the optimal configuration of countries maximizes total welfare, enough total income might be generated so that transfer schemes between winners and losers could make the optimal number of countries sustainable.[1]

However, in practice, these transfers schemes may be difficult to implement, for a variety of reasons discussed below. Therefore the question is whether or not the optimal configuration of borders generates a distribution of welfare among individuals that will make the borders themselves sustainable. In this chapter we study the case where transfers and side payments do not exist, and we will show that without transfers for citizens of the same country optimal borders may not be sustainable. In chapter 4 we consider transfers among citizens.

The reason why optimal borders are not sustainable is that the distribution of welfare among citizens of a country are uneven. Consider the optimal configuration of borders. If everyone has the same income, a fiscal system that does not allow transfers implies that everybody pays the same income tax. But individuals living near the middle of the country (i.e., in preferences and in location near to the public goods and policies provided by the central government) will be better off than those at the borders. But then the latter will have an incentive to vote for separation and for a reorganization of borders. Without transfers from the center to the borders, the latter may object to the existing optimal borders. The "objection" may take several forms: one is unilateral secession, in order to form an independent country or join an already existing one; another is voting in a referendum to rearrange borders. As a result, in equilibrium, there will be smaller countries relative to the optimum. In other words, the optimal configuration of borders implies countries that are too big to be sustainable without transfers from the center to border regions.

3.2 The Size of Countries in a Democratic Equilibrium

To fix ideas, let us assume that the world can be characterized by a linear segment of length 1. Obviously land is bidimensional, but the mathematical complications of moving to two dimensions is not worth the gain in realism. For the reasons discussed in chapter 2, we assume that the locations of two individuals capture both an ideological dimension and a geographical one and that the locations of individuals are fixed. That is, if two individuals are far from each other, they live far from each other geographically and have very different policy preferences.

A country is identified by two borders, that is, two points on the segment and by a choice of public goods/public policy. For simplicity we assume that each country has one and only one public good with a fixed cost, denoted by k.[2] This implies that economies of scope and transaction costs are so high that it is simply impossible to have a multilevel organization of overlapping jurisdictions.

The per capita tax needed to finance this public good is equal to the total cost of the good, k, divided by the size of the population denoted s, that is, k/s. Clearly the larger the country is, the lower is the per capita tax, since more individuals pay for a fixed cost k. This is the simplest possible way of capturing the economies of scale effect. Individuals derive benefits from the public good, but these benefits decrease with distance from the public good. Remember that with the term "distance," we capture both an ideological and a geographical concept. Thus being "far" from a public good can be interpreted as living a long travel distance from it, and being "far" from a public policy can be interpreted as preferring a different policy from the one implemented. Individuals' net of taxes income is obviously decreasing in the tax they have to pay to finance the public good.

In chapter 2 we discussed the question of what is the optimal number of countries that maximizes the sum of individuals' welfare in the world, which is a reasonable criterion in this example since everyone is identical. Let us briefly review what we found. First of all, all countries would have the same size. Given the uniformity of the distribution of the population and the fact that everyone is identical, there is no reason why certain countries should be small, with high taxes and low average distance from public goods, and others should be large, with low taxes and high average distance from the public good. This resulting equal size of countries is not meant to be realistic, of course. It does suggest, however, that some form of "nonuniformity" is needed to obtain countries of different size, such as different levels of density or different degrees of "heterogeneity" in the distribution of preferences in different parts of the world.[3] In the technical part of this chapter we explore the case of a nonuniform distribution of individuals and show how one obtains countries of different size. Second, the total world welfare is maximized by a well-defined "optimal" number of countries, call that N^*.

From the solution of this problem we obtained two important insights

1. The optimal number of countries is decreasing in the cost of the public good, k. That is, the more costly the public good, the larger is the incentive to share it among more taxpayers.

2. The optimal number of countries is increasing in the disutility from distance from the public good. That is, the more costly it is to be far from the public goods, the more individuals are willing to pay to be close to it. This implies that the lower (average) distance achievable in small countries is a sufficient reward for the higher taxes.

Now we can move away from an ideal world of optimality and ask the following question: What happens when decisions over public policy and political borders are made by democratic vote? Will those decisions lead to efficient or inefficient borders? For the moment we can continue to assume that all individuals have the same income and that everyone in the same country pays the same taxes.[4]

The first question to address is the location of the "government" for these political borders. Let us consider, for the moment, the borders of a country as definite, and that all citizens can vote. Our goal is not to pursue any innovative or creative voting theory; we will proceed by the well-traveled path of the median voter theorem. The public good will be located somewhere at the middle of the country where its position corresponds to that of the median voter; this is the voter who splits the population into two equally sized groups. The median voter theorem implies that the median position is the only one that cannot be upset by a majority vote for an alternative proposal, in this case a different site for the public good.[5] A middle location of the public good minimizes the average (and total) distance of citizens from the public good. This is likewise the position that maximizes total welfare for the costs of the public good. In our example the median voter coincides with the middle of the distribution, which is the middle of the country.[6]

From just a glance at a world map, it is apparent that the capital cities, which is where many public goods are located and public policies are decided, tend to be around the middle of the country. Of course, where the "middle" is depends on the distribution of individuals at the time when the capital was chosen. In the United States, for instance, a permanent capital was chosen on the Potomac with the explicit goal of placing it in the middle of the federation of states, as a passage from the *Federalist Paper* 14 (Madison) clearly emphasizes: "As the natural limit of a democracy is that distance from the Central Point which will just permit to the most remote citizens to assemble as often as their public function demand ... so the natural limit of a republic is that distance from the center which will barely allow the representatives to meet as often as may be necessary for the administration of public affairs." As we have pointed out, a capital set in the middle minimizes the traveled distance of individuals living in the country. In fact the early political debate in the American Republic is splendid evidence that supports the assumption of a very close connection between geographical distance and ideological distance. By knowing where an individual lived, north or south of the Potomac and how far from it, one could predict his views on virtually every policy issue facing the federation!

In Australia, the capital (Canberra) was located exactly midway between Sidney and Melbourne, which, at the time of the creation of Australia, could be considered close to the "middle" of the distribution of the population.[7] The transfer of the Nigerian capital from Lagos to Abuja in 1991 was motivated by the desire to locate the capital within the geographical *and* ethno-linguistic/religious "middle" of a fragmented country. Of course, we do not claim that the location of a country's capital is uniquely determined by median considerations. Obviously multiple additional factors such as the geographic character of the country, its coastline, issues of internal and external security, miscalculations, and idiosyncratic historical events enter into the picture. However, the experiences of numerous "new" or "democratizing" countries are suggestive of a tendency to place the capital in the middle. Deviations from a middle position are likely to reflect significant differences in the political weight of different regions within a country.

We are now ready to think about the number and size of nations. In the absence of regional transfers, the benefits of belonging to a larger country are unequally distributed, with the larger share going to the individuals who live close to the government in ideology and geographical location. These individuals pay as much as everyone else but do not bear the higher heterogeneity costs; in fact they are close in preference to the policies chosen, and close in distance to the public good. By contrast, individuals far from the government bear a disproportionate share of the heterogeneity costs, and hence do not fully internalize the benefits of belonging to a larger country. When allowed to vote over borders, those individuals close to the borders may favor a breakup, even if this would imply a configuration of borders that does not maximize total welfare. This is an application of a more general result, namely that the one person–one vote majority does not always produce outcomes that maximize everyone's welfare.

In section 3.3, which we have starred for its technical focus, though it can be easily followed by a nontechnically inclined reader, we show a simple example whose outcome does not regard the optimal configuration of borders for two reasons:

1. The majority of voters may prefer to break up the country and form two countries, each half the original size, although total welfare is not maximized at the new equilibrium.

2. The breakup is motivated by the desire of people far from the central government to create governments close to their own preferences, even if this means larger taxes for *everyone* (including those who were happy with the one large country).

The fact that majority vote can lead to "inefficient" breakup is not special to the example in section 3.3, as the rest of this chapter provides a more general discussion. In particular, we will define a "democratic equilibrium" in which borders are freely determined through referenda, and we will see that the "optimal number of nations" is not a democratic equilibrium: if a social planner were to divide the world optimally, *in each country* we would have a majority in favor of a change of borders, and specifically, in favor of the formation of smaller countries. When borders are determined via majority vote, "too many" countries are created: the "democratic equilibrium" implies a number of countries *larger* than the optimal one.

Let us illustrate these results by a graphic example. In figure 3.1 we have an optimal number of five countries, that is, $N^* = 5$.

In the middle country, where the public good is located at 1/2 (the middle of this country), everyone pays the same tax, equal to $k/(1/5)$. The individuals with the average utility are located midway between the center and the borders, thus at points 9/20 and 11/20 in the figure.

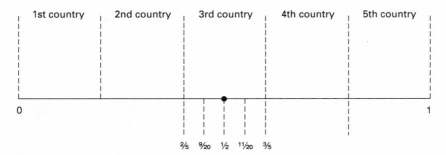

Figure 3.1
A five-country world

Everyone else between points 2/5 and 9/20 and between 11/20 and 3/5 gets a less than average utility. The question is whether these "below average" individuals will choose to stay in this country.

In general, as we will show formally in the next section, the optimal number of countries ($N^* = 5$ in our example) will not be sustainable, and, in equilibrium there will be a larger number of smaller countries, say, $\tilde{N} = 7$. The reason is that individuals close to the borders of a country, those located between 2/5 and 3/2 (or 11/20 and 3/5) pay the same tax as everyone else but do not internalize the full benefits of the "optimality" of the N^* solution because they are far from the public good. These individuals may prefer to rearrange borders in such a way that the new borders make them the net "winners." Equilibrium is ended when the world is divided into an inefficiently large number of small countries.

An interesting point is that while borders in the voting equilibrium do not maximize average utility, they do maximize the utility of the individuals at the border. That is, the democratic outcome maximizes the utility of individuals who are the farthest away from the government. Since such individuals are those with the lowest utility, the voting equilibrium satisfies an alternative "ethical" criterion: it maximize the *minimum* utility, meaning the utility of the worst-off individual. This is called the Rawlsian criterion, as it is based on the philosophical argument that John Rawls (1971) made in his celebrated book *A Theory of Justice*.[8] The fact that the voting equilibrium maximizes the utility of the individual at the border confirms the intuition that the breakup of "efficient" countries is due to the incentives to secede faced by the individuals who are most far from the center.

Since in a voting equilibrium the average utility is not maximized, there is a potential for alternative arrangements that—if side payments can be introduced—would improve everybody's utility.[9] Since the optimal allocation of borders ($N^* = 5$ in our example) maximizes average and total welfare, in principle, the winners should compensate the losers.[10] There are two ways in which the losers can be compensated. One is with decentralization of policies. That is, the public goods and public policies could be decentralized. (We return to this issue later in chapter 9; here we continue to focus on the type of public goods and public policies that cannot be decentralized.) The second is a system of regional transfers in favor of border regions. In the criteria of our model this implies that the tax rate on income would be directly related to the distance to the public good: individuals closer to the middle would pay a higher tax, and those who are farther away would pay a lower tax. If we interpret distance in a geographic sense, then this system of transfers or of differential taxation could be relatively easy to design.[11] To the extent that distance captures ideological differences, the design of an appropriate transfer system may be more problematic. We return to this issue in chapter 4.

To sum up, we can conceive of a country's optimal size as a trade-off of the benefits of scale versus the costs of heterogeneity. The larger the economies of scale, the larger is the country's optimal size; the more heterogeneous are individual preferences, the smaller is the optimal size. In equilibrium we do not necessarily observe the optimal number of countries. An uneven distribution of net benefits within a country introduces tension, and border regions will have an incentive to break away and redraw borders. As a result the equilibrium configuration involves smaller jurisdictions than the optimal size.

*3.3   Majority Voting and (In)Efficient Size: A Simple Example[12]

Consider the following simple example. As in chapter 2, the world population has mass equal to one and is uniformly distributed over the $[0, 1]$ interval, which, as always, has both a geographical and an ideological interpretation. There exists only one public good, which costs k. Each individual i has income y and pays taxes per capita t_i that depend on the size of the country (as discussed above, in a country of size s, taxes per capita are k/s). Hence utility is due to the benefits from the public good, which decrease with an individual's distance from the government l_i, plus that individual's net income:

$$u_i = g - al_i + y - t_i. \tag{3.1}$$

Suppose that this world is one unified country (i.e., $N = s = 1$) and that everyone pays taxes equal to k.[13] Since the population is distributed uniformly between 0 and 1, and the government is located at $\frac{1}{2}$ (i.e., in the middle), the average distance from the government is $\frac{1}{4}$. Hence average utility in a one-country world is

$$u_{N=1} = g - \frac{a}{4} + y - k. \tag{3.2}$$

What if the world is divided in two countries of size $\frac{1}{2}$ each? Then everyone will pay higher taxes (i.e., $2k$), while the average distance will go down to $\frac{1}{8}$, since the two new governments will be located at $\frac{1}{4}$ and

$\frac{3}{4}$ respectively. Hence the average utility in a two-country world will be

$$u_{N=2} = g - \frac{a}{8} + y - 2k. \tag{3.3}$$

Immediately we can see that average utility is higher in the one-country world than in the two-country world if and only if

$$k > \frac{a}{8}, \tag{3.4}$$

that is, if and only if benefits from economies of scale—measured by k—are large enough to offset the costs associated with a higher distance from the government—measured by $a/8$.

Suppose that actually $k > a/8$ so that the average utility is higher in the one-country world. Say a referendum takes place whereby individuals are to choose between living in this one-country world or allowing it to break up to form two countries of equal size. Obviously the individual who lives at $\frac{1}{2}$ (the "capital" of the unified country) will not agree to a breakup since his taxes will go up and he will end up farther from the government (his new distance from the government going from 0 to $\frac{1}{4}$). But what about the individuals in the new country capitals? Their taxes will go up as well, but their distance from the public goods will be reduced from $\frac{1}{4}$ to 0. The reduction in distance will be sufficient to compensate for the higher taxes if and only if

$$k < \frac{a}{4}. \tag{3.5}$$

Now, what if we have the case where k is smaller than $a/4$, and the individuals at $\frac{1}{4}$ and $\frac{3}{4}$ do want to break up the country? Then all individuals between 0 and $\frac{1}{4}$ and all individuals between $\frac{3}{4}$ and 1 will also vote for a breakup (their average distance also decreases by $\frac{1}{4}$, while their taxes go up by k). In other words, the inequality above is sufficient to guarantee a 50 percent majority vote in favor of a breakup, although the breakup will *reduce* average utility.[14] In other words, majorities in favor of the breakup of an efficient country are observed for all values of the parameters that satisfy

$$\frac{a}{8} < k < \frac{a}{4}. \tag{3.6}$$

This result, as we discussed in the previous section, stems from the unequal distribution of the benefits in a large country. Since the individuals at the margins pay a disproportionate share of heterogeneity costs, and do not fully internalize these benefits, they will gain in a breakup of the country despite the higher taxes per capita this would mean for everyone and the reduction of average utility overall.

*3.4 The Number of Countries: A Formal Analysis[15]

3.4.1 The Model

We continue to model the world as a segment of whose length is normalized to 1. The segment is divided into intervals called "countries." The distribution of the population is uniform and has a total mass of 1. Every country needs a single "government," (or, equivalently, public good). By the word "government," we identify an entity that provides all the public goods and controls all policies. A country's government is financed only by its citizens, and benefits only its citizens.

The world has at least one government; thus $N \geq 1$, where N denotes the number of countries in the world. For simplicity, and without loss of generality, we assume that a country's government costs k, regardless of the size of the country. In other words, we assume that $\gamma = 0$ relative to the notation of equation (2.2) in chapter 2. As before, every individual has the same, exogenous income y and pays tax t_i, where the i subscript identifies the individual. Migrations are not allowed, as an individual's position on the line is fixed. The utility of individual i is

$$u_i = g - al_i + y - t_i, \tag{3.7}$$

where g and a are two positive parameters and l_i is the distance from individual i to his government. Thus the utility function is linear in private consumption. The parameter g measures the maximum utility of the public good at $l_i = 0$. The parameter a measures the loss in utility that an individual suffers when the type of government is far from his preferred type. A sufficient condition to ensure that a higher g increases utility for every type of government is $a < 1$. This is not necessary for our results, but it is a natural assumption if we interpret g as a measure of "government services" and a as reduction in the "marginal utility" of government services located at a distance l_i from the individual's preferred type. If, for reasons discussed above, we identify the "line" both in a geographical and in an ideological sense, l_i represents distance both geographically and ideologically.

Following the discussion of the previous chapter, we immediately obtain that a social planner maximizing the sum of individual utilities would choose the number of countries of equal size[16]

$$N^* = \sqrt{\frac{a}{4k}}.$$ (3.8)

In this case the public good or government is located in the middle of each country.

3.4.2 The Equilibrium Number of Countries

We begin by imposing two assumptions:

1. The location of the public good within each country is decided by majority rule. The vote on the type of public good is taken after the borders of the country are established.

2. Taxes in each country are proportional to income, with the same tax rate for every citizen.[17]

We can further assume that no one is "forced" to belong to a country against his or her will:[18]

RULE A   Each individual at the border between two countries can choose which country to join.

We will say that a configuration of N countries is:

1. An A-equilibrium if the borders of the N nations are not subject to change under rule A.

2. A-stable if it is an A-equilibrium and it is stable under rule A.

We use the following standard notion of stability: an equilibrium is stable if borders are perturbed so that as a small mass of individuals "moves" from one country to the country bordering it, by virtue of rule A the equilibrium distribution of borders is reestablished. We find that a necessary condition of stability is that the countries be of equal size. (We develop this discussion in the appendix at the end of this chapter.) Therefore we focus on countries of equal size, unless we note otherwise.

We are now ready to consider border rearrangement involving majority voting. Borders can be changed if a majority of the citizens of the countries affected by the border change are in favor of it. We introduce

RULE B   A new nation can be created, or an existing nation can be eliminated, if the modification is approved by majority rule in each of the existing countries affected by the redrawn borders.

We say that N countries have the following configuration:

1. A B-equilibrium if it is A-stable and no new country is created or no existing country is eliminated under the A-stable application of rule B. That is, any A-stable proposed modification to create or eliminate a country is rejected by majority vote in at least one of the affected countries.

2. B-stable if it is a B-equilibrium and it is stable under rule B.

The critical point here is that citizens be allowed to vote only on border rearrangements that are A-stable. That is, no votes on borders are considered if they do not satisfy rule A.[19] The immediate implication here is that only border rearrangements that lead to countries of equal size can be voted upon.[20] This conclusion follows from the fact we noted above that only countries of equal size are A-stable. The proof is fairly elaborate and thus is described in the appendix; it leads to the following result:

PROPOSITION 3.1 A configuration of equally sized countries is a B-equilibrium if and only if their number $\tilde{N}$ is given by the largest integer smaller than

$$\sqrt{\frac{a}{2k}}. \tag{3.9}$$

We have now reached the crucial result of this chapter: that *the equilibrium number of counties* ($\tilde{N}$) *is larger than the optimal number* (N^*). The intuition of this result is that which we have noted earlier: without compensatory schemes the majority voting equilibrium is not efficient. Individuals far from the center of government obtain a low level of utility when taxes are the same for everyone. When these individuals who are "far" from the public good vote, they do not appropriately take into account the aggregate loss of efficiency in moving beyond the optimal number of countries.

From a "positive" perspective it is useful to know that voting on a configuration of borders does not maximize the "size of the pie." A reconfiguration of the borders could produce a surplus that, *if* side payments were available, could be redistributed in a way that makes everybody better off. But would an efficient number of countries be desirable when side payments are *not* available? Is there anything wrong with having an "inefficiently" large number of countries? To be sure, an "efficient" equilibrium does not make everyone better off.[21] As we saw earlier, those individuals very far from the center of government would be worse off in the efficient equilibrium than they would be in the voting equilibrium. The losers' aggregate losses would be smaller than the winners' aggregate gains, but that would be of little consolation to the losers themselves.

In social welfare theory a possible justification for "socially" preferring the efficient solution even when that results in winners and losers is Harsanyi's (1953, 1955) "veil of ignorance" argument. Suppose that an individual does *not* know his location on the [0, 1] line but has to choose a configuration of borders based on the assumption that he could be anywhere along that line. He would have to maximize his expected utility, given that he could be in any location. In this context this is equivalent to maximizing average utility.[22] Hence, behind a veil of ignorance, a utility-maximizing individual would choose the efficient equilibrium, and not the voting equilibrium. This provides a strong "normative" argument in favor of average-utility maximization.[23]

However, maximization of average utility is not the only appropriate "social goal" from an ethical perspective. An alternative normative approach was elaborated by John Rawls (1971) in his famous *Theory of Justice*. A utilitarian interpretation of Rawls's approach should not maximize expected utility behind a veil of ignorance but rather the utility of the individual who will be *worst off* for each possible choice. In other words, the Rawlsian criterion requires the maximization of the *minimum* utility in each possible configuration.

In our model the worst-off individual in each configuration is the individual who lives farther away from the capital—that is, the individual at the border. Suppose, as before, that the world is divided into N countries of equal size, $s = 1/N$, since equal size is a necessary condition to maximize minimum utility.[24] The worst-off individual's utility is then

$$u_{\min}(N) = g - a\frac{s}{2} + y - \frac{k}{s} = g - \frac{a}{2N} + y - kN. \tag{3.10}$$

It is easy to verify that the number of countries that maximizes this utility (abstracting from the integer constraint) is

$$N^R = \arg\max u_{\min} = \sqrt{\frac{a}{2k}}, \tag{3.11}$$

which is identical to the voting equilibrium $\widetilde{N}$.

Clearly, the voting equilibrium does not maximize average utility, but it *does* maximize the utility of the individual living at the *border*. If, for ethical reasons, one wants to minimize the losses of the "worst-off individual," one should choose the voting equilibrium. This result supports the intuition that an "inefficiently" large number of countries in a voting equilibrium is due to the incentives to secede of the individuals far from the center.

3.4.3 Unilateral Secessions

We now consider the effect of unilateral secessions. We are interested in whether the configuration of countries survives as an equilibrium if we allow for a group of citizens to unilaterally break away. We begin by defining the following criterion:

RULE C   A new nation can be created when a connected set of individuals belonging to an existing country unanimously decides to become its citizens.

DEFINITION   A country of size s is C-stable if there exist no groups of citizens of size z that would want to break away and form a new country of size z, by rule C, for any z.

As shown in the appendix to this chapter, the following proposition holds:

PROPOSITION 3.2   A country of size s is C-stable if and only if

$$s \le (\sqrt{6} + 2)\sqrt{\frac{k}{a}}. \tag{3.12}$$

Proposition 3.2 implies that a configuration of N countries of equal size is C-stable if and only if

$$N \ge \frac{1}{\sqrt{6} + 2}\sqrt{\frac{a}{k}}. \tag{3.13}$$

The intuition behind this result is that if countries are too big, it is advantageous to border groups to unilaterally break away, even absent a majority driven reallocation of borders as implied by rule B.

We can add to this a more sophisticated type of secession in which individuals belonging to adjacent countries break away from their countries of origin. The calculations are analogous to those we used to prove proposition 3.2, and lead to a more stringent condition, that is,

$$N \geq \frac{1}{\sqrt{2}+2}\sqrt{\frac{\alpha}{k}}. \tag{3.14}$$

Note that both the efficient number of countries $\widetilde{N}$ and the optimal number of countries N^* satisfy conditions (3.13) and (3.14). So neither efficient borders nor democratically determined borders would be destroyed by unilateral secessions.[25]

3.4.4 Countries of Different Size

The result that in equilibrium all the countries have equal size (an obviously unrealistic implication) is an artifact of the assumption that individuals are uniformly distributed. By this assumption, the model is tractable in closed form. In what follows, we briefly show how one can extend the model to the nonuniform case.

Define the cumulative distribution of the world population as $F(z)$. The population of country x, p_x is thus given by $p_x = F(\bar{b}_x - F(\underline{b}_x)$, where $\bar{b}_x(\underline{b}_x)$ is the upper (lower) border of country i. As above, the government is located at the median in each country, except that now the median does not coincide with the middle of the country. Define as $\underline{d}_x$ the distance from the median of country x to its lower border, and $\bar{d}_x$ the distance from the median to the upper border. The conditions of indifference at the borders, implied by rule A, are as follows:

$$\underline{d}_{x+1} - \bar{d}_x = \frac{k}{a}\frac{p_{x+1} - p_x}{p_x \cdot p_{x+1}} \qquad \text{for } x = 1, \dots, N, \tag{3.15}$$

if N is the number of countries, and the countries are numbered in increasing order from left to right. In addition to the $(N-1)$ conditions (3.15), we have that $\sum_{x=1}^{N} p_x = 1$. For uniform distributions expression (3.15) reduces to $s_{x+1} = s_x$ for $x = 1, \dots, N$.[26] A simple examination of (3.15) shows that, in general, countries will have different population sizes and geographical extensions.

As for rule C, the results can (conceptually at least) easily be extended to the nonuniform case. In this case as well the secession threat is highest for individuals at the borders. Clearly, the no-secession conditions analogous to equations (3.13) and (3.14) would depend on the shape of the distribution $F(z)$. Finally, the application of rule B would certainly be computationally very demanding. As for the uniform case, one would allow voting only on proposals that are A-stable, except that now the condition for A-stability does not necessarily imply countries of equal size, but must satisfy the system of conditions in equation (3.15).

3.5   Conclusions

Under the assumption that economies of scope induce a single government to provide the entire bundle of public goods and policies that characterize each country, we have discussed the equilibrium configuration of countries emerging from the basic trade-off of the benefits of scale versus the costs of heterogeneity of preferences. We started with the "optimal" number of countries that maximizes average welfare, given this trade-off. We then asked the question of whether a decentralized, democratic equilibrium would always generate this optimal number. The answer is: not necessarily. For given country size the distribution of benefits among its citizen is in fact uneven: those closer in preferences and location to the government have higher welfare. Those located further away from the government have incentive to break up the country and redraw borders through one-person, one-vote majority voting. Lacking an appropriate system of compensatory transfers among citizens of a country, voting over borders breaks down the configuration of optimally sized countries. We have also seen that the voting equilibrium, while it does not maximize average utility, leads to the configuration of borders that—in the absence of compensation schemes—is the *least* costly for the individuals who are the *most far away* from their government.

In the next chapter we investigate whether and how an appropriate system of transfers within a country can enforce superior outcomes.

3.6   Appendix: Derivations

3.6.1   Derivation of the A-stable Configuration of Equally Sized Countries

An individual at the border between two countries of sizes s_1 and s_2 is indifferent if

$$g - \frac{a s_1}{2} + y - \frac{k}{s_1} = g - \frac{a s_2}{2} + y - \frac{k}{s_2}, \tag{A3.1}$$

which is satisfied if either the countries have equal size, that is,

$$s_1 = s_2, \tag{A3.2}$$

or the two countries have different size, and their product is given exactly as

$$s_1 s_2 = \frac{2k}{a}. \tag{A3.3}$$

Perturb the equilibrium so that two bordering countries now have size $s + \varepsilon$ and $s - \varepsilon$ respectively, where ε is an arbitrarily small positive number. The original equilibrium is A-stable if and only if the individuals at the new border strictly prefer the smaller country to the larger country, that is, if and only if

$$g - \frac{a\,(s_1 + \varepsilon)}{2} + y - \frac{k}{s_1 + \varepsilon} < g - \frac{a\,(s_2 - \varepsilon)}{2} + y - \frac{k}{s_2 - \varepsilon}. \tag{A3.4}$$

This expression implies that at the limit,

$$\lim_{\varepsilon \to 0} (s_1 - \varepsilon)(s_2 + \varepsilon) = s_1 s_2 > 2\frac{k}{a}, \tag{A3.5}$$

since equations (A3.3) and (A3.5) cannot hold simultaneously, two countries of different size cannot be A-stable. By contrast, two countries of equal size $s_1 = s_2 = s$ are A-stable if and only if they satisfy condition (A3.5), that is, if and only if $s^2 > 2k/a$, which is equivalent to

$$N < \sqrt{\frac{a}{2k}}. \tag{A3.6}$$

■

3.6.2 Proof of Proposition 3.1

Since we have shown that only countries of equal size are A-stable, we will now focus on such configurations. In what follows "number of countries" will therefore mean "number of countries of equal size." Let $l_i\{N'\}$ denote the distance of individual i from the government when the total number of nations is N'. Let $d_i\{N, N'\} = l_i\{N'\} - l_i\{N\}$ denote the change in individual i's distance from the government when the world goes from N countries to N' countries. An individual i will prefer N to N' as long as

$$g - a l_i\{N\} + y - kN > g - a l_i\{N'\} + y - kN', \tag{A3.7}$$

that is,

$$a d_i\{N, N'\} + k(N' - N) > 0 \tag{A3.8}$$

Let $d_m^x\{N, N'\}$ denote the median distance change in nation x, where $x = 1, 2, \ldots, N$. Nation x will have a majority that prefers N to N' if and only if

$$ad_m^x\{N, N'\} + k(N' - N) > 0. \tag{A3.9}$$

We define rules B1 and B2 as follows:

RULE B1   A new country can be created when the change is approved by majority rule in each existing country whose territory will be affected by the border redrawing.

RULE B2   An existing country can be eliminated when the change is approved by majority rule in each existing country whose territory will be affected by the border redrawing.

A configuration of N nations is:

• A B1-equilibrium if no nation is created under A-stable applications of rule B1. That is, any A-stable proposed modification to increase the number of countries by one is rejected by majority voting in at least one of the affected countries.

• A B2-equilibrium if no nation is extinguished under A-stable applications of rule B2. That is, any A-stable proposed modification to decrease the number of countries by one is rejected by majority voting in at least one of the affected countries.

Clearly, a configuration of nations is a B-equilibrium, as defined in section 3.4, if and only if it is both a B1-equilibrium and a B2-equilibrium.

By the definitions above, we have that a configuration of N countries is a B1-equilibrium if and only if in at least one country x (where $x = 1, 2, 3, \ldots, N$) we have

$$ad_m^x\{N, N+1\} + k[(N+1) - N)] > 0. \tag{A3.10}$$

As we show below, for every N and every x,

$$d_m^x\{N, N+1\} = \frac{1}{2}\left[\frac{1}{N+1} - \frac{1}{N}\right]. \tag{A3.11}$$

Hence, by substituting (A3.11) into (A3.10), we get that N is a B1-equilibrium if and only if

$$N(N+1) \geq \frac{a}{2k}. \tag{A3.12}$$

Likewise we have that N is a B2-equilibrium if and only if in at least one country x ($x = 1, 2, \ldots, N$) we have

$$ad_m^x\{N, N-1\} + k[(N-1) - N)] > 0. \qquad (A3.13)$$

That is,

$$d_m^x\{N, N-1\} > k. \qquad (A3.14)$$

Since each country must have a majority in favor of the change of borders, a necessary and sufficient condition for B2-stability is that the country where the median voter (i.e., the individual who experiences the median distance change) "suffers" the most should oppose the move from N to $N-1$ countries. Hence we must consider the maximum distance for every N, which is given as follows (see below)

$$d_m^x\{N, N-1\} = \frac{1}{2}\left[\frac{1}{N-1} - \frac{1}{N}\right]. \qquad (A3.15)$$

After substituting (A3.15) into (A3.14), we get that N nations are a B2-equilibrium if and only if the following condition holds:

$$(N-1)N \leq \frac{a}{2k}. \qquad (A3.16)$$

Therefore a "democratic equilibrium" that satisfies both A-stability and B-stability is a configuration of N countries of equal size such that

1. $N < \sqrt{a/2k}$ (condition for A-stability derived above).
2. $N(N+1) \geq a/2k$ for $N+1 < a/2k$ (condition A3.12).
3. $N(N-1) \leq a/2k$ for $N-1 < a/2k$ (condition A3.16).

The largest integer smaller than $\sqrt{a/2k}$ is the only integer that satisfies all three properties. ∎

Derivation of Median Distance Changes
We now derive equation (A3.11). We want to show how the median distance change $d_m^x\{N, N+1\}$ is given by $(s' - s)/2$ where $s = 1/N$ and $s' = 1/(N+1)$.

Consider a nation x of size $s = 1/N$. Call M the midpoint. When $N+1$ nations are formed, the citizens of nation x are divided in two new nations of size $s' = 1/(N+1)$. Call the two midpoints of the two new nations M' and M''. Call A and B the points on the left and right of M, respectively, such that individuals at A and B experience the median distance change. That is,

$$d_m^x\{N, N'\} = |AM'| - |AM| = |BM''| - |BM| \tag{A3.17}$$

and

$$|AB| = \frac{s}{2}. \tag{A3.18}$$

Equation (A3.17) defines the change of distance, while (A3.18) ensures that A and B represent median points.

Since

$$|M'M''| = |M'A| + |AB| + |BM''| = s' \tag{A3.19}$$

by construction, straightforward algebraic manipulations imply that

$$d_m^x\{N, N + 1\} = \frac{s' - s}{2}. \tag{A3.20}$$

Analogous geometrical constructions can be used to derive equation (A3.15), that is, to show that the maximum median distance change $d_m^x\{N, N - 1\}$ is given by $(s'' - s)/2$ with $s'' = 1/(N - 1)$ and $s = 1/N$.[27]

3.6.3   Extension: An Alternative to Rule B

Rule B requires a majority in each of the N existing nations in order to modify their borders. In this section we show that our characterization of the stable number of nations is the same under an alternative rule B' requiring a majority in each of the N' *new nations*. Assume that from N nations, N' new nations can be formed if in the territory of each of the proposed N' nations there exists a majority in favor of the change. As in our previous discussion, we will define the concepts of B1'-equilibrium, B2'-equilibrium, and B'-stability as follows:

• A configuration of nations is a B1'-equilibrium (B2'-equilibrium) if no new nation is created (canceled) under A-stable applications of rule B1' (B2'). That is, any A-stable proposed modification to increase (decrease) the number of countries by one is rejected by majority voting in at least one of the new countries whose territory is affected by the change.

• A B'-stable equilibrium if it is both a B1'-equilibrium and a B2'-equilibrium, and it is stable under rules B1' and B2'.

The following result shows that rule B' implies the same characterization of the stable number of countries as rule B: a configuration of countries of equal size is B'-stable if and only if its number satisfies conditions 1 through 3 above, and is therefore identical to the stable configuration of countries as defined and characterized in section 3.4.

Proof Consider the proposal of forming $N - 1$ nations. It will be rejected by majority voting in nation $x(x = 1, 2, \ldots, N - 1)$ as long as

$$a d_m^x \{N - 1, N\} + k[N - (N - 1)] > 0. \tag{A3.21}$$

But we already know from our previous derivation that

$$d_m^x \{N - 1, N\} = \frac{1}{2} \left(\frac{1}{N} - \frac{1}{N - 1} \right).$$

Hence the proposal of moving from N to $N - 1$ will be rejected by a majority of voters in each of the potential $N - 1$ countries if and only if $N(N - 1) \leq a/2k$, which is identical to (A3.16). Conversely, we will find that the proposal of moving from N to $N+1$ countries will be rejected by majority voting in at least one of the potential $N + 1$ nations if and only if in every country we have

$$a d_m^x \{N + 1, N\} + k[N - (N + 1)] \geq 0. \tag{A3.22}$$

Hence, by substituting

$$\max d_m^x \{N + 1, N\} = \frac{1}{2} \left(\frac{1}{N + 1} - \frac{1}{N} \right),$$

we have $N(N + 1) \geq a/2k$, which is identical to condition (A3.15). ∎

3.6.4 Proof of Proposition 3.2

Suppose that z connected individuals in a country of size s are considering whether to secede unilaterally. Obviously the group would never include the individual at the center of the country who would pay higher taxes in a smaller country and whose distance from the government, which is already zero, could not be improved. Hence $z < s/2$. A secession of size z will be unanimously agreed upon by all z individuals if and only if the individual who is least well-off in a secession agrees. By construction, such individual is the one at distance $s/2 - z$ in the original country. Such individual would *not* go along with a secession if and only if[28]

$$g - a \frac{z}{2} + y - \frac{k}{z} \leq g - a \left(\frac{s}{2} - z \right) + y - \frac{k}{s}, \tag{A3.23}$$

which can be rewritten as

$$a\frac{s}{2} + \frac{k}{s} \leq a\frac{3z}{2} + \frac{k}{z}. \tag{A3.24}$$

For s to be robust to unilateral secessions, the equation above must hold true for every $z < s/2$, which is true if and only if it holds true for the value of z that minimizes $a(3z/2) + (k/z)$, which is $z' = \sqrt{2k/3a}$. By substituting z' into (A3.24) and solving for s, we get (3.12). ∎

4   Transfers

4.1   Introduction

In chapter 3 we saw that when borders are determined democratically, countries may be "too small." The reason is that people far from the government—that is, distant in preferences or in location from the political and geographic middle of the country—have to contribute to the financing of the government in the same proportion as people who are closer in preference to the government's policies and geographically close to centrally located public goods. Hence people far from the government may have an incentive to break up the existing configuration of countries even when that configuration maximizes the total of everybody's utilities. But what if individuals far from the center could be compensated for staying in jurisdictions that are not close to their preferences? Would the optimal number of countries be sustainable through compensation schemes in which people far from the government pay lower taxes, or even receive net positive transfers? These are the questions that we address in this chapter.

One can think of several examples in which border regions receive a relatively favorable treatment. An often-cited example is Quebec in Canada; in Italy, five regions with "special status" that are at the northern borders with linguistic minorities, or are islands, receive much larger transfers relative to other regions with similar levels of incomes. Northern regions in Sweden receive favorable fiscal treatments.

The question is whether and how these transfers enforce an equilibrium number of countries which is more efficient than the case with no transfers. The answer is, as it is often the case, it depends. There are two important considerations that play a role here. One is feasibility: the implementation of these transfer schemes may be economically costly, for several reasons. For instance, they require high taxes on part of the population, creating tax distortions (i.e., discentives to work, save, or invest). The second one is more subtle and has to do with the credibility of transfer scheme. Suppose that a region is enticed to join (or to remain in) a country with the promise of a favorable treatment. Once the region has acceded, the central government can break its promises.

Transfers across regions could assume an additional dimension when individuals differ not only in preferences and location but also in productivity and income. In this configuration of countries, as pointed out by Bolton and Roland (1997), the equilibrium is even more directly influenced by the design of transfer schemes.

4.2   Transfers from the Center to the Periphery

In the previous chapter we noted how, when everyone pays the same taxes, the distribution of welfare is not uniform. Those closer to the government are better off than those at the pheriphery. Now we explore the possibility of compensatory transfers from the center to the borders. Some simple geometry helps the intuition. Imagine that the world can be described as a linear segment of length 1 as in figure 4.1, with individuals uniformly distributed over such segment.

Suppose that the world is divided into two countries with a border at point $\frac{1}{2}$, and assume that this is the optimal number, meaning it maximizes the average and total utility in the world. Each country's public good (the government) is located in the middle. This means that the government of the country at the left of point $\frac{1}{2}$ is located at point $\frac{1}{4}$, while the government of the country at the right is located at point $\frac{3}{4}$. To fix ideas, let us consider the country at the left. Who in this country is above or below average in terms of welfare? Since we assume that everyone pays the same taxes, those at a distance below average from the public good are those with a welfare above average, and vice versa. It is easy to see that the individuals who are at the *average* distance from

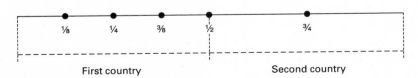

Figure 4.1
A two-country world

the public good are located at $\frac{1}{8}$ and $\frac{3}{8}$.[1] Now let us consider those who receive less than average utility. Clearly, these individuals are located between 0 and $\frac{1}{8}$ and between $\frac{3}{8}$ and $\frac{1}{2}$. Since we have constructed this example for the case where two is the number of countries that maximizes world welfare, there must be enough resources to compensate the "losers." Specifically, in our case one can find enough resources to finance transfers from individuals located between $\frac{1}{8}$ and $\frac{3}{8}$ to the disadvantaged individuals to enforce the optimal size of the country, which in our case is $\frac{1}{2}$, and make sure that no citizen would prefer a different configuration of countries. In other words, it should be possible to transfer resources from those individuals close to the public good to those farther away in order to compensate them. The Coase theorem predicts that if those transfers were costless, they would be agreed upon by all individuals, and an efficient configuration of borders would result.[2]

An important assumption of the Coase theorem is, however, that the implementation and administration of these transfer schemes be costless, and that there be no waste associated with them. In reality this is not the case. These redistributive schemes imply transfers of fiscal resources. Therefore someone has to suffer the costs of distortionary taxation. Indeed, standard public finance theory shows that tax distortions grow more than proportionally with the tax rates. Distortions (i.e., disincentives to work) are introduced by income taxes, and the higher the tax rates are, the higher are the distortions. Thus, in the "regions" around the middle, the additional tax distortions would more than compensate the reduction of tax distortions at the periphery.

Moreover the administration of these transfer systems can be complex. If the only relevant dimension of heterogeneity were costs from geographical distance, then the interregional transfer system could be constructed relatively easily. Land price could serve as a market mechanism to ensure an appropriate distribution of costs and benefits. Land and real estate prices would be higher near the public good because individuals who highly value closeness would be willing to pay more for land close to the public good. However, compensation schemes are more difficult to implement when individuals differ along the preference dimension. It may be impossible to measure how much to compensate different individuals since preferences are not observable.[3] It may not be possible for the central government to extract truthful revelations of how "unhappy" certain regions are, and to compensate them appropriately. The incentives for regions to overstate their grievances are obvious. In the real world the issue of interregional transfers within countries has often become highly charged politically, as in Canada, Italy, and Spain. Matters are especially difficult when complex cultural or linguistic cleavages separate regions.

There is an additional difficulty in the implementation of these transfer schemes. Country breakups by unilateral secession or national referendum are costly and lengthy processes. A region may be induced to abandon this process in exchange for a favorable fiscal treatment. As the hypothetical regions "settle in," the central government may renege on its promises, counting on the cost and difficulty of a secession. In other words, promises of favorable treatment if a border region stays in are not always credible. Aware of this possibility, a border region may choose to break away. By the same token, a small region or country may be reluctant to join a big country, or group of countries, into a new, larger country if the potential entrant does not find the promises of favorable treatment credible.[4]

Whether or not this credibility problem can be overcome depends on the specifics of institutional arrangements. In general, credibility problems can be overcome by building a reputation in repeated interactions among the agents involved repeatedly in the same strategic situation. However, it is hard to imagine a "repeated game" between a region and the rest of the country: "repeated" sequences of "secession games" may be an appealing concept for a game theorist, but it does not seem realistic.

More realistically, if a national government wants to retain a region, or induce a region to join, it may set up institutional structures to ensure commitment. For instance, as the United States federation developed and new territories in the west were admitted, there was much discussion related to how their rights would be guaranteed in the federation. For instance, the structure of Senate representation guarantees the rights of less populated western states. In the European Union as well, smaller countries have a disproportionally high voting power for the same reason.

The discussion of transfers becomes even more important if one considers differences in income across regions. This same difference in income may be at the root of differences over public policies. Bolton and Roland (1997) studied the case where people do not differ in their preferences over government types but rather differ in their incomes, and therefore differ in their preferences over redistribution policies. Thus poorer individuals and poorer regions would vote for high taxes, implying a larger redistributive government, and richer individuals and richer regions would have opposite preferences. Other things being equal, regions that differ from the central government in their preferred redistribution policies have an incentive to break away, and the central government may choose tax rates and redistributive schemes with an eye toward avoiding undesired secessions. In particular, to the extent that secessions are costly, poorer regions have some leverage to extract redistributions from the wealthier ones. Regional redistributions between rich and poor regions can be relatively large as the cases of Germany, Italy, and Spain clearly show. It may be more difficult to enforce this kind of redistribution within local governments, however. For example, in the United States, the lower cost of migration and the lower cost of secession of a suburb from an inner city makes it much more difficult for the poor to extract redistributions from the rich. This is precisely why in federal states redistributive policies are in the largest part a prerogative of the federal rather than local governments.

Note that redistributions from richer to poorer regions do not require direct and explicit interregional transfers. Any feature of the fiscal system that redistributes resources from rich individuals to poorer ones in a sense redistributes from rich regions to poor regions, since more wealthy individuals are concentrated in the former. However, it is the exact nature of redistributive schemes that determines the distribution of winners and losers.[5]

In summary, a system of interregional transfers could, in principle, support the optimal configurations of countries, but it must overcome three important obstacles to a successful implementation. First, tax-transfer schemes may introduce inefficient economic distortions and large administrative costs. Second, tax-transfer schemes require knowledge of individual preferences and willingness to pay for public goods. Third, credibility problems may generate a suboptimal equilibrium where regions break away for lack of a fiscal commitment to compensations. The optimal size of countries, as characterized in chapter 3, may not be sustainable through a system of interregional or interpersonal transfers.

*4.3 A Formal Model of Transfers

As in chapter 3, we assume that individuals are uniformly distributed along the linear segment [0, 1], and that each individual i at a distance l_i

from the government has utility given by

$$u_i = g - al_i + y - t_i. \tag{4.1}$$

As in chapter 3, we let everyone have the same pre-tax income y.[6] However, unlike in chapter 3, we now set a tax rate that is dependent on the location of an individual. As we discussed above, this is less of a problem if we interpret distance in a purely geographical sense. If we interpret distance as also capturing a preference dimension, having tax rates dependent on individual tastes is much more problematic. In particular, we will consider a linear "scheme" of compensation so that individuals who are far from the public good may pay lower taxes:

$$t_i = \overline{q} - ql_i, \tag{4.2}$$

where $\overline{q}$ and q are nonnegative parameters, and $0 \leq q \leq a$.

As usual in the literature, we will assume that transfers are costly. In particular, we assume that to transfer \$1 to an individual, the government needs to raise \$$[1+(\gamma q/2)]$. The parameter γ measures the extent of such deadweight losses. That is, the costs of the transfers ("deadweight losses") are proportional to the level of the compensation q. Hence the net revenues that the government extracts from each individual i, net of transfer costs, is[7]

$$r_i = \overline{q} - q\left(1 + \frac{\gamma q}{2}\right)l_i. \tag{4.3}$$

As in chapter 3, we assume that a government must provide a public good with cost k. Hence the budget constraint for a country with borders b and b' with $b' > b$, and size s is

$$\int_b^{b'} r_i \, di = k. \tag{4.4}$$

By substituting (4.2) into (4.3) and rearranging terms, we obtain

$$\overline{q} = \frac{k}{s} + \left(q + \frac{\gamma q^2}{2}\right)\overline{l}_i, \tag{4.5}$$

where $\overline{l}_i$ denotes the average distance, that is,

$$\overline{l}_i \equiv \frac{\int_b^{b'} l_i \, di}{s}. \tag{4.6}$$

Hence the utility function of an individual i at a distance l_i from the government is

$$u_i = g - al_i + y - \frac{k}{s} - \left(q + \frac{\gamma q^2}{2}\right)\bar{l}_i + q l_i. \tag{4.7}$$

Before proceeding, the following immediate observations are in order:

1. If $q = a$ compensation is complete and every individual achieves the same level of utility. Compensation is incomplete for $0 \le q < a$. In particular, if $q = 0$ there is no compensation and the model is identical to the one in chapter 3.[8]

2. For *any* positive γ, a social planner interested in maximizing total utility would choose N^* countries of equal size, each with the government in the middle and no compensation at all, that is, $q = 0$.

The second point follows immediately from the fact that any compensation scheme would reduce the total amount of resources, and that utilities are linear.

Now, would a majority of voters agree to such a compensation scheme? That is, would the voters choose a $q > 0$? To answer, one must know when the decision about the parameter q is taken. Suppose that the decision about q is taken after the country borders have been decided. This is reasonable since a tax rule can be changed (by majority role) more frequently and with fewer costs and delays than a secession or a merger with another country. To put it differently, a majority can always "promise" compensation to a minority if the latter accepts to join (or stay in) certain borders. However, ex post, tax laws can be changed relatively easily. Under this assumption we can show that, when individuals are uniformly distributed, the following is true:

PROPOSITION 4.1 For any positive γ, $q = 0$, and the government is located in the middle of the country.

The proof is simple. Each individual's ideal q_i is obtained by maximizing (4.5) with respect to q:

$$q_i = \max\left\{0, \min\left(\frac{l_i - \bar{l}_i}{\gamma \bar{l}_i}, a\right)\right\}. \tag{4.8}$$

The intuition is straightforward: an individual would prefer no "compensation scheme" if his distance from the government is less than the average distance. On the other hand, if his distance is more than average, he will like some compensation, and at the limit, if he is far enough from the government and the deadweight losses are small enough, complete compensation ($q_i = a$).

It is easy to verify that individual i's preferences over q are single peaked at q_i. We can apply the median voter's theorem and obtain the equilibrium compensation scheme that is preferred by the individual located at the median distance from the government.[9] Let l_m denote the median distance from the government. Then we have

$$q_m = \max\left\{0, \min\left(\frac{l_m - \bar{l}_i}{\gamma \bar{l}_i}, a\right)\right\}. \tag{4.9}$$

In the case of a uniform distribution, $l_m = \bar{l}_i$, and therefore $q_m = 0$. More generally, we will see no compensation schemes implemented whenever $l_m \leq \bar{l}_i$.

Hence, adding linear compensation schemes to our model in chapter 3 does not help to bridge the gap between efficiency and stability. With the linear scheme above, more than 50 percent of the population pays more with a positive q than with a zero q. Therefore, when the minority has accepted to stay in a country, the only majority voting solution is $q = 0$.

If one could envision institutions that lead to an ex ante commitment to a transfer scheme, then one could sustain a different (smaller) number of countries. In that case, could one support the optimal number of countries, as an equilibrium? A formal answer to this question would require solving a rather complicated issue of multidimensional majority voting, in which three issues are at stake: the location of the public good, the compensation scheme, and the country borders. In general, there is no reason why the answer should always be affirmative. For example, if the "deadweight losses" in the redistribution scheme, or analogously, the distortionary costs of taxation, are too high, then it may simply be not feasible (i.e., too costly) to set up the redistributive schemes that enforce the optimal number of countries N^*. If in addition we consider revelations of population preferences, the issue becomes even more complex.

4.3.1 Transfers and Polarization

The compensation scheme discussed above refers to a linear tax-transfer system with a uniform distribution of individuals. Two recent papers by Haimanko, LeBreton, and Weber (2000) and by LeBreton and Weber (2001) have explored generalizations of this problem.

Let us take, for example, a nonuniform distribution of individuals, in which the median distance (l_m) is different from the average distance $(\bar{l}_i)$. In particular, we assume $l_m > \bar{l}_i$. As is common in the literature, we will call the difference between the median and the average a measure of polarization.[10] This formalization comes from an analogy with redistributive schemes along income lines, as in Romer (1977) and Meltzer and Richard (1981). In the context of an income ladder, the assumption that the median is poorer (thus has lower welfare) than the mean is natural and consistent with real world income distributions. The analogous assumption here that the median has a larger distance (thus has lower welfare) than the mean is less obviously grounded.

Haimanko, LeBreton, and Weber (2000) showed that in polarized societies where $l_m > \bar{l}_i$ one can support some redistributive scheme even without ex ante commitment. However, there is still no assurance that the feasible redistributive scheme enforces the optimal size of countries. We illustrate this point by reviewing, and slightly modifying, an example from Haimanko, LeBreton, and Weber (2000).

Consider the following nonlinear distribution of locations in the world (figure 4.2):

3/10 of the population is located at 0.

4/10 of the population is located at 1/2.

3/10 of the population is located at 1.

It should be obvious that the total utility in a one-country world is given by

$$u_u = g - \frac{6}{10}\frac{a}{2} + y - k. \tag{4.10}$$

If three independent countries are formed, utility in each of the peripheral countries—meaning the country at 0 and the country at 1—is

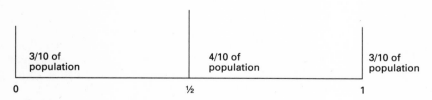

Figure 4.2
Nonuniform distribution

given by

$$u_p = g + y - k\frac{10}{3},\tag{4.11}$$

while utility in the central country (i.e., the country at $\frac{1}{2}$) is given by

$$u_c = g + y - k\frac{10}{4}.\tag{4.12}$$

Finally, if individuals located at $\frac{1}{2}$ form a country with either individuals at 0 or at 1, the total utility in the country would be given by

$$u_{cp} = g - \frac{3}{10}\frac{a}{2} + y - k\frac{10}{7}.\tag{4.13}$$

Suppose that the efficient solution is given by everyone living in just one country. By comparing sums of utilities, it is immediate to verify that

1. *the one-country solution is efficient if and only if* $k > 3a/20$.

Is the efficient one-country equilibrium stable in the absence of compensation? A necessary condition for stability is that the individuals at 0 and 1 should not be willing to breakup unilaterally (our rule C in chapter 3). By comparing utilities again, it is immediate to verify that

2. *a breakup would occur, in the absence of compensations, if and only if* $k > 3a/8$.

Together these results imply the following:

3. *for all* $3a/20 < k < 3a/8$, *in the absence of compensation we have the breakup of an efficient country.*

Result 3 confirms, for this nonuniform example, the general proposition that in the absence of compensation, inefficient countries could break up when people are free to redraw political borders.

The question now is: Can compensation prevent such breakup? The answer is: Not necessarily. In this example, when the world is but a single country, the median distance is $\frac{1}{2}$, while the average distance is $\frac{3}{10}$. Hence the compensation scheme implemented in equilibrium will be $q = \min\{2/5\gamma, a\}$. Should we then expect stability? Again, not necessarily. On the one hand, if γ is very high, the compensation may not be sufficient to prevent people at 0 or 1 from breaking up. On the other hand, if γ is very small, the resulting "excessive" compensation may induce a "secession of the center." For example, consider the extreme case of $\gamma = 0$.[11] Then we have $q = a$, which means *full compensation*. In other words, individuals at the periphery are fully compensated for being far from the government, and each individual in the country obtains the *same utility*, independently of his location. Now consider the utility of an individual located in the central region. If the country is unified, this utility will be $g - 3a/10 + y - k$, while in an independent center all individuals located at $\frac{1}{2}$ would get $g + y - k(10/4)$. Hence the center will secede as long as $k < a/5$.

Therefore we have that

4. *for all $a/5 < k < 3a/8$ a breakup of an efficient country will occur even when there is full compensation.*

This example highlights, once again, the difficulty in designing transfer schemes that induce an optimal number of countries, even with more general assumptions about the distribution of individuals.

LeBreton and Weber (2001) explore the case where a nonlinear transfer scheme can prevent unilateral secessions (our rule C of chapter 3) in a country of optimal size. They characterize an equilibrium where partial compensations prevent unilateral secessions. This solution, however, does not address the issue of credibility and commitment discussed above.

4.3.2 Income Differences and Transfers

Thus far we have focused on transfers as a way to compensate individuals who are situated "far" from the government. We maintained the assumption that everyone has the same income, and that the only relevant differences among individuals stem from different preferences over types of government. In reality people do have different incomes, and different regions in a country have different income distributions. This very same difference in income may create differences over public policies, especially with respect to redistribution.

A large literature on local public finance covers these issues in the context of fixed national boundaries.[12] In an important paper Bolton and Roland (1997) discuss how different regional distributions of income may lead to secessions. They analyze the different preferences for types of governments of different income groups, and their different preferences on redistribution policies. In particular, if taxes are proportional to income, individuals with different incomes would differ on their favored tax-transfer policies. Hence differences between median voters

across regions may generate incentives to break up, even in the absence
of other forms of heterogeneity.

Following Bolton and Roland (1997), we consider two exogenously
defined regions of a country whose population is normalized to 1.
Region A includes s_A individuals, while region B includes $s_B = 1 - s_A$
individuals. Individuals have different incomes and y_i denotes individual i's income. The distribution of income in region A is represented by
a probability density function $\phi_A(y_i)$, while the distribution of income
in region B is denoted by a probability density function $\phi_B(y_i)$. Income
distribution in a unified country formed of region A plus region B is defined by $\phi_{AB}(y_i)$. Average income levels in regions A and B are defined
as $y_A = \int y_i \phi_A(y_i)\, dy_i$ and $y_B = \int y_i \phi_B(y_i)\, dy_i$, while average income in
the unified country is defined as $y_{AB} = \int y_i \phi_{AB}(y_i)\, dy_i$.

As in our previous analysis we maintain our assumption that governments provide a pure public good with fixed cost equal to k. Therefore a
union of the two regions, other things being equal, implies lower costs
for public good provision (economies of scale). However, we extend
government's functions to include redistribution of income across individuals. That is, each individual i receives transfers R. Public good
provision and transfers are financed by a proportional income tax at
rate τ. Analogously to the case of "compensation schemes" studied in
the previous sections, we will assume that taxation is costly and involves
"deadweight losses:" a dollar of tax revenues provides only $(1 - \gamma\tau/2)$
dollars for transfers and public goods.

In this section we abstract from heterogeneity of preferences over
types of public goods, and focus on heterogeneity of income. In our
previous notation this implies that all individuals are located at the same
distance from the government, which we set at zero. Hence individual
i's utility will be given as follows:

$$u_i = g + y_i - \tau y_i + R. \tag{4.14}$$

The level of transfers will depend on the tax rate, the average income in
the country, and the country's size. As in Meltzer and Richard (1981) we
consider a tax-transfer scheme in which the revenues of a proportional
income tax are redistributed lump sum. If region A is independent, each
individual who belongs to region A will receive the following level of
transfers:

$$R_A = \left(\tau - \frac{\gamma\tau^2}{2}\right) y_A - \frac{k}{s_A}. \tag{4.15}$$

Analogously, in an independent region B, we have

$$R_B = \left(\tau - \frac{\gamma \tau^2}{2}\right) y_B - \frac{k}{s_B}. \tag{4.16}$$

In a unified country transfers will be given as

$$R_{AB} = \left(\tau - \frac{\gamma \tau^2}{2}\right) y_{AB} - k. \tag{4.17}$$

In a democracy we assume that the tax rate is decided endogenously through majority vote. It is easy to see that the median voter theorem applies. Under majority vote the equilibrium tax rate is that preferred by the individual with the median income in the country. Let the median incomes in region A, region B, and in the unified country AB be denoted respectively as y_A^m, y_B^m, and y_{AB}^m. Moreover, to simplify notation, let us normalize $\gamma = 1$. Henceforth, assuming that the median income is lower than average income (as it is usually the case empirically), we have that if regions A and B are independent, their tax rates are respectively

$$\tau_A = \frac{y_A - y_A^m}{y_A} \tag{4.18}$$

and

$$\tau_B = \frac{y_B - y_B^m}{y_B}. \tag{4.19}$$

In a unified country (regions A and B), the tax rate will be

$$\tau_{AB} = \frac{y_{AB} - y_{AB}^m}{y_{AB}}. \tag{4.20}$$

Will individuals prefer unification or separation? For each individual in region A the answer depends on the sign of the difference between his utility if region A is independent, given by

$$u_A(y_i) = g + y_i + \frac{y_A - y_A^m}{2y_A}\left[(y_A - y_i) + \left(y_A^m - y_i\right)\right] - \frac{k}{s_A}, \tag{4.21}$$

and his utility in the unified country, given by

$$u_{AB}(y_i) = g + y_i + \frac{y_{AB} - y_{AB}^m}{2y_{AB}}\left[(y_{AB} - y_i) + \left(y_{AB}^m - y_i\right)\right] - k. \tag{4.22}$$

A majority of individuals in region A will prefer separation to unification if and only if separation is preferred by the individual with median income in region A, that is, if an only if

$$u_A\left(y_A^m\right) - u_{AB}\left(y_A^m\right) > 0. \tag{4.23}$$

After substituting y_A^m into (4.21) and (4.22), condition (4.23) can be rewritten as

$$\left\{\frac{\left(y_A - y_A^m\right)^2}{2y_A} - \frac{k}{s_A}\right\} - \left\{\frac{y_{AB} - y_{AB}^m}{2y_{AB}}\left[\left(y_{AB} - y_A^m\right) + \left(y_{AB}^m - y_A^m\right)\right] - k\right\} > 0. \tag{4.24}$$

By rearranging terms in equation (4.24), we can immediately obtain the following

PROPOSITION 4.2   Separation will be preferred by a majority of voters in region A if and only if

$$\frac{\left(y_{AB}^m - y_A^m\right)^2}{2y_{AB}} + \left[\frac{y_A - y_{AB}}{2} + \frac{\left(y_A^m\right)^2}{2y_A} - \frac{\left(y_A^m\right)^2}{2y_{AB}}\right] - \frac{1 - s_A}{s_A}k > 0. \tag{4.25}$$

Three effects are at work in proposition 4.2:[13]

1. The first term $(y_{AB}^m - y_A^m)^2/2y_{AB}$ captures what Bolton and Roland call *political effect,* that is, the difference in desired fiscal policy between the median voter in region A and the median voter in the unified country. Such effect is always positive (unless $y_{AB}^m = y_A^m$): a separation would lead to a policy "closer to the people" (i.e., to the median voter) in region A.

2. The second term $[(y_A - y_{AB})/2 + (y_A^m)^2/2y_A - (y_A^m)^2/2y_{AB}]$ captures the *tax base effect.* It is positive if region A is richer than the unified country ($y_A > y_{AB}$), and negative if region A is poorer than the unified country. In other words, this term captures the intuitive effect that a richer region, all other things being equal, would not benefit from joining a poorer region in a union, while a poorer region would benefit from forming a union with a richer region.

3. The third term is always negative, $-[(1 - s_A)/s_A]k = -(s_B/s_A)k$, since it captures the *economies of scale* associated with forming a union. It is larger, in absolute value, the larger k is, and the larger the other region (region B) is with respect to region A.[14]

An analogous equation holds for region B.

Following Bolton and Roland (1997), the analysis could be extended to study whether, in the face of a possible secession, tax policies in a unified country could be changed to prevent breakup. While the national median voter may sometimes forestall a secession by using a "compensatory fiscal policy," large differences in desired policies in the two regions may prevent the feasibility of such strategy.

In summary, when regions have different income distributions (in particular, their median voters have different incomes) and therefore different preferences over taxation and redistribution policies, a majority of voters in a region may have incentives to form independent political units in order to pursue more preferred fiscal policies. These incentives will be stronger in the relatively rich regions because of the tax-base effect. However, a sufficiently big "political effect" may induce the median voter of a poor region to break with the relatively rich unified country. In general, a breakup will occur unless the incentives to break up (the political effect in all regions, and the tax-base effect in rich regions) are offset by economies of scale. Consequently, within this framework, tax and transfer policies will tend to lead to political fragmentation rather than contribute to political unification.

4.4   Conclusions

Transfer schemes may not be enough to guarantee the stability of an efficient number of countries in a political equilibrium. In general, we can expect compensation schemes to be voted on ex post (i.e., after borders are decided) and to reflect the political equilibrium of the country. Only in the presence of credible commitments can transfers be reasonably promised to minority groups.

There is no guarantee that a political equilibrium will deliver appropriate side payments sufficient to prevent some groups from breaking up an efficient country and forming a different jurisdiction. In cases where a country is less polarized, no compensation will be given in equilibrium, and the analysis of chapter 3 carries through even where linear compensation schemes are available. In cases of high polarization, some compensation is sustainable but may not be appropriate to maintain efficient borders. Compensation schemes become even more complicated if one allows for differences in incomes between individuals and regions. Redistribution then becomes a policy goal besides being compensation for distance from the public good, and this may become an additional force that leads to the break up of countries.

5   Leviathans and the Size of Nations

5.1   Introduction

In the last few decades of the twentieth century there was a sharp increase in the number of independent nations and in the share of democracies. The most striking breakup was, of course, that of the former Soviet Union following the collapse of communism.

One may wonder whether there is something systematic in this trend. Should we always expect that democratization and secessions go hand in hand? In order to answer this question, we need to think more about how borders are determined in a world in which governments may rule against the will of a majority of their subjects (dictators). This is the task that we take on in this chapter.[1]

In this chapter we consider neither ideal social planners who maximize social welfare nor free citizens who can vote over government policies and political borders. By contrast, we assume that decisions are taken by rent-maximizing governments who care about their own welfare, and that of their close associates, rather than the welfare of their citizens. Following a tradition that goes back to Thomas Hobbes (1651), we will call such governments "Leviathans." While Leviathans do not care about their subjects directly, their policies may be indirectly influenced by the well-being of the population.[2] Even a dictator who does not need the support of the majority of the population to stay in power will nonetheless need to provide some minimum level of well-being to at least a fraction of his subjects in order to ensure his political survival.

The basic insight of this chapter is that dictators prefer large empires to small countries. This is because they can extract larger total rents from larger populations. However, dictators themselves have to face a trade-off between size and heterogeneity. As size increases and the population becomes more heterogeneous, dictators may find that thwarting insurrections becomes an increasingly costly affair. This trade-off determines the equilibrium size of empires. Precisely because more heterogeneity makes large empires unstable and costly, the Leviathan may try to reduce heterogeneity by creating, more or less artificially, a sense of "unity." This way some dictators portray themselves as flag-waving nationalists. By promoting patriotism they may succeed at reducing the costs of preventing a large heterogeneous populations from revolt and breakup of the country.

5.2 The Size of Nations in a World of Leviathans

5.2.1 Rent-Maximizing Leviathans

Consider a world run by a rent-maximizing Hobbesian Leviathan whose only objective is to extract as many resources as possible from his subjects in order to enrich his small circle of government. As in Brennan and Buchanan (1980) thus, we posit that this ruler maximizes his wealth, or rent, at the expense of his population. What would be the ideal solution from the point of view of this Leviathan? That is, what would be the configuration of borders that would maximize the Leviathan's net rents?

In the absence of constraints, the Leviathan's rents will be maximized if he controls the entire world, and expropriates all the income of every individual through taxation. In other words, the "first best" from a Leviathan's perspective is a world empire. A Leviathan who does not face constraints of border derivations and/or reasonable taxation levels would supply only the minimum possible amount of the public service and tax at the maximum feasible level. In other words, dictators can extract large rents if they rule a large number of territories and individuals, and provides few public goods.[3]

However, it is unlikely that any government can be completely insensitive to the welfare of its citizens. Even dictators have to guarantee some minimum level of welfare to at least part of the population to stay in power. No dictator has ever managed to conquer and run the entire world precisely because empires that are too big become unmanageable, and various internal or external challenges lead to their collapse.[4]

As empires enlarge, and encompass more distant populations (both geographically and ideologically) avoiding insurrections becomes a tricky problem for the Leviathan. The dictator who wants to maintain the large revenue will need to make costly concessions to these regions, such as reduce taxes or expend more of his intake in revenue on military police.

Let us denote by δ the fraction of the population that a dictator has to maintain above a certain minimum level of welfare to continue his rule. Let us assume, for simplicity, that if a fraction δ of the population is kept above a certain level of welfare an insurrection never occurs and the Leviathan can rule undisturbed.

That is to say, if δ is zero, the Leviathan faces no constraint at all. On the other hand, a δ equal to 1 means that the Leviathan would need to guarantee a certain minimum level of welfare to all his citizens, including the disadvantaged groups. The Leviathan can be defined as a true dictator where δ is much lower than half. That is, the dictator must satisfy a fraction of the population quite smaller than $\frac{1}{2}$. Typically dictators rule with a very narrow elite of privileged groups—think, for instance, of the aristocracy in the *ancient regime*, the high-ranked members of the communist party in the former Soviet bloc, or the friends and family of Saddam Hussein in Iraq.

How do the borders in a world of Leviathans depend on δ? As we show in the formal section, the number of countries in a world of Leviathans is *increasing* in δ. The larger the fraction of population that has to be relatively "pleased" by the Leviathans, the larger is the number of countries in a world of Leviathans. The intuition for this result goes as follows: for small $\delta's$, Leviathans have few constraints and do not care much about individuals' (heterogeneous) preferences. By ignoring heterogeneity costs, rulers can take full advantage of economies of scale. In other words, Leviathans would want to rule over large countries. In a low-δ equilibrium Leviathans will choose to rule large countries, regardless of whether some citizens will be thus very far from the public good and obtain very low utility.[5] But what if δ were to increase? An increase in the share of population that the dictator has to satisfy to prevent insurrections makes heterogeneity costs more important compared to economies of scale: a larger δ implies that the preferences of a larger number of individuals have to be taken into account by a rent-maximizing Leviathan. Hence Leviathans will obtain less gain in ruling large populations, and may allow far away regions to break up rather than confront an insurrection and/or reduce those chances through costly concessions, such as lower taxes.[6]

The point is that in a world of Leviathans, for δ less than $\frac{1}{2}$, which is when dictators can "ignore" the welfare of more than half of the population of their state, *the number of countries is lower than the efficient number*. A fortiori, the size of countries with dictators is larger than in the "democratic" equilibrium. The intuition is clear: when unconstrained by people's preferences, Leviathans prefer large countries because they can expropriate more citizens, providing fewer public goods per capita. On the other hand, when δ is higher than $\frac{1}{2}$, "democratic" Leviathans will rule countries that are smaller than the efficient number. Interestingly, when $\delta = 1$ (i.e., Leviathans must take into account everyone's preferences), the borders under Leviathans will coincide with the borders that would have been chosen in free referenda, as defined in chapter 3. In summary, dictatorships are associated with inefficiently large countries, while democratization leads to breakups of empires and secessions.

Leviathans may try to influence (and repress) individual behavior. For instance, they typically try to reduce heterogeneity and make their population more "homogeneous" by means of public education, propaganda, repression of minority languages, religions, or cultures. Historical examples abound, from the Franco dictatorship in Spain, which repressed regional movements; to the Soviet communist party, to repression of other religions and ethnic groups in Taliban Afghanistan. Moreover, by spending on domestic military repression, a Leviathan could reduce δ, but a trade-off still remains because the Leviathan would have to use a portion of his rents to reduce δ. An alternative strategy for Leviathans might be to decentralize power; this, however, may run counter to the very nature of a dictatorial government. Interestingly, Ades and Glaeser (1995) find that nondemocratic countries tend to have larger capital/main cities, a symptom of centralization of power, an issue to which we return in chapter 9.

When the "no insurrection constraint" becomes more binding, that is, with an increasing δ, the Leviathan has a greater incentive to spend money on activities that increase homogeneity. A threatened Leviathan may have to engage in more or less peaceful activities to include all of the minorities. In fact an increase in δ may be the beginning of the end for dictators, for they have to devote resources to satisfy their more rebellious populations.

In this chapter we treat δ as a parameter. However, our analysis could be extended to allow for an "endogenous" determination of δ as a function of a full-fledged theory of insurrections. For example, Acemoglu and Robinson (2000) interpret the extension of voting rights to larger and larger fractions of the population as consequence of a problem of insurrections for absolute monarchs in the nineteenth century. Note that an extension of voting rights can be interpreted as an increase in the fraction of the population that the ruler will have to satisfy in order to remain in office. In fact, as the fraction of the population with a political voice increases, the more political weight their demand will have. One could think of a dynamic version of the size/heterogeneity trade-off—in which δ changes along with size—as underlying the history of collapse of large dictatorial empires: as δ becomes larger, the sustainable size of empires declines.

In summary, this chapter's main message is that in moving from a world of Hobbesian dictators to a world of democracies, the average size of countries should shrink.

5.2.2   How Did Leviathans Become Big?

Competing Leviathans may try to increase their territories and populations at the expense of one another. So how does one reach an equilibrium whereby these Leviathans' rents are maximized in a bellicose world? In an original analysis David Friedman (1977) argued that Leviathans will prevail that have more to gain in conquering territories and people and have better technologies to do so, and the world, in the end, would be allocated "efficiently" to these Leviathans. Note that the efficiency criterion relevant here is the maximization of wealth of the rulers, subject to the no insurrection constraint discussed above.

The process that leads to the rent-maximizing distribution of territories among Leviathans may be exceedingly complex. It is, of course, influenced by a host of other factors, special shocks and human personalities. A key element is the economies of scale in war technology, an issue that we explore in chapter 11. In the feudal period from the so-called dark ages to about the fifteenth century, it was relatively easy for lords to establish control over relatively small territories and extract rents from the small population. The war technology of the time, with relatively small economies of scale and fixed costs, allowed for relatively free entry of new lords. As in the theory of firm location in industrial organization, competition among lords reduced their per capita rents, and led to a large number of lords, each partially controlling small populations.

As the technology of war evolved and economics of scale and fixed costs became more relevant, more powerful lords consolidated their holdings, smaller lords lost out, and entry became much more difficult. The most powerful lord of all, the king, finally established a monopoly of power internally and engaged in conflicts with other kings. The analogy of industrial organization is again useful: as fixed costs and economies of scale prevented entry, the kings established a monopoly of coercion, and their rents substantially increased since they controlled large territories, the same way in which a monopolist controls a large fraction of a market, or even an entire market. The equilibrium informally proposed by Friedman (1977) and formally studied in this chapter may be interpreted as one in which the kings have directed the "market" for territories and rents in the way that maximizes their joint profits (i.e., rents).

*5.3   The Size of Nations in a World of Leviathans: A Formal Analysis

5.3.1   The Basic Model

Consider the model of chapter 3. Recall that individuals are uniformly distributed over the segment [0, 1], and have utility u_i equal to

$$u_i = g - al_i + y_i - t_i, \tag{5.1}$$

where l_i is the individual's distance from his government, t_i denotes his taxes, y_i is his income, and g and a are positive preference parameters.

Now we assume that borders are determined in order to maximize governments' joint net revenues. This is the cooperative solution that would be adopted by a class of Leviathans (a group of individuals who can become country rulers) if they could transact at no costs and use unrestricted side payments.

Friedman (1977) argues that this is a reasonable assumption to predict long-run equilibrium borders in a world of rent-maximizing governments. Although explicit cooperative behavior by rulers may be rare (and mainly limited to those areas of the world run by related aristocracies or homogeneous nomenclatures), one could expect that even noncooperative behavior would, under appropriate assumptions, lead to such a solution. The idea is that—through peaceful bargaining, war, dynastic alliances, and the like—each portion of land and population will be allocated to the Leviathan who values it more. This is the Leviathan who is able to obtain the highest net revenues from the acquisition. Consequently the drawing of borders will be consistent with the maximization of the Leviathan's joint net revenues. This is a stylized assumption, but the basic message of this chapter does not hinge on it. It is the simplest possible way of capturing the rather general implications of the model. In chapters 7 and 8 we discuss issues of noncooperative behavior in conflict resolutions, including wars.

As in chapter 3 we assume that each individual pays the same tax t. That is, Leviathans are unable to tax individuals as a function of their preferences over the type of government.[7] Therefore governments' joint revenues R are given by

$$R \equiv \int_0^1 t_i - kN = t - kN. \tag{5.2}$$

We assume that each Leviathan must guarantee at least a utility level of u_0 to a fraction δ of his citizens. Therefore a Leviathan who rules a country of size $s = 1/N$ faces the following constraint:

$$g - \frac{a\delta s}{2} + y - t \geq u_0. \tag{5.3}$$

This means that the utility of an individual at a distance equal to $\delta s/2$ from the government must be at least as high as u_0. Clearly, if constraint (5.3) is satisfied, at least δs individuals will have utility larger or equal to u_0, and the Leviathan's "no insurrection" constraint is satisfied. Also the government must be located at a distance not larger than $\delta s/2$ from each border. This condition is easily satisfied for every $\delta \leq 1$ if the Leviathan locates the government in the middle of the country.

Clearly, the Leviathan will not choose to increase welfare of its citizens above the minimum level that satisfies the noinsurrection constraint. Any additional welfare would come at the expense of the Leviathan's rents. Thus equation (5.3) will hold with equality. Substituting this equation into (5.2), we obtain

$$R = g - \frac{a\delta}{2N} + y - u_0 - Nk, \tag{5.4}$$

which is maximized at[8]

$$N_\delta = \sqrt{\frac{a\delta}{2k}}. \tag{5.5}$$

Taxes are given by

$$t_\delta = g - \frac{a\delta}{2N_\delta} + y - u_0. \tag{5.6}$$

Several observations are in order.

1. The minimum level of utility u_0 affects equilibrium taxation but not the equilibrium number of countries.

2. The equilibrium number of countries in a world of Leviathans depends on the by now familiar trade-off between heterogeneity costs (measured by the parameter a) and economies of scale (measured by the parameter k): N_δ is increasing in a and decreasing in k.

3. The number of countries in a world of Leviathan is increasing in δ. A larger δ implies a larger number of countries the larger is a and the smaller is k. In other words, a more extensive noinsurrection constraint brings about more countries, and the effect is larger when heterogeneity costs are higher and/or economies of scale are smaller.

4. When we compare N_δ with the efficient number of countries N^* and with the equilibrium number of countries in a voting equilibrium $\widetilde{N}$, we obtain

if $\delta < \frac{1}{2}$, $N_\delta < N^*$.

if $\delta = \frac{1}{2}$, $N_\delta = N^*$.

if $\frac{1}{2} < \delta < 1$, $N^* < N_\delta < \widetilde{N}$.

if $\delta = 1$, $N_\delta = \widetilde{N}$.

Note in the results above that for any value of δ strictly less than one, there are fewer countries with rent-maximizing Leviathans than in a democratic world. When Leviathans are dictatorial, meaning they can rule without the consent of a majority ($\delta < \frac{1}{2}$), the number of countries with Leviathans is below the efficient number. The implication is that in a world of dictatorial Leviathans there are too few countries; that is, the countries are inefficiently large.

Therefore, if we think of "democratization" as a process that brings the number of countries from N_δ with $\delta < \frac{1}{2}$ to a number $\widetilde{N}$, we formally obtain the most important implication of this chapter, namely that *democratization leads to an increase in the number of countries.*

5.3.2   Endogenous Heterogeneity

Suppose now that the Leviathan can invest resources in reducing the heterogeneity of preferences. Here we want to think of "distance" in the ideological dimension. One could also think of distance as in a geographical sense, in which case the Leviathan's investment could be interpreted as an investment in transportation to better link the middle of the country to the periphery. Formally, this means investing resources in reducing a, which is the parameter that measures heterogeneity in preferences. Suppose that the heterogeneity parameter a in a population is given by the following function:

$$a = a(m),$$ (5.7)

where m is the Leviathan's public spending in "heterogeneity-reducing" activities (educational programs, national schooling system, repression of minority languages and cultures, political propaganda and indoctrination, etc.). Henceforth $a(m)$ is decreasing in m:

$$a'(m) < 0.$$ (5.8)

We can also reasonably assume that heterogeneity-reducing activities have nonincreasing returns—namely each additional unit of resources spent on heterogeneity reduction has a smaller impact on the level of heterogeneity. This is consistent with the idea that the Leviathan will first reduce the "easier" forms of heterogeneity, and then move to the more ingrained differences of preferences among his subjects. Formally, $a(m)$ is a convex function:

$$a''(m) \geq 0.$$ (5.9)

The Leviathan faces a new budget constraint in which fiscal revenues have to be devoted to supply the public good and finance m. For simplicity, and without much loss of generality, we will assume the following specification:[9]

$$a(m) = a_0 + \frac{a_1}{m}.$$ (5.10)

Therefore, by making the appropriate changes in equation (5.4), we obtain

$$R = g - \frac{a_0\delta}{2N} - \frac{a_1\delta}{2mN} + y - u_0 - m - Nk.$$ (5.11)

From (5.11) we have the following first-order conditions for N and m:

$$\frac{\partial R}{\partial N} = \frac{a_0\delta}{2N_\delta^2} + \frac{a_1\delta}{2m_\delta N_\delta^2} - k = 0,$$ (5.12)

$$\frac{\partial R}{\partial m} = \frac{a_1\delta}{2m_\delta^2 N_\delta} - 1 = 0.$$ (5.13)

These formulas characterize a unique equilibrium number of countries N_δ and an equilibrium level of investment in heterogeneity-reducing activities m_δ. The comparative statics associated with a higher level of the democratic constraint δ are given by the derivatives[10]

$$\frac{dN_\delta}{d\delta} = \frac{\delta}{N} \frac{2a_0 m + a_1}{4a_0 m + 3a_1} > 0, \tag{5.14}$$

$$\frac{dm}{d\delta} = \frac{m_\delta}{\delta} \frac{2a_0 m + 2a_1}{4a_0 m + 3a_1} > 0. \tag{5.15}$$

These expressions show that a stricter "no insurrection" constraint leads to (1) smaller countries and (2) larger spending in heterogeneity-reducing activities by rent-maximizing governments.

In other words, as the constraint includes increasing fractions of the population, we should expect two consequences: Leviathans will have to reduce the size of the countries, as predicted in the previous section, and they will attempt to reduce heterogeneity costs by investing more heavily in those activities that can induce homogeneous preferences within their borders. The reasoning is simple: to a rent-maximizing Leviathan heterogeneity is more costly in countries in which a large fraction of the population must be satisfied. Therefore a higher δ increases the incentives to reduce heterogeneity, if possible, in each country. By contrast, a fully autocratic Leviathan who is oblivious to his subjects' preferences can survive within a large heterogeneous population and not waste resources on reducing his subjects' heterogeneity.

This finding shed insights into some actual historical developments. For example, a traditionally autocratic empire such as the Ottoman empire could tolerate widely ranging heterogenous and multicultural minorities, while the process of democratization in the nineteenth and twentieth century was often accompanied by attempts at nation-building and cultural homogenization by (relatively smaller) central governments.

5.4   Conclusion

In a world of dictators we should observe larger countries than in a democratic world. Unconstrained Leviathans take maximum advantage of economies of scale by spreading small amounts of public goods over large populations, which pay high taxes. As the threat of insurrection increases, the Leviathans may choose to engage in propaganda and other activities to reduce discontent and heterogeneity among the population. But the main long-term effect stemming from democratization should be a breakup of existing empires and the formation of smaller countries.

The democratization result is important since, historically, the formation of existing countries has been determined largely in a nondemocratic world. As the world becomes more democratic, we should observe secessions, or, at least, increasing pressure for decentralization and local autonomy.

6

Openness, Economic Integration, and the Size of Nations

6.1 Introduction

The five largest countries (by population) in the world are China, India, the United States, Indonesia, and Brazil. Among them, only the United States is a rich country. By contrast, many of the richest countries in the world are small. Of the ten richest countries in the world, in terms of GDP per capita, only four have populations above one million. They are the United States (260 million people), Switzerland (7 million), Norway (4 million people), and Singapore (3 million people). Of these four, two are below average in terms of population. Singapore experienced the second highest growth rate in the world between 1960 and 1990: 6.3 percent per year. During that same period, the fastest growing economies outside East Asia were Botswana (1 million people), with a growth rate of 5.7 percent per year, and Malta (300,000 inhabitants), which, with 5.4 percent, had the highest growth rate in Europe. Size and prosperity do not seem to go hand in hand. More generally, when and how does the size of a country matter for the economic prosperity of its inhabitants? Are small countries economically "viable"? What does the relationship between size and prosperity imply for the equilibrium number and size of countries?

In the previous chapters we maintained the simplifying assumption that income per person in a country does not depend on the country's size. In this chapter we extend our analysis and explore the links of country size, production, and economic growth. The main point of this chapter is that *whether country size matters for economic prosperity depends on a country's degree of economic integration with the rest of the world.*

We emphasize a distinction between the political size of a country and the size of its market. How much these two concepts coincide is a function of the degree of openness of international markets. In a world of complete autarky the two concepts of size coincide. In a world of complete economic integration across borders the two are entirely independent. Thus the "economically viable" size of countries depends on the trade regime. While small countries may not be viable in a world of trade barriers, they may be prosperous in a world of free trade and global markets.

This implies that the trade-off between size and heterogeneity is influenced by the trade regime. As the trade regime becomes more open, it is more viable for relatively small regions or groups to seek independence. On the other hand, since small countries have more to gain from free trade and openness, general support for free trade is higher in a world of small countries. Henceforth one should expect economic integration and political disintegration to go hand in hand, in a mutually reinforcing process.

6.2 Political Size and Market Size

Does a large market size matter for economic success? Because of specialization, externalities, and other mechanisms, interaction among a large number of individuals may increase productivity.[1] These mechanisms have been extensively studied in the literature on the determinants of income per capita and growth. For example, Romer (1986), Lucas (1988), and Grossman and Helpman (1991) pioneered models of growth in which a larger economic size may, in principle, increase productivity. The extent of the market also plays a key role for models of industrialization, as in Murphy, Shleifer, and Vishny (1989). In such models a certain size of the market (defined by the size of demand) is necessary for entrepreneurs and investors to step in, overcome fixed costs, and spur development.[2]

A country's market size coincides with its domestic size only if the country's economy is perfectly integrated domestically but completely closed to the rest of the world. In other words, the size of the market in each country coincides with its political size only in a world of complete autarky, that is, in a world without any economic relationships among the countries. It follows that only in an autarkic world a country that is small has a small market and thus low demand for output and low production. Note that from the point of view of market size, what matters may not be total population but total income.

In an economically integrated world, on the other hand, the market size of a country is larger, and even much larger, than its political size.

In the extreme case where borders are totally irrelevant for economic interactions, the market size of each country is the world. In a world of free trade, political borders are economically irrelevant. As Keynes (1920, p. 99) put it: "In a regime of Free Trade and free economic intercourse it would be of little consequence that iron lay on one side of a political frontier, and labor, coal, and blast furnaces on the other. But as it is, men have devised ways to impoverish themselves and one another; and prefer collective animosities to individual happiness." In other words, political size and political borders play an economic role insofar as they are associated to barriers to trade and obstacles to economic exchanges. In summary, at one extreme (autarky), market size and political size coincides, while at the other extreme (perfect free trade) political size does not affect market size, which is given by the whole world. In general, a country's market will be given by its domestic market and *part* of the world market, depending on the country's degree of international openness. If there are economies of scale to the size of the market, larger countries can be expected to do better economically than smaller countries (all other things being equal) when international openness is low, but political size should become less relevant as economic integration increases. Thus the "viable" size of country decreases with international openness.

Perfect economic integration among countries is rarely observed in the real world. Borders do matter even when trade is free from formal protectionist policies and financial market are liberalized. A vast empirical literature has documented this point. McCallum (1995) looked at trade across the notoriously open US–Canadian border, using a gravity model of trade that relates trade flows to distance between countries,[3] and found that trade between Canadian provinces is much larger than trade between Canadian proxies and the United States. More recent work by Anderson and van Wincoop (2001) showed that the border effect is smaller than the one suggested by McCallum's results but still significant: these authors found that borders reduce trade among industrialized countries by about 30 percent. Portes and Rey (2000) consider the effects of borders in financial markets, and attribute the size of these effects to information costs.[4] In general, the evidence shows that the economic costs of crossing borders decrease as trade restrictions and capital controls are removed, but they do not go to zero, even with borders free from policy-induced transaction costs.

Since the economic costs of being small fall as economic integration increases, one should observe that ethnic minorities and border regions of larger countries may prefer to split away as international openness and economic integration increase. While in a world of closed economies the economic benefits of size may keep certain regions together, international openness reduces the benefits of political size. This may rise the demand for political autonomy. In a nutshell, economic integration should go hand and hand with political disintegration.

It is not coincidental that the existence of NAFTA has made Quebec separatism more viable and less costly. Regionalism in Europe appears to be fostered by the European common market, an issue that we will revisit in chapter 12.

Whereas economic integration may lead to separatism and smaller countries, small countries should be particularly keen on maintaining free trade and open financial markets. The process is thus self-sustaining: more economic integration favors the creation of smaller countries, and small countries aim to support integration, and the two effects reinforce each other. In fact we can think of two configurations of trade and size of countries. One is characterized by large and closed economies that have relatively little interest in promoting trade liberalization. The other consists of small countries and trade liberalization.

Recall that in chapter 5 we argued that in a world of dictators, countries are inefficiently large. Combining the argument of chapter 5 and of the current chapter, we should conclude that dictators ruling large countries should not be particularly interested in promoting free trade. It follows that both democratization and opening of international markets should accompany political separatism and the breakup of large countries. In particular, to the extent to which free trade makes it more appealing and feasible for small regions to be independent, it makes it harder for dictators to hold together large and heterogeneous states. The last few decades have witnessed a vast process of democratization, breaking up of countries, and deepening economic integration. By our analysis, we should not be surprised that these three phenomena go hand in hand. We return to this empirical discussion in chapters 11 and 12.

Our emphasis on the relationship between economic integration and political disintegration is in contrast to "functionalist" theories in international relations, which stress the complementarity between political and economic integration. According to classic functionalism, an increase in economic integration would lead to political integration at both the regional and global levels. For example, Mitrany (1966) argued that in an economically integrated world countries would need to delegate more tasks to international institutions, and form large and increasingly centralized political unions. Along the same lines, Haas (1958a, b, 1964) argued that increasing economic integration would lead to more extensive and centralized governing mechanisms and deeper political integration.[5] These views were based on the idea that international economic integration would give a larger role to central governments and foster political cooperation, while they underplayed heterogeneity costs and conflicts of interest across different communities.

We are not denying that integrated economies need supranational institutions that ensure the proper functioning and openness of markets. However, political centralization or close policy coordination of government functions are not necessary preconditions for the functioning of the international economy. The view that the operation of markets needs a heavy machinery of domestic supervision and international policy coordination is largely misplaced. Our emphasis here is that free trade and open capital markets allow small countries to prosper. We will return to these issues in chapter 12.

*6.3 A Simple Model of Country Size and Economic Integration

6.3.1 The Basic Structure
So far we have modeled income as exogenous. In this section we treat income as a function of human capital. Human capital, in turn, will depend on the size of the country and its contact with the outside world.

Define H_j as the aggregate human capital in country j, and y_j as output per capita in country j, where $j = 1, 2, \ldots, N$. Suppose that output per capita is given by the production function

$$y_j = A_j f(x_j), \tag{6.1}$$

where $f(.)$ is a function of a several inputs measured in per capita terms, and A_j is total factor productivity. We assume that the latter will depend on the total level of "knowledge" in the economy. This is just one possible formalization of the idea that size matters. In this discussion "size" has to do with the pool of ideas and total accumulated education or knowledge available in an economy.

Let us take an extreme where each domestic economy is completely insulated from the rest of the world. In this world, total factor productivity depends only on the domestic level of human capital. A simple specification for a world of autarchy is

$$A_j = H_j. \tag{6.2}$$

By contrast, in a world of complete economic integration and international openness, everyone can learn from everyone else, independently of political borders. In a world of perfect economic integration, we have that for every country j,

$$A_j = \sum_{m=1}^{N} H_m;$$ (6.3)

that is, every country can benefit from the productivity of human capital throughout the world. In this world there are also no barriers to the international transmission of knowledge.[6]

For simplicity, let us assume that the degree of openness in the world is uniform across countries. That is, every country j shows the same degree of openness with respect to every other country.[7] Let ω measure this degree of openness such that the following holds:

$$A_j = H_j + \omega \sum_{m=1;m\neq j}^{N} H_m,$$ (6.4)

where $0 \leq \omega \leq 1$. When $\omega = 0$ (no openness), we are back to autarky where only domestic human capital matters. When $\omega = 1$, we are in a fully integrated world where each country's productivity depends only on the world stock of human capital. Values of ω between 0 and 1 capture the more realistic intermediate situations.

6.3.2   Economic Integration and the Number of Countries

Let us return to the model of chapter 3, with the difference that now income per capita in each country is given by the production function described above. For simplicity, we can assume that every individual in this world is endowed with the same vector of inputs x and, in particular, with the same amount of human capital h. For notational simplicity, we normalize $f(x) = 1$. Then we have that individuals living in a country j of size s_j have incomes equal to

$$y_j = s_j h + \omega(1 - s_j)h = h\omega + hs_j - h\omega s_j.$$ (6.5)

Equation (6.5) shows how in a politically divided world ($s_j < 1$) without an integrated economy ($\omega < 1$), we could have that for each country income per capita is increasing both in openness and in country size, but that the benefits from country size are smaller the larger the degree of international openness, and, conversely that

the benefits from openness are smaller the larger the size of the country.

The fact that benefits of political size decrease with international openness has important implications for the determination of the equilibrium number and size of countries.

We are now ready to consider country formation. For the reasons discussed in chapters 3 and 4 we will confine ourselves to countries of equal size and identical taxes for everyone. Then utility can be written as

$$u_i = g - a l_i + h\omega + h(1 - \omega)s - \frac{k}{s}. \tag{6.6}$$

Following the steps of chapter 3, we can derive the efficient number of countries and the equilibrium number in the presence of imperfect economic integration. The number of equally sized countries that maximizes average utility is[8]

$$N^* = \sqrt{\frac{a - 4(1 - \omega)h}{4k}}. \tag{6.7}$$

For the same reasons given in chapter 3, the efficient number of countries N^* may not be an equilibrium outcome when secessions and voting on borders are allowed. From the proof in the appendix to chapter 3, we can establish that the equilibrium number of countries $\widetilde{N}$ is[9]

$$\widetilde{N} = \sqrt{\frac{a - 2(1 - \omega)h}{2k}}. \tag{6.8}$$

As in our basic model of chapter 3, the equilibrium number of countries $\widetilde{N}$ is larger than the efficient number of countries. The new result here is that both N^* and $\widetilde{N}$ are increasing in the degree of openness, ω.

The intuition is that a breakup of countries is more costly if it implies smaller economies. However, the benefits of remaining large are fewer if small countries can freely trade and economically interact. This result suggests that economic integration is associated with regional political separatism. In other words, an increase in openness and economic integration influences the trade-off between heterogeneity and scale.

Now, extending the analysis developed in chapter 5, we can derive the number of countries in a world of Leviathans:

$$N_\delta = \sqrt{\frac{a\delta - 2(1 - \omega)h}{2k}}.$$ (6.9)

Again, we see that the number of nations is increasing in the degree of openness ω: with more openness, all other things being equal, we have more small countries. As in chapter 5, we have that in a nondemocratic world (i.e., when $\delta < \frac{1}{2}$) the number of countries is "too small," meaning that the countries are "too large" from an efficiency perspective.

6.3.3   Economic Integration and Welfare

In our model, more openness (i.e., a higher ω) always increases total factor productivity and income per capita if borders remain unchanged. However, when the number and size of countries may change as a consequence of higher economic integration, "perverse" effects may occur. First, consider the equilibrium income per capita

$$y = h\omega + h(1 - \omega)\bar{s}(\omega),$$ (6.10)

where $\bar{s}(\omega) = 1/\widetilde{N}$. Taking the derivative of output with respect to openness, we get:

$$\frac{dy}{d\omega} = h(1 - \bar{s}) + h(1 - \omega)\frac{d\bar{s}}{d\omega}.$$ (6.11)

The first term in the equation, $h(1 - \bar{s})$, is always positive, and captures the effect of increasing openness for given political borders. The second term is negative because more openness reduces the equilibrium size of countries.

If we consider the fact that the number of countries must be an integer, and treat $\bar{s}$ as a continuous variable, we have that the derivative $dy/d\omega$ is positive if and only if the equilibrium country size is below a critical value that depends on a, h, and ω (but not on k), that is,

$$\frac{dy}{d\omega} > 0 \quad \text{if and only if} \quad \bar{s} < \frac{a - 2(1 - \omega)h}{a - (1 - \omega)h}.$$ (6.12)

The intuition of this result is as follows: An increase in international openness increases income per capita in a world of smaller countries but may reduce income per capita in a world of large countries. When there are already many small countries, openness brings about large gains to

every country (the gains are larger for smaller countries), which makes
the costs incurred in the creation of new countries relatively small. By
contrast, in a world of a few large countries, more openness brings fewer
gains, and following any breakups of the large countries, substantial
additional costs that offset the (small) gains from openness. Even if
openness brings about higher productivity and higher income, when
borders are endogenous the effect on income will be smaller than it
would have been in the case of fixed, exogenous borders. In this respect,
the fact that increasing economic integration may bring about more
political disintegration tends also to reduce the economic benefits of
openness.

In this model income is not the same as welfare. Individual utility
depends not only on pre-tax income but also on the costs and benefits of
public goods provided by the government. A higher income is neither
necessary nor sufficient for a higher average utility. In fact it is possible
that increasing openness, by reducing the size of countries, brings about
a decrease in average utility even if average income increases. Economic
integration makes countries smaller. When countries are already very
small, the average welfare loss due to the shrinking size can outweigh the
income effects due to higher economic integration. This is an application
of the second-best principle.

Formally, a change from some ω to a higher ω' (greater economic
integration) that increases the equilibrium number of nations from $\tilde{N}$ to
a larger $\tilde{N}'$ will cause the following change in average utility:

$$u' - u = \frac{a}{4}(\tilde{s} - \tilde{s}') + (y' - y) - k(\tilde{N}' - \tilde{N}). \qquad (6.13)$$

The first term, $a\,(\tilde{s} - \tilde{s}')/4$, measures the reduction in the average distance
from the government due to the smaller country size. The second term,
$y' - y$, measures the change in income, and the third term, $-k(\tilde{N}' - \tilde{N})$,
measures the increase in taxation.

The income change $y' - y$ is given by two terms:

$$y' - y = (\omega' - \omega)(1 - \tilde{s}')h - (\tilde{s} - \tilde{s}')(1 - \omega)h. \qquad (6.14)$$

The first term, $(\omega' - \omega)(1 - \tilde{s}')h$, measure the direct effect of more openness: the effect of foreign human capital, $(1 - \tilde{s}')h$, is now bigger because
of the increase in openness. The second term, $(\tilde{s} - \tilde{s}')(1 - \omega)h$, measures
the reduction in productivity due to the fact that domestic human capital
is now smaller in each country.

These analytical results raise two sets of issues:

1. How likely is it that in practice an increase in openness may reduce welfare because of increasing political disintegration?

2. What are the policy implications of this result? Should one oppose increasing economic integration if political disintegration should follow?

On the first issue, the point is that breakup is more likely to decrease welfare in a configuration of borders where the countries are already inefficiently small. That is the equilibrium outcome in the absence of transfer schemes, and when borders are decided by voting. Historically borders have been determined nondemocratically. In that case, as we saw earlier, countries can be too large. When countries are too large, an increase in openness, by reducing the size of countries, unambiguously increases welfare. Therefore, in the past, in a world of Leviathans openness was likely to increase welfare even more insofar as it did result in breakups of countries.

To the extent that democratization and trade liberalization are related phenomena, they both should lead to the breakup of countries and to increases in welfare. In a democratic world, if the initial configuration of countries has been inherited from a past of empires and dictatorships, chances are that economic integration and (peaceful) political disintegration, up to a point, would jointly increase welfare. After that point, if the process of secessions continues, the political fragmentation would offset the gains from more openness. In such a case the policy implication is not to slow down economic integration, since the welfare loss stems from inefficient political borders and not from excessive economic integration. The first-best response to such inefficiency is to design appropriate mechanisms (transfers and other compensation mechanisms) that can prevent harmful secessions without compromising the freedom of economic exchanges.

*6.4   Size of Countries, Trade, and Growth

In the simple model of the previous section we built on the idea of productivity spillovers; we did not model trade explicitly. In this section we present a model that explicitly allows for trade both within and among countries.[10] The model developed in this section provides the microfoundations for the benefits of size. The model is explicitly dynamic, and it will provide a useful framework for our empirical work on the relationship of country size to openness and economic growth in chapter 10.

6.4.1 Trade and Production

Again, individuals are located on a continuum $[0, 1]$, and the population of the world is normalized to 1. Let us assume that each individual living at location i obtains utility from consumption according to the following function:

$$\int_0^\infty \ln C_i(t)e^{-\rho t}\, dt, \tag{6.15}$$

where $C_i(t)$ denotes consumption at time t, and $\rho > 0$.[11] At time t total capital and labor at location i are denoted, respectively, by $K_i(t)$ and $L_i(t)$. Both inputs are supplied inelastically and are not mobile. At each location i a specific intermediate input $X_i(t)$ is produced using the location-specific capital according to the linear production function $X_i(t) = K_i(t)$.

There exists a unique final good $Y(t)$. Each region i produces $Y_i(t)$ units of the final good, according to the production function

$$Y_i(t) = \left(\int_0^1 X_{ij}^\alpha(t)\, dj\right) L_i^{1-\alpha}(t) \tag{6.16}$$

with $0 < \alpha < 1$. $X_{ij}(t)$ denotes the amount of intermediate input j used in location i at time t.

Intermediate inputs can be traded across locations that belong to the same country at no cost (i.e., we assume no internal barriers to trade). By contrast, if one unit of an intermediate good i' is shipped to a location i'' that belongs to a different country, only $(1 - \beta)$ units of the intermediate good will arrive, where $0 \le \beta \le 1$.

Let $D_i(t)$ denote the units of an intermediate input i used domestically (i.e., either at location i or at another location that belongs to the same country as location i). Let $F_i(t)$ denote the units of input i shipped to a location that does not belong to the same country as location i. By assumption, only $(1 - \beta)F_i(t)$ units will be used for production. In equilibrium, as the markets are perfectly competitive, each unit of input i will be sold at a price equal to its marginal product both domestically and internationally. Therefore

$$P_i(t) = \alpha D_i^{\alpha-1}(t) = \alpha(1 - \beta)^\alpha F_i^{\alpha-1}(t), \tag{6.17}$$

where $P_i(t)$ is the market price of input i at time t. At each time t the resource constraint for each input i is

$$s_i D_i(t) + (W - s_i)F_i(t) = K_i(t), \tag{6.18}$$

where s_i is the size of the country to which location i belongs.

We define

$$\omega \equiv (1 - \beta)^{\alpha/(1-\alpha)}. \tag{6.19}$$

This means that the lower the barriers to international trade are, the higher is ω. Hence ω can be interpreted as a measure of "international openness." Again, as in the previous section, $\omega = 0$ (i.e., $\beta = 1$) means complete autarky, while $\omega = 1$ (i.e., no barriers to international trade: $\beta = 0$) means complete openness.

The equations above imply that

$$D_i(t) = \frac{K_i(t)}{(1 - \omega)s_i + \omega} \tag{6.20}$$

and

$$F_i(t) = \frac{\omega K_i(t)}{(1 - \omega)s_i + \omega}. \tag{6.21}$$

Households' net assets in region i are identical to the stock of region-specific capital $K_i(t)$. Since each unit of capital yields one unit of intermediate input i, the net return to capital is equal to the market price of intermediate input P_{it} (for simplicity, we assume no depreciation). From standard intertemporal optimization we have[12]

$$\frac{dC_{it}}{dt} \frac{1}{C_{it}} = P_i(t) - \rho = \alpha[(1 - \omega)s_i + \omega]^{1-\alpha} K_i^{\alpha-1}(t) - \rho. \tag{6.22}$$

Hence the steady-state level of capital at each location of a country of size s_i will be

$$K_i^{ss} = \left(\frac{\alpha}{\rho}\right)^{\alpha/(1-\alpha)} [(1 - \omega)s_i + \omega]. \tag{6.23}$$

The steady-state level of output in each unit of a country of size s_i is given by

$$Y_i^{ss} = s_i \left(D_i^{ss}\right)^\alpha + \sum_{j \neq i} s_j(1 - \beta)^\alpha \left(F_j^{ss}\right)^\alpha. \tag{6.24}$$

By substituting D_i^{ss} and F_j^{ss}'s with their expressions from the equations above, we can obtain the following

PROPOSITION 6.1   The steady-state level of output per capita is

$$Y_i^{ss} = \left(\frac{\alpha}{\rho}\right)^{\alpha/(1-\alpha)} [(1-\omega)s_i + \omega]. \tag{6.25}$$

Hence output in the steady state is increasing in ω and in s_i. The effect of s_i is smaller for the larger ω.

In steady state the growth rate of output can be approximated by

$$\frac{dY}{dt}\frac{1}{Y} = \xi e^{-\xi}(\ln Y^{ss} - \ln Y(0)), \tag{6.26}$$

where

$$\xi \equiv \frac{\rho}{2}\left[\left(1 + \frac{4(1-\alpha)}{\alpha}\right)^{1/2} - 1\right]$$

and $Y(0)$ is initial income.[13] Hence we will also have

PROPOSITION 6.2   The growth rate of income per capita around the steady state is increasing in size, increasing in openness, and decreasing in size times openness.

These results show how the economic benefits from size are decreasing in openness and the economic benefits from openness are decreasing in size. These are precisely the empirical implications of the model that we test in chapter 10.

6.4.2   Equilibrium Number and Size of Nations

We can now use the model to derive the equilibrium number and size of countries. To simplify the analysis, we will focus on steady-state utility. Again, following the analysis of chapter 3, we focus on countries of equal size and taxes identical across individuals. Hence the relevant steady-state utility for an individual living at location i is

$$u_i = g - al_i + \left(\frac{\alpha}{\rho}\right)^{\alpha/(1-\alpha)} [(1-\omega)s + \omega] - \frac{k}{s}. \tag{6.27}$$

Equation (6.27) is formally identical to equation (6.6) if we substitute h with $(\frac{\alpha}{\rho})^{\alpha/(1-\alpha)}$. Hence all results about the number and size of countries that we derived in the previous section extend to this model.

In particular, we have

$$N^* = \sqrt{\frac{a - 4(1 - \omega)(\alpha/\rho)^{\alpha/(1-\alpha)}}{4k}}, \tag{6.28}$$

$$\widetilde{N} = \sqrt{\frac{a - 2(1 - \omega)(\alpha/\rho)^{\alpha/(1-\alpha)}}{2k}}, \tag{6.29}$$

$$N_\delta = \sqrt{\frac{a\delta - 2(1 - \omega)(\alpha/\rho)^{\alpha/(1-\alpha)}}{2k}}. \tag{6.30}$$

Hence, again, we have that the efficient number of countries, the number of countries in a voting equilibrium, and the number of countries in a world of Leviathans are all increasing in international openness ω.

6.5   Conclusion

This chapter established two important results. First, we discussed the relationship of country size, openness, and income per capita. We provided a model in which the benefits of country size decrease as international economic integration increases. Conversely, the benefits of trade openness and economic integration become larger for smaller countries. Second, we argued that economic integration and political integration go hand in hand. As the world economy becomes more integrated, one of the benefits of large countries (the size of markets) vanishes. As a result the trade-off between size and heterogeneity shifts in favor of smaller and more homogeneous countries.

One could also think of the reverse source of causality: small countries have a particularly strong interest in maintaining free trade because so much of their economy depends on international markets. Indeed, we could think of two possible worlds. One world of large and relatively closed economies, and another of many more smaller and more open economies.[14]

In chapter 11 we will argue that this broad pattern of correlations is consistent with the evolution of trade and the configuration of political borders over the last several centuries.

7   Conflict and the Size of Nations

7.1 Introduction

Issues of conflict, defense, and security have historically been important factors in the determination and redrawing of political borders. Plato wrote that "the number of citizens should be sufficient to defend themselves against the injustice of their neighbors," (*Laws*, Book V). In his study of federalism Riker (1964, p.) argued that historically the external military threats and the need for defense were critical conditions for federal consolidation in the United States and elsewhere. He wrote that politicians are willing to give up some independence to form a federation only when they face "some form of external military-diplomatic threat or opportunity. Either they desire protection from an external threat or they desire to participate in the potential aggression of the federation." Along the same lines, Gilpin (2001) notes: "The few examples of successful federal experiments have been motivated primarily by national security concerns. Indeed, the two most successful federal republics—Switzerland and the United States—were created in response to powerful external security threats. . . . The German federalist state resulted from conquest by one nation (Prussia) of other German political entities."

In this chapter we study how the size of countries is influenced by the need for government to protect the interests of its citizens in an unfriendly world. Even in the absence of declared wars, the military power of a country matters in the settlement of international disputes. In turn military power depends on defense spending and other protective sources that can be used to foster the interests of a country's citizens.

Defense and national power are public goods, and in principle, larger countries can provide better and cheaper security for their citizens. In a more bellicose world, large countries have an advantage, but when the need to use military force is reduced internationally, defense becomes less important and smaller countries more safe.

We begin by focusing on *one* aspect of the connection between international conflict and the equilibrium number and size of countries: the benefits that individuals obtain from belonging to a strong country when dealing with nationals of other jurisdictions where disputes cannot be mediated by "impartial" supranational institutions.[1] That is, the underlying power of a country positively influences the standings of its citizens in international transactions. For example, in the absence of neutral supranational institutions, one can expect a US citizen to see resolved in his favor a dispute over trade or resources with a citizen of, say, Panama, than vice versa. A reasons why the United States has such power internationally is its superior military capability. We are interested in this chapter only in bilateral conflict, that between (citizens of) two countries. We do not consider coalitions of countries or multilateral conflicts and negotiations.

The model of this chapter is closely connected with the spatial model of country formation that we have used so far. In the next chapter we present several extensions.

7.2   Conflicts and Size

7.2.1   Military Spending and International Conflict

Consider all types of interactions that occur between individuals, firms, or groups of different countries. These relationships involve trade in goods, services, and factors of productions and include trade, financial transactions, and political initiatives. There exists a fundamental difference between interactions that take place within a country and those that take place across countries. Potential conflicts between citizens of a country can be resolved within a common legal framework, enforced by a government, which has the monopoly of legal coercion within its own territory. By contrast, international exchanges take place in a less regulated world. In other words, due to reasonably well-functioning legal systems, norms, and monopoly of coercion, domestic interactions between individuals are generally resolved without the use of violence or "power" of the individuals or groups. By contrast, on the international level, absent a supranational sovereign, national armies provide the necessary support to defend private and national interests. There have been periods in history when a particular country had hegemonic power, but generally international relations occur in a world without a sovereign with the monopoly of the legal use of violence.

If a conflict arises between nationals of two countries, there is no guarantee it will be resolved peacefully by international law and international social norms. In the absence of an international authority (or some other coordinated way of resolving international conflict without the use of national power), the defense of the interests of each national depends on the relative strength of his country. All other things equal, the stronger (militarily) that a particular government is, the more favorable will be the outcome of an international confrontation. Therefore the need to protect the interests of a country's citizens internationally is an important component of the incentives to form large, militarily powerful nations. Of course, not all international transactions result in use of force, but in general, the allocation of benefits on international bargaining tables is directly related, and proportional to, the military strength of the countries and different military alliances.

Therefore governments provide an additional public good to their nationals: defense and power in international conflicts. The higher a country's military strength, the more powerful is the protection of its nationals' interests should they get involved in an international conflict. That is, other things being equal, the nationals of a more militarily powerful government usually obtain favorable treatment when in conflict with foreigners.

Defense is a public good that requires the investment of national resources, and it embodies an element of economies of scale. In per capita terms it is cheaper to "buy" defense in a larger country. Empirically, the relationship between defense spending and country size is complex because of the existence of international alliances, and because of the fact that some large countries may provide defense for small countries that have low defense spending in per capita terms. An example is the role of the United States in NATO. Defense spending as a share of GDP is higher in the United States than in European countries, including the smallest countries. This is because small European countries free ride on US military spending.[2] Over the past thirty years US defense spending has gone from about 6 percent of GDP to the current minimum of 3.1 percent. In no European country has defense spending ever been above 3 percent of GDP. On the other hand, by virtue of its size and its share of military spending, the United States has en-

joyed a hegemonic role. In our formal analysis we abstract from military
alliances, and we assume that each country has to provide its own defense. We briefly return to military alliances in the conclusion of this
chapter.

Defense spending depends on the likelihood that international interactions are resolved through the use of national power. Muscle flexing
and threats of military intervention buy advantageous settlements in international disputes. The higher the likelihood that a conflict will arise,
the higher are the benefits of belonging to a large, powerful country,
where defense is cheaper in per capita terms. It follows that the number
and size of nations will depend on the probability of conflict. That is,
in a more bellicose world the trade-off between economies of scale and
heterogeneity costs is tilted in favor of the former, since defense spending is particularly valuable, and there are economies of scale in defense
spending.

7.2.2   International Conflict and the Size of Countries

Following the analysis of previous chapters, we consider two types of
worlds:

1. One where equilibrium borders are *not* determined through force
but consensually, via voting and agreement. Analogously, decisions
over public goods (including defense spending) within jurisdictions
are made consensually. As we will see, even in such an ideal situation, once borders are established, relative power and defense will have
a role, stemming from the need to defend one's nationals in potentially
conflictual exchanges across different countries.

2. A world of Leviathans, where provision of public goods and defense
spending are decided by rent-maximizing governments.

Consider a situation in which, first, borders are formed and changed
as in chapter 3. Specifically, in equilibrium no border change is approved
by majority vote in any of the existing countries. Second, once borders
are formed, within each country voters decide over the type of government and the amount to expend for defense. Third, individuals from
different jurisdictions interact and conflicts arise. International conflicts
are resolved by using national power ("defense").

In a bellicose world where international conflict is high, individuals will prefer to live in large countries, for two reasons. One is that
defense is cheaper (in per capita terms) in a large country. The sec-

ond reason why large nations are preferred in our model is that we are assuming that military conflicts occur only across national borders. That is, the experiment we are running is an increase in the propensity of "across border conflict," holding constant heterogeneity of preferences within countries of a certain size. The opposite argument applies where the world becomes more peaceful. When the probability of international conflict is small, the incentive to remain in a large country is reduced. So the model predicts a breakup of large countries in a peaceful world.

Interestingly, almost by definition, when countries break up the number of interactions that are "international" (crossborder) increase. Think of a country splitting in two. The trade between these two new countries is now international, whereas before it was interregional. With international interactions conflict may increase because there are more opportunities for conflict in a world where a large fraction of interactions among individuals is international. In other words, for small countries there is potential for more conflict because fewer interactions would be resolved domestically. Or, to put it differently, a smaller number of interactions can take place within the political jurisdiction of the central government. Conversely, interactions among individuals who do not share a monopolist of coercion—the central government—increase.

Does a reduction in the probability of conflict (i.e., the probability that an international exchange is solved by the use of force) mean a reduction in the *observed number* of international conflicts? The answer is: not necessarily. In fact a reduction in the probability of conflict across jurisdictions has two effects. For a given number and size of countries, as the probability of conflict goes down, defense and national strength become less important, and therefore more countries may be created. This way a lower probability of conflict could increase the number of international exchanges. Then exchanges that used to take place within the same jurisdiction are added to the mass of international conflicts. This second effect may offset the first effect: a reduction in the probability that every international exchange cannot be resolved without conflict may lead to more observed conflicts because those are more international exchanges when the average country size is small.

For the same reason the amount of resources per capita spent on defense does not always follow a reduction in the probability of conflict. A reduction in the probability of conflict may even result in an increase in defense spending per capita, since the populations of small countries are small. More generally, then, political disintegration reduces the extent to which a reduction in the probability of conflict translates into lower defense spending.

In a world of Leviathans, as we saw in chapter 5, the countries are larger when there are fewer so-called democratic constraints. Democratization induces smaller countries to form. So there are two forces, potentially correlated, that lead to a reduction of country size: democratization and a reduction of the probability of war. To the extent that being a democracy also makes it less likely that brute force is used in international confrontations, then the process of democratization has a direct and an indirect effect both pushing toward a reduction in the size of countries.

In summary, this chapter contains three main messages:

1. International conflict provides an important incentive to form larger jurisdictions.

2. Since a *lower* probability of having to use force in international relations brings about more jurisdictions, it can be associated with an overall *increase* in the number of international transactions that are resolved through conflict and the use of national power.

3. Democratization and a reduction in the use of force in international transactions are interrelated forces both leading to a reduction in country size.

These three results seem consistent with the events triggered by the collapse of the Soviet Union. This event triggered the formation of many new countries not only within the former Soviet Union, but also in Eastern Europe and Yugoslavia. NATO has not yet broken apart, but its role is vastly reduced.

While the "global" risk of conflict has decreased, localized confrontations have certainly not disappeared. In some cases conflicts have taken the form of international wars between separate countries (e.g., Iraq versus Kuwait), in others they have been the results of the process of countries disintegration, as in the case of the Balkans.

In the formal analysis that follows, we reach these conclusions with two different formalizations. In this chapter we maintain a very simple model of conflict and wars, but we retain the same level of generality in the modeling of borders and number of countries that we had thus far. In the other model explored in chapter 8, we formalize more deeply and precisely the war game, but we have to simplify other aspects of the model.

*7.3   Conflict and the Size of Nations

7.3.1   The Model

We extend the model in chapter 3 to study the role of defense spending in international conflict. As in the previous chapters, the world is modeled as a segment of length normalized to one. The world population has mass 1 and is uniformly distributed on the segment [0, 1]. We assume that the utility of each individual i is given by

$$u_i = g - al_i + z_i - t_i, \tag{7.1}$$

where g and a are two positive parameters and l_i is the distance from individual i to his government. Again, l_i represents distance both geographically and ideologically. Every individual has resources z_i and pays tax t_i. In contrast to chapters 3 to 5, individual resources are not exogenous but depend on the resolution of conflict.[3] Specifically, we assume that individual resources z_i are divided into two components:

$$z_i = y + e_i, \tag{7.2}$$

where y is individual income (equal for everybody) which is *safe* from the consequences of conflict, while e_i is the amount of resources of individual i after a conflict is resolved.

Conflict stems from the distribution of resources. National jurisdictions provide clearly defined control rights for their citizens, but transactions across jurisdictions take place in a situation in which military strength influences the resolution of conflicts. Specifically, individuals are randomly matched pairwise. When a pair (i, j) meets, the two individuals generate a pool of resources equal to $2e$, which has to be divided. There are two possible states: conflict (c) and no conflict (nc). In a state of nc resources are distributed peacefully and equally:

$$e_i = e_j = e. \tag{7.3}$$

In a state of conflict, the share of individual i depends on the "power" of his country, which is measured by his country's defense spending d_i-relative to defense spending of the country of individual j,[4]

$$e_i = \frac{d_i}{d_i + d_j} 2e, \tag{7.4}$$

and, analogously,

$$e_j = \frac{d_j}{d_i + d_j} 2e. \tag{7.5}$$

In the rest of this chapter we will assume that *when two individuals who belong to the same country meet, they are always in a state of no conflict.* That is, we rule out domestic conflict. We can interpret this assumption as meaning that each government has complete control over means of coercion within its own jurisdiction.

By contrast, when two individuals who do not belong to the same country meet, they can be either in a state of no conflict—in which case equation (7.3) applies—or in a state of conflict—in which case equations (7.4) and (7.5) apply. In the rest of this chapter we will assume that the probability of a state of conflict between two individuals who belong to different jurisdictions is equal to p.

It is worth remembering that "conflict" in this chapter should be interpreted as any situation in which international law and social norms are insufficient to ensure a peaceful division of resources between members of different countries, and the division takes place by involving the "relative strengths" of the two countries. The resolution of a state of conflict through relative force does not imply the direct use of violence but may simply reflect military "muscle flexing" or the weight in international bargaining tables arising from a country's strength. Thus the potential conflict between two individuals may stem from a trade relationship, or from conflicting interests on natural resources and/or other economic and noneconomic issues.

The parameter p is related to the availability of alternative means of resolution that do not involve a country's strength—such as the applicability of international law collectively enforced by the community of nations, or of self-enforcing social norms. In other words, p is related to the regime of international relations. In a world of effective international law and shared social norms, p is small; in an anarchic world in which individuals' payoffs from international exchanges mainly depend on the relative strength of one's country, p is large.

Defense spending is costly, and is paid through general taxation. As in chapter 3 we assume that all individuals living in the same country pay the same taxes. For example, all individuals living in a country of size s_x pay the same taxes t_x. Therefore the budget constraint for a government of a country of size s_x with a defense spending equal to d_x is given by

$$s_x t_x = k + d_x. \tag{7.6}$$

In the rest of this chapter, for the reasons discussed in chapter 3, we will focus on countries of equal size. In the appendix we formally derive the equal-size result from equilibrium and stability conditions.

7.3.2 The Choice of Defense Spending

If the world is divided into N countries of equal size $s = 1/N$, the payoff of an individual i living in country x is given by

$$u_i^x = g - al_i + y + [1 - (1 - s)p]e + ps \sum_{x' \neq x} \frac{d_x}{d_x + d_{x'}} 2e - \frac{k + d_x}{s},$$

$$x = 1, 2, \ldots, N. \quad (7.7)$$

The first-order condition which determines the desired amount of defense by each individual of country x can be obtained immediately from the utility above:

$$ps \sum_{x' \neq x} \frac{d_{x'}}{(d_x + d_{x'})^2} 2e = \frac{1}{s}. \quad (7.8)$$

This equation shows that the marginal costs of an extra unit of defense spending, equal to $1/s$, have to equal the marginal benefits in terms of a higher "prize" in case of conflict.

In equilibrium, each of the N equal-sized countries will choose the same level of defense spending, which is given as follows:

$$\tilde{d} = \frac{s(1 - s)pe}{2}, \quad (7.9)$$

where we have used the fact that $N = 1/s$. Several observations are in order. First, the equilibrium amount of defense is increasing in the probability of conflict p. Not surprisingly, it is also increasing in the amount of the payoff from conflict e. Second, defense spending is zero when there is only one country in the world, since, by definition, there is no conflict. Third, defense per capita, which is

$$\frac{\tilde{d}}{s} = \frac{(1 - s)pe}{2}, \quad (7.10)$$

is decreasing with country size.[5] Fourth, since defense is, from the point of view of global efficiency, pure waste, individual utility would be maximized at $\tilde{d} = 0$. Thus in this model defense spending is the result of a "prisoner's dilemma" type of situation.

7.3.3   The Equilibrium Number of Countries

By following the steps of chapter 2, we can derive the equilibrium number of countries that would result through majority voting as follows:[6]

$$\widetilde{N} = \sqrt{\frac{a - pe}{2k}}, \tag{7.11}$$

while the equilibrium size of countries is

$$\widetilde{s} = \frac{1}{\widetilde{N}} = \sqrt{\frac{2k}{a - pe}}. \tag{7.12}$$

The equilibrium number of countries is decreasing with the probability of conflict, and the equilibrium size of countries is increasing with the probability of conflict.

This is one of the critical results of this chapter. It implies that a decrease in the probability of conflict would result in a breakup of countries. Two forces underlie this inverse relationship between p and $\widetilde{N}$. First, if p increases, an individual would like to belong to a larger country in order to reduce the probability of being matched with foreigners. Second, since defense spending increases in p and defense per capita is decreasing in larger countries, the benefits of size increase.

7.3.4   Country Size and Observed International Conflict

The mass of observable conflict M can be defined as follows:

$$M(p) = p[1 - \widetilde{s}(p)]. \tag{7.13}$$

That is, the mass of international conflict is given by the probability that an international relationship results in a conflict multiplied by the share of interactions that are international. It follows that

$$\frac{dM}{dp} = 1 - \widetilde{s}(p) - p\frac{d\widetilde{s}}{dp}, \tag{7.14}$$

which, by substituting $\widetilde{s}(p)$ and $d\widetilde{s}/dp$ implies the following result: the mass of international conflicts is increasing in p if and only if

$$\widetilde{s}(p) < \frac{a - pe}{a - pe/2}. \tag{7.15}$$

The intuition for (7.15) is that a reduction in p has two effects. For a given size of countries, it reduces the mass of international conflict. The direct effect is larger, the smaller is the size $\widetilde{s}$, namely the larger is the mass of international matches relative to domestic matches. The second, and indirect, effect is that a reduction in p reduces the size of countries, thus increasing the mass of international interactions that can potentially lead to conflict. Thus, for small $\tilde{s}$ the direct effect dominates; for large $\tilde{s}$ it does not. Clearly, starting from a world with a few large countries, a reduction in p that leads to the formation of many new countries may actually increase the number of observed conflicts.

A similar intuition underlines the effect of a reduction of p on defense spending per capita. From equation (7.10) it follows that

$$\frac{d(\tilde{d}/\tilde{s})}{dp} = \frac{(1-\tilde{s})e}{2} - \frac{pe}{2}\frac{d\tilde{s}}{dp}. \tag{7.16}$$

The first term of (7.16) is the direct positive effect of a change in p on defense per capita: a lower p leads to lower defense. The second term, with the opposite sign, is the indirect effect due to the consequences of a change of p on the size of countries. The equation above leads to the same condition as for M: defense per capita is increasing in p if and only if

$$\tilde{s}(p) < \frac{a - pe}{a - pe/2}. \tag{7.17}$$

Thus, a reduction of p may actually lead to an increase in defense spending per capita because countries become smaller. More generally, one may summarize the argument by stating that the "peace dividend" that one may expect by the reduction of international conflict is mitigated by the fact that the latter leads to smaller countries, with larger defense spending per capita.

*7.4 Conflict and Size in a World of Leviathans

Consider an extension of the model of Leviathans developed in chapter 5. Once borders are formed, each Leviathan chooses defense spending in order to maximize his rents. Since he must satisfy his no insurrection constraint (a fraction δ of the population must obtain utility higher or equal to u_0), we have that the Leviathan can charge the following taxes per capita:

$$t = g - a\frac{\delta s}{2} + z_i - u_0. \tag{7.18}$$

He will collect the following net rents per person

$$R = t - \frac{d+k}{s}. \tag{7.19}$$

Hence Leviathans in equilibrium will choose

$$\frac{\tilde{d}}{s} = \frac{(1-s)pe}{2}.$$

The equilibrium size of countries in a world of Leviathans will maximize total rents, given by

$$R = g - a\frac{\delta s}{2} + y + e - u_0 - \frac{(1-s)pe}{2} - \frac{k}{s}. \tag{7.20}$$

Hence that size will be

$$s_L = \sqrt{\frac{2k}{a\delta - pe}}. \tag{7.21}$$

Hence as in chapter 5, higher δ (democratization) means smaller countries.

Notice that

$$\frac{\partial^2 s_l}{\partial \delta \partial p} < 0, \tag{7.22}$$

which means that at higher levels of conflict democratization has small effects on the size of countries, and vice versa. In other words, in a world of high conflict democratization is "less important" in reducing the size of countries, and in a world of more widespread democracy, conflict is less important in determining the size of countries.

7.5   Conclusion

External threats lead to the consolidation of countries. In a less peaceful world, large countries provide better "protection" to their citizens. Therefore in a world in which international transitions often result, directly or indirectly, in the use of force, large nations have advantages. Thus the reduction of the likelihood of international conflict, captured by the probability that any interaction between members of different countries results in a conflict, has two effects. On the one hand, it reduces conflict for given country borders. On the other hand, it induces the formation of smaller countries so that more interactions become cross-border. The result is that observed conflict may actually increase.

While the relationship between democracy and conflict is at the heart of a vast literature in the field of international relations,[7] the connection between democratization, conflict, and the size of countries is relatively unexplored.[8] In this chapter we have moved a step into the direction of a formal analysis of those important issues, by focusing on the effects of conflict and democratization, and their interaction, on the size of countries. However, we have maintained the assumption that the probability of international conflict is independent of the degree of "democratic responsiveness" of different governments. An interesting avenue of research would be to extend the analysis in order to explore endogenous links between conflict and democratization.

We also have vastly ignored the issue of military alliances and multinational unions of countries.[9] Several small countries could form a military alliance, share a common defense policy of national assistance, and retain political independence in other policy areas. Thus, when we speak of "breakups of countries" in this area, we could also be talking of "breakups of military alliances." Future work could incorporate the two. We return in chapter 12 to a discussion of multicountry unions, with specific reference to the European Union.

7.6 Appendix: Discussion of Equilibrium and Stability

It is immediate to show that countries of equal size, with the government located in the middle and the same amount of defense spending satisfy the requirement that individuals located at the borders are indifferent between belonging to either country.

How about stability? As we did in chapter 3, we define a configuration of countries as A-stable if and only if, after a small perturbation of the border, the original equilibrium is re-established.

The following result holds:

7.6.1 Result 7.A

Given a configuration of N equally sized countries, if all $N-2$ countries not affected by the border change maintain their level of defense fixed, the smallest size of countries that is stable is a function of p—call it $s(p)$—such that for $p > 0$,

$$s(0) \leq s(p) \tag{A7.1}$$

and

$$\frac{\partial s(p)}{\partial p} \geq 0. \tag{A7.2}$$

The result above indicates that the minimum stable size is (weakly) increasing in p. If p is high, small countries are not stable. The reasoning is that if a perturbation makes a country larger, the citizens of a neighboring smaller country will want to join the bigger country because defense is too expensive in the smaller country. Therefore, leaving aside majority vote considerations, an increase in conflict leads to a higher minimum stable size. An increase in conflict requires larger countries to keep borders "stable."

To prove this result we need to derive a lemma. Define d_1' and d_2' as the defense spending in country 1 and 2 after a small perturbation ε. By definition, $s_1' = s - \varepsilon$ and $s_2' = s + \varepsilon$, whereas in all other countries of size $s = 1/N$, defense is $d = s(1-s)pe/2$.

LEMMA   Aggregate defense is smaller in the smaller country, but defense per capita is larger in the smaller country, that is,

$$d_1' < d_2' \tag{A7.3}$$

and

$$\frac{d_1'}{s_1'} < \frac{d_2'}{s_2'}. \tag{A7.4}$$

Proof   The first-order conditions for the determination of defense imply the following two equations:

$$(s+\varepsilon)\left[(1-2s)\frac{d}{(d_2'+d)^2} + (s-\varepsilon)\frac{d_1'}{(d_1'+d_2')^2}\right] = \frac{1}{2pe}, \tag{A7.5}$$

$$(s-\varepsilon)\left[(1-2s)\frac{d}{(d_1'+d)^2} + (s-\varepsilon)\frac{d_2'}{(d_1'+d_2')^2}\right] = \frac{1}{2pe}. \tag{A7.6}$$

We differentiate both sides with respect to ε, evaluate the two expressions at $\varepsilon = 0$, and obtain

$$\frac{\partial d_1'}{\partial \varepsilon} = \frac{(2s-1)d}{s(1-s)} > 0 \tag{A7.7}$$

and

$$\frac{\partial d_2'}{\partial \varepsilon} = -\frac{(2s-1)d}{s(1-s)} < 0. \tag{A7.8}$$

Using (A7.6) and (A7.7) and evaluating at $\varepsilon = 0$ again, we obtain

$$\frac{\partial(d_1'/s_1')}{\partial \varepsilon} = -\frac{d}{s(1-s)} < 0 \tag{A7.9}$$

and

$$\frac{\partial(d_2'/s_2')}{\partial\varepsilon} = \frac{d}{s(1-s)} > 0. \qquad (A7.10)$$

This proves the lemma. ∎

We are now ready to prove our stability result 7.A. We already know from chapter 3 that for $p = 0$, a stable size $s(0) = 1/N$ must satisfy $N < \sqrt{a/2k}$. By definition of stability, at $p = 0$ the individual in the smaller country prefers to move to the larger country after a perturbation. Now consider some $p > 0$. Can we have $s(p) < s(0)$? No, that would be a contradiction, since aggregate defense is smaller but defense per capita is larger in the smaller country. A similar argument can be made for $p' > p$. Hence the function $s(p)$ is weakly increasing in p. ∎

7.6.2 Voting Equilibria

If we restrict voting on configurations of equally sized countries we can apply the results we obtained in chapter 3 about median distance changes. We know that defense spending per head when all countries have equal size $s = 1/N$ is given by $(1 - s)pe/2 = (N - 1)pe/sN$, while when $s' = 1/(N + 1)$, it is $(1 - s')pe/2 = Npe/2(N + 1)$. Hence, when the number of countries is increased from N to $N + 1$, the change in utility for the individuals who experience the median distance change $d_m\{N, N + 1\}$ is given by

$$a d_m\{N, N+1\} + K[(N+1) - N] + \frac{pe}{2}\left[\frac{N}{N+1} - \frac{N-1}{N}\right]. \qquad (A7.11)$$

Since $d_m\{N, N + 1\} = -1/2N(N + 1)$, as shown in the appendix to chapter 3, we have that (A7.10) is positive (no majority in favor of a breakup) if and only if

$$-\frac{a}{2N(N+1)} + K + \frac{pe}{2N(N+1)} \le 0, \qquad (A7.12)$$

which implies that

$$N(N+1) \ge \frac{a - pe}{2k}. \qquad (A7.13)$$

Note that this is the condition for B1-stability.

By the same token, to obtain the necessary and sufficient condition for B2-stability in this framework, we can use the fact (shown in the appendix to chapter 3) that the maximum median distance change from N to $N - 1$ equally sized countries is $1/2N(N - 1)$, and the fact that defense spending per capita with $N - 1$ countries is $[1 - (1/N - 1)]pe/2$. So we have

$$N(N - 1) \leq \frac{a - pe}{2k}.$$

(A7.14)

It is immediate to see that the number of countries that satisfies both (A7.13) and (A7.14) is the integer closer to

$$\sqrt{\frac{a - pe}{2k}},$$

(A7.15)

which is in fact the "equilibrium" number of countries we used in the text of this chapter.

8

War, Peace, and the Size of Nations

8.1 Introduction

This chapter provides further discussion of the relationships of conflict, defense, and size. On the one hand, we will complicate our model of conflict and size by focusing on a more general conflict-resolution technology, in which both international peaceful bargaining and nonpeaceful confrontations between nations are explicitly modeled. On the other hand, we will simplify our framework, by departing from the basic spatial model in which individuals are distributed over a continuum. We will assume that discrete regions may join in political union and enter into conflict with other political unions. While the results of this chapter are obtained within a more extensive and detailed analysis of the resolution of conflict, they are consistent with the effects of conflict on country formation and secessions studied in chapter 7 (the reader who is interested only in the main intuition and not in the technical details and extensions can skip this chapter entirely). In particular, we will see again that a higher probability of having to use defense capabilities in international relations increases the incentives to form larger countries. In this chapter we will see that this effect comes in two parts: (1) a higher probability of facing an international conflict increases the incentives to form a larger country even if the conflict is solved peacefully and no war results in equilibrium, because a country's bargaining power will depend on its military capability; (2) a positive probability that the conflict will turn violent (actual war) will further increase the incentives to form larger political unions. In the first part of the analysis we will assume that relations between nations are completely "anarchic," and depend exclusively on the potential or actual use of force. In the second part of the analysis we will introduce the possibility that some conflicts between states can be resolved independently of relative military strength through international law (as enforced by a supranational authority or by international norms). If the enforcement of international law were perfect, defense spending would become irrelevant, and conflict would play no role in country formation. However, the enforcement of international law is in fact imperfect, so defense and conflict will affect country formation. We will see that the stronger the "extension" of international law, the less relevant will be defense, and hence the smaller will be the sizes of countries in equilibrium. Hence stronger international law brings about breakup of countries. Interestingly, such breakup, in increasing the number of countries, and hence the number of potential conflicts that may take place among independent political units, may lead to wars. Of course, the paradoxical result is that a more effective and extensive enforcement of international law may increase conflict and wars in equilibrium. Such results—while obtained within different contexts—are reminiscent of the effects studied in chapter 7.

At the end of this chapter we discuss the links among conflict, international trade, and the determination of political borders.[1] A central idea is the inverse relationship between international conflict and international trade. Conflict reduces trade between countries. Hence a cost of conflict comes from the lost gains from trade.[2] Our discussion explores the implications of this relationship for the formation and breakup of countries. The main conclusion is that a world of larger countries should be associated with higher protectionism and more conflict, while a world of smaller countries should be associated with freer trade and less international conflict.

*8.2   War and Bargaining

In this section we present a simple model of conflict resolution between two countries. The purpose of this section is not to provide a rational theory of wars but a simple foundation for conflict resolution—in which military capabilities play a key role—on which to base the study of border formation in the rest of the chapter. We will model conflict as distributional in the sharing of an economically valuable pie. More specifically, we will assume that international conflict may arise when international control rights over some valuable resource are not specified or not enforceable. While this specific reason for wars is not uncommon, our model of conflict can be interpreted more generally, in an "ideological" interpretation, presented in the appendix A at the end of this chapter.

Consider two countries, j and j'. Suppose that there exists a resource R on which both countries have claims, such as oil reserves located in international waters between the two countries. The countries may resolve their potential conflict with war or bargaining. Wars are costly: if country j goes to war, its aggregate cost is given by $c_j \geq 0$. For simplicity, and without much loss of generality, we assume that war costs are constant across countries, $c_j = c_{j'} = c \geq 0$.

For simplicity, we will also assume complete information in this model. That is, we will assume that the governments of the two countries know each other's preferences, constraints, and military capabilities. As usual in this book, we do not make this assumption because we think it is realistic but for analytical simplicity. We are aware that a large and influential literature in international relations has plausibly argued that uncertainty and asymmetric information should play a central role in order to explain war outbreaks as rational outcomes.[3] We agree with such assessment, but we think that as it is often the case in economics, important insights about an "uncertain" phenomenon can be achieved by building simplified deterministic models. In particular, we will provide a model in which wars can emerge in equilibrium, even in the absence of uncertainty and asymmetric information, because of commitment problems: countries may be unable to credibly commit *not* to go to war, even when the no war outcome is mutually advantageous. In this respect our analysis is consistent with Fearon (1995), who has argued that only *two* mechanisms can claim empirical relevance as explanations for why rationally led states may go to war over divisible resources: "(1) the combination of private information about resolve or capability and incentives to misrepresent these, and (2) states' inability, in specific circumstances, to commit to uphold a deal." (Fearon 1995, p. 409).[4] Our model uses the second mechanism.

Each country has a strategy set of two elements: $\sigma_j = \sigma_{j'} = \{$fight; bargain$\}$.[5] The payoffs are as follows. When both countries decide to fight, the net payoffs are

$$u_{ff}^{j} = \frac{d_j}{d_j + d_{j'}} R - c, \tag{8.1}$$

$$u_{ff}^{j'} = \frac{d_{j'}}{d_j + d_{j'}} R - c, \tag{8.2}$$

where d_j ($d_{j'}$) is military spending in country j (j').

If both countries choose to bargain, we adopt a Nash bargaining solution to share the pie. For the disagreement point we choose, quite naturally, the war outcome. Under these assumptions the Nash bargaining solution implies allocations shares α_j^* and $(1 - \alpha_j^*)$, such that

$$u_{bb}^j = \alpha_j^* R, \tag{8.3}$$

$$u_{bb}^{j'} = (1 - \alpha_j^*)R, \tag{8.4}$$

where

$$\alpha_j^* = \arg\max \left[\alpha_j R - \frac{d_j}{d_j + d_{j'}} R + c \right] \left[(1 - \alpha_j)R - \frac{d_{j'}}{d_j + d_{j'}} R + c \right] \tag{8.5}$$

s.t. $\quad \alpha_j R \geq \dfrac{d_j}{d_j + d_{j'}} R - c, \quad (1 - \alpha_j)R \geq \dfrac{d_{j'}}{d_j + d_{j'}} R - c,$ $\qquad$ (8.6)

which gives[6]

$$\alpha_j^* = \frac{d_j}{d_j + d_{j'}}. \tag{8.7}$$

For $c = 0$, the two countries obtain the same net payoffs no matter whether they engage in open warfare or in Nash bargaining. For any $c > 0$, the bargaining outcome Pareto dominates the fight outcome. However, that outcome (bargain, bargain) may not be an equilibrium. To illustrate this point, we need to specify the payoffs for (bargain, fight) and (fight, bargain) outcomes. When country j chooses to fight while country j' chooses to bargain, we denote their respective payoffs as

$$u_{fb}^j = \frac{d_j}{d_j + d_{j'}} R + E_j - c, \tag{8.8}$$

$$u_{fb}^{j'} = \frac{d_{j'}}{d_j + d_{j'}} R - e_{j'} - c. \tag{8.9}$$

The idea is that while one country's decision to fight will always trigger an open conflict in which both countries will eventually engage, the first country to mobilize for war may enjoy a "first-strike advantage." $E_j \geq 0$ denotes the first striker's advantage: it measures the additional gain that country j can obtain by engaging in open warfare while country j' proposes to bargain.[7] Conversely, $e_{j'} \geq 0$ denotes for country j' the "surprise loss," meaning the loss that country j' would suffer should that country propose to bargain while the other country attacks.

One could think of E_i as the sum of three components: (1) the benefits stemming from a higher probability of winning because of a surprise attack, (2) lower war costs (hence E_i may be a function of c), and (3) other economic and political benefits. Analogously, e_i includes the costs due to (1) a lower probability of winning when a country is taken "by surprise," (2) higher war damage, and (3) other economic and political costs. Analogously, if country j decides to bargain but country j' "strikes," the respective payoffs are

$$u_{bf}^j = \frac{d_j}{d_j + d_{j'}} R - e_j - c,\tag{8.10}$$

$$u_{bf}^{j'} = \frac{d_{j'}}{d_j + d_{j'}} R + E_{j'} - c.\tag{8.11}$$

It can be immediately verified that:

RESULT 8.1   The strategy profile (fight, fight), is always a Nash equilibrium.[8] It is the unique Nash equilibrium if and only if $\max\{E_j, E_{j'}\} > c \geq 0$. The strategy profile (bargain, bargain) is also a Nash equilibrium if and only if $\max\{E_j, E_{j'}\} \leq c$.

That is, open conflict is the only Nash equilibrium if and only if the advantage of a surprise strike more than offsets the costs of open warfare for at least one country. Note that in equilibrium there will be no surprise attack, so for any $c > 0$ both countries will be worse off than they would be had they bargained (the game is a standard prisoner's dilemma).[9] If the "temptation" is high enough to induce a strike, open conflict would be the unique suboptimal equilibrium.

Nevertheless, bargaining can be sustained as an equilibrium if and only if the costs of open conflict are higher than the temptation to strike for *both* countries. When $\max\{E_j, E_{j'}\} \leq c$, (fight, fight) is still a Nash equilibrium. However, for any $c > 0$, (bargain, bargain) Pareto dominates (fight, fight).[10] The strategy profile (bargain, bargain) also dominates the mixed equilibrium that exists for $\max\{E_j, E_{j'}\} \leq c$.

What is the most reasonable prediction of how this game will be played? Clearly, if the first-striker's advantage is high enough, the only Nash equilibrium is given by "both countries fight," and open warfare is the only noncooperative equilibrium outcome in a one-shot game. When the first striker's advantage is lower than direct war costs, open warfare and peaceful bargaining are both Nash equilibria. So is a mixed equilibrium in which each country fights and bargains with positive probabilities. However, this multiplicity of equilibria is reduced to a unique equilibrium when the refinement of *coalition-proofness* is introduced (Bernheim et al. 1987).[11] When we restrict our attention to coalition-proof equilibria, only the Pareto-dominant (bargain, bargain) equilibrium is robust to coordinated deviations. The following holds:

RESULT 8.2   If $\max\{E_j, E_{j'}\} > c > 0$, the strategy profile (fight, fight) is the unique coalition-proof Nash equilibrium. If $\max\{E_j, E_{j'}\} \leq c > 0$, the strategy profile (bargain, bargain) is the unique coalition-proof Nash equilibrium.

In summary, by the coalition-proof refinement, this game has an unambiguous outcome: war if the first striker's advantage is higher than war costs in at least one country, and peaceful bargaining otherwise. The concept of coalition-proof equilibrium is a natural choice when we embed our model of conflict into a model of endogenous country formation and defense spending.

*8.3 Wars, Defense, and Borders in an Anarchic World

Now we use our model of international conflict within a framework in which both defense spending and country borders are endogenous. To keep the model tractable, we find it useful to simplify our description of the world. We consider the case of an exogenously given maximum number of countries, four being the lowest number of countries necessary in order to have more than one country breakup. It also becomes more convenient to model the world as a circle rather than a line.

The "world" is a set of regions, each inhabited by a (discrete) number of homogeneous individuals. For simplicity, we normalize the number of individuals in each region to one. Each region borders two others. Two regions are located in the west (region $W1$ and region $W2$) and two are located in the east (region $E1$ and region $E2$). Western regions are contiguous, and so are eastern regions. To fix ideas, we assume that the four regions are distributed as points on a circle (figure 8.1).

The segment connecting a pair of regions measures the areas of the world to which both regions have access (i.e., the seas between them). Regions cannot split by assumption, but regions can merge to form countries composed of more than one region. Therefore, if two regions merge, the area of the world that lies between them becomes part of the unified country.

A "country" is defined as an independent political unit in which (1) defense is completely and credibly centralized, (2) a unified government takes decisions over bargaining and war strategies, and (3) the net returns from conflict are distributed across its citizens.[12]

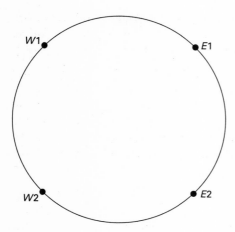

Figure 8.1
A world composed of four regions

Consistently with our discussion in the previous chapters, we assume that the formation of a larger, less homogeneous country implies some heterogeneity costs. Part of these costs may come from the expected losses associated with the possibility of a civil war, or other major domestic upheavals due to high heterogeneity within a country. For simplicity, we assume that the heterogeneity costs of forming a country including both an eastern and a western region are prohibitive. By contrast, if $E1$ and $E2$ form a unified country, each individual in each region will bear a cost $0 \leq h_e < \infty$. Analogously, if $W1$ and $W2$ form a unified country, each individual in each region will bear a cost h_w. Without loss of generality, we impose $0 \leq h_w \leq h_e$. We also assume that heterogeneity costs are the same for every member of a country, namely they do not depend on the location of each individual within the country. This assumption is simpler than the setup in the spatial model, where the heterogeneity costs depended on individuals' location on an ideological and/or geographical line.

The utility function for each individual i is

$$u_i = y_i - t_i + r_i - \delta_i h_i, \tag{8.12}$$

where y_i is the individual's income, t_i measures the individual's taxes, r_i measures the individual's net returns from conflict resolution, as specified below (including direct war costs and surprise gains or losses, if any), δ_i is a binary index which takes value 0 if the individual lives in an independent region and value 1 otherwise. Finally, we have $h_i = h_w$ if the individual lives in a western region, whilst $h_i = h_e$ if the individual lives in an eastern region.

Borders, taxes, and returns from conflict resolution are endogenously determined as equilibrium outcomes of an extensive game that we will specify below.

Let d_j denote defense in country j. One unit of defense costs one unit of income and is financed through a proportional income tax. The tax rate is denoted with τ_j. Let S_j denote the set of individuals in country j. Then we have that

$$\tau_j \sum_{i \in S_j} y_i = d_j. \tag{8.13}$$

Each individual in the world has the same income (*before* taxes and *before* conflict resolution): $y_i = y$. Therefore the budget constraint (8.13) simplifies to

$$\tau_j s_j y = d_j, \tag{8.14}$$

where $s_j \equiv |S_j|$ is the number of individuals in country j.

Defense is used to deal with potential conflicts with neighboring countries. Consistently with the model presented in the previous section, we consider a simple distributional conflict: somewhere on the circle there exits a valuable natural resource that will be discovered with probability π after political borders and defense allocations have been decided. This order of moves underlies a "timing" that we regard as realistic. That is, we assume that borders are set before defense spending is decided, and defense must be in place before actual conflict arises. This timing makes sense within a dynamic framework by noting that (1) border changes are more costly than changes in defense spending, and are observed more rarely, and (2) building defense takes time.

Finally, we also assume that when borders and defense are decided, individuals do not know whether any conflict over them will be resolved through bargaining or through war. It seems appropriate to assume that the precise features of potential conflicts and their resolution are uncertain when borders and defense investments are decided. Specifically, we assume a three-stage game.

In the first stage, the individual in each region decides on whether its region should form a unified country with the neighboring region ($E1$ with $E2$ and $W1$ with $W2$) or should form an independent country.[13] Borders are decided accordingly; a country is formed if and only if citizens in both regions contemplating to form a country agree. In other words, in stage 1 each region can choose from an action set of two. The action space of each player in each region is: {decide for union, decide for independence}. If at least one eastern (western) region prefers independence, the two eastern (western) regions will form two independent countries.

In stage two (i.e., after borders have been decided), a government is elected in each country. After the election the government acts as a unified "agent." It is the unique player for each country in the following stages of the game. In countries formed by one region, the government's objective function is identical to citizens' utility. In countries formed by two regions, the government's objective is given by a weighted average of the utilities of the citizens in the two regions.

In each country j, the government chooses the level of defense spending d_j, where $0 \leq d_j \leq \sum_{i \in S_j} y_i$. Defense spending d_j can take any real value between zero and the maximum amount of resources available in the country.[14] As we will see, preferences over defense are identical across individuals within each country. Therefore our assumption that defense is chosen by utility-maximizing governments is equivalent to having defense chosen through direct voting within each country.

In stage three, after defense is decided, uncertainty is resolved, for the location of R and the value of E are revealed. In particular, we assume that with probability π, a pie of size R is found on a point along the circle. We assume that the probability that R will be located between any two given regions is $\pi/4$. With probability ρ, the specific conflict at hand implies a first striker's advantage E larger than c, while, with probability $1 - \rho$, we have $E < c$. The difference $E - c$ captures the incentives to unilaterally start a war. Those incentives will depend on technological, economic, and political factors known only when the location and the nature of the conflict are revealed.[15] Depending on the location of the resource, at most two countries may lay a claim on it.[16] The resource R is allocated through bargaining or conflict. In this final stage each government involved in conflict chooses fight or bargain in order to maximize the utility of its citizens as specified above. Each government's objective is equivalent to the maximization of conflict returns, which we will specify consistently with our analysis in section 8.2. In particular, conflict returns to country j facing country j' are

$$\frac{d_j}{d_j + d_{j'}} R \tag{8.15}$$

when both countries bargain,

$$\frac{d_j}{d_j + d_{j'}} R - c, \tag{8.16}$$

when both countries fight,

$$\frac{d_j}{d_j + d_{j'}} R + E - c, \tag{8.17}$$

when country j chooses to fight a bargaining opponent, and

$$\frac{d_j}{d_j + d_{j'}} R - e - c, \tag{8.18}$$

when country j proposes bargaining but country j' chooses to fight.[17]

We narrow our analysis to coalition-proof Nash equilibria. More precisely, we use the extensive-form refinement of perfectly coalition-proof Nash equilibrium as defined in Bernheim et al. (1987).

In coalition-proof equilibria we need to consider deviations by coalitions of players.[18] Our game has a unique perfectly coalition-proof Nash equilibrium, which we can derive as follows:

First, we restrict all possible pairs of governments to play Pareto undominated equilibria in all two-player subgames of the terminal stage. In other words, governments will play "bargain" if $E \leq c$ and "fight" if $E > c$.

We will then consider the subgames consisting of the terminal two-stage games. We will show that given the payoffs supported by stage three equilibria, for each possible configuration of countries, there exists a unique Nash equilibrium in which each government chooses a specific level of defense. We will show that the unique Nash equilibrium in the terminal two-stage subgame is coalition-proof. We will then consider the game played by the four regions in the first stage. In the first stage, each strategy profile implies a given configuration of the world, to which unique equilibrium payoff vectors are associated. Each region will play coalition-proof equilibrium strategies. We will show that those equilibrium strategies characterize a unique equilibrium configuration of the world for given values of the parameters.

In summary, for a given vector of parameters $(h_e, h_w, \pi, R, \rho, c)$ we can find unique values for (1) the equilibrium number and size distribution of countries, (2) the equilibrium distribution of defense levels per capita across countries, and (3) the equilibrium probabilities of international conflict and war. Note that π measures the probability of a "potential" conflict, and ρ the probability that any conflict will be resolved through war. The probability of observing an international conflict and the probability that war will occur are both endogenous variables within our model, since they depend on the size distribution of countries.

We will now derive the equilibrium levels of defense spending and the equilibrium returns from conflict for each possible configuration of countries.

LEMMA 8.1   Equilibrium defense spending per capita in country i is given by

$$d_i = \frac{\pi R}{8s_i}. \tag{8.19}$$

Proof   See appendix B.   ∎

This result shows that equilibrium defense per capita is reduced by countries forming a larger union. By defining "expected conflict returns" for each country as its expected share of R minus expected war costs, we have the following lemma:

LEMMA 8.2   For every configuration of countries and for every country of size s_i, expected conflict returns per capita in equilibrium are given by

$$\frac{\pi R}{4} - \frac{\pi}{2} \frac{\rho c}{s_i}. \tag{8.20}$$

Thus, in equilibrium, when wars are impossible ($\rho = 0$) or costless ($c = 0$), individuals within each country will obtain the same expected returns from conflict, regardless of whether they live in a large country or in a small country. However, because of lemma 1, individuals living in a large country enjoy a benefit of size: their expected return comes at a lower cost in terms of defense per capita. In other words, a larger size brings about net economies of scale in defense. In addition, when wars are possible ($\rho > 0$) and costly ($c > 0$), a larger size reduces the expected war costs.

This analysis of equilibrium defense spending and equilibrium expected returns from conflict points to a scale advantage: large countries can exploit economies of scale in defense. However, these benefits have to be weighted against the higher heterogeneity costs. We are now ready to study under what conditions the benefits from size associated with conflict resolution are larger or smaller than the heterogeneity costs.

LEMMA 8.3   Given heterogeneity cost h_k ($k = $ w, e), and given the equilibrium payoffs associated with all possible configurations of countries (i.e., with all terminal two-stage subgames), individuals will (strictly) prefer to live in a two-region country rather than in an independent region if and only if

$$\frac{\pi}{4}\left(\frac{R}{4} + \rho c\right) > h_k. \tag{8.21}$$

Proof   See appendix B.   ∎

The term $\pi[(R/4) + \rho c]/4$ can be interpreted as net conflict benefits from unification, because these are the benefits stemming from lower defense spending per capita and lower expected war costs in a larger country. Lemma 8.3 states the intuitive result that unification will be likely to be preferred to independence given a higher probability and/or relevance of a potential conflict, a higher probability that the conflict leads to open warfare, but lower heterogeneity costs associated with unification.

PROPOSITION 8.1   For all $0 < h_w \leq h_e$, $\pi \geq 0$, $c \geq 0$ and $0 \leq \rho \leq 1$, in equilibrium we will have

1. four independent regions ($N = 4$) if and only if

$$\frac{\pi}{4}\left(\frac{R}{4} + \rho c\right) \leq h_w, \tag{8.22}$$

2. a unified west and two independent countries in the east ($N = 3$) if and only if

$$h_w < \frac{\pi}{4}\left(\frac{R}{4} + \rho c\right) \leq h_e, \tag{8.23}$$

3. a unified west and a unified east ($N = 2$) if and only if

$$\frac{\pi}{4}\left(\frac{R}{4} + \rho c\right) > h_e. \tag{8.24}$$

Proof   See appendix B.   ∎

Proposition 8.1 is intuitive. When the conflict benefits from unification are lower than the lowest heterogeneity costs (i.e., $\pi[(R/4) + \rho c]/4 < h_w$), independence is the equilibrium strategy in each region. If $h_w < \pi[(R/4) + \rho c]/4 < h_e$, the benefits from unification are high enough to compensate western regions for their (lower) heterogeneity costs but too small to make unification worthwhile in the east, where heterogeneity costs are assumed to be higher. If $\pi[(R/4) + \rho c]/4 > h_e$, unification is the equilibrium strategy everywhere.[19]

We will now study the implied comparative statics for different values of the fundamental parameters. Proposition 8.1 states that the equilibrium number and size of countries will endogenously depend on the probability of a potential conflict (π), the payoff from conflict (R), and the heterogeneity costs (h_e and h_w). For given heterogeneity costs, a high π and/or a high R tend to be associated with large countries, whereas a low π and/or a low R tend to be associated with small countries.

Moreover proposition 8.1 shows that the number of countries depends positively on the probability that conflict will be resolved through military confrontation (ρ) times the direct costs of military confrontation (c). Recall that a more bellicose world implies a world of large countries, and a reduction in the probability of war and/or its costs induces country breakup.

Note that the probability of observing an actual *international* conflict depends not only on the probability that a potential conflict arises (π) but also on the number of countries, which depends endogenously on π. This endogenous link may generate a paradoxical result: a *lower* probability of potential conflict may be associated with a *higher* probability of actually observing an international conflict in equilibrium.

Let χ denote the probability of an international conflict. By definition, it will be given by

$$\chi = \frac{\pi N}{4}. \tag{8.25}$$

By proposition 8.1, we can immediately derive the following corollary:

COROLLARY 8.1   For any $h_w \leq h_e$ such that $\pi' > 16 h_w/(R + 4\rho c)$, consider a lower $\pi'' < 16 h_e/(R + 4\rho c)$. Let $\chi(\pi')$ denote the probability of an international conflict associated with $\{\pi', R, h_e, h_w, \rho, c\}$, and let $\chi(\pi'')$ denote the probability of an international conflict associated with $\{\pi'', R, h_e, h_w, \rho, c\}$. Then $\chi(\pi') > \chi(\pi'')$ if and only if $\pi'/\pi'' > 2$.

Put differently, for every vector of parameters such that there exists two countries in equilibrium, there exists a range of *smaller π's*, such that for the same R and h, (1) four countries will result in equilibrium and (2) the probability of international conflict will be *higher* than in the equilibrium with the *higher* π.[20] The intuition is straightforward: while a smaller π reduces the probability of international conflict for given borders, the smaller chance that a conflict may arise reduces the incentives to form larger countries and therefore increases the number of countries in equilibrium. Some conflicts that would be resolved within domestic borders are now resolved through international confrontation. This indirect effect may offset the direct effect of a reduction in π, and bring about an *increase in the probability of observing an international conflict.*

On the other hand, note that with a lower π, international conflict may be more likely but it will also be more *local* (in our example, each conflict involves only half the world rather than the whole world). A reduction in the probability that a conflict be resolved by open warfare (lower ρ), due to a breakup of countries, may even raise the probability of war occurring.

The endogenous reduction in the number and size of countries that may be brought about by a lower probability of potential conflict can generate an additional paradoxical effect: a *lower* π may induce *higher* defense per capita in equilibrium. Certainly defense per capita is increasing in π for a given configuration of countries. Therefore a reduction in the probability π, for given borders induces a "peace dividend": lower probability of conflict would translate into lower defense per capita in each country. However, a lower π, by inducing a reduction in the equilibrium size of countries, may lead to *higher* defense per capita in equilibrium. Moreover, even when defense per capita does not increase because of a higher π, any endogenous reduction in size implies a level of defense per capita higher than the level that would be observed if borders remain unchanged. In other words, the endogenous link of probability of conflict with defense spending and size of countries points to reasons why a "peace dividend" may be reduced or completely offset by a breakup of countries. Formally, we can state the following:

COROLLARY 8.2   For any $h_w \le h_e$ such that $\pi' > 16h_w/(R + 4\rho c)$, consider a lower $\pi'' < 16h_e/(R + 4\rho c)$. By lemma 8.1, we have that defense per capita at the higher level of π is given by

$$d(\pi') = \frac{\pi' R}{16}.$$ (8.26)

In contrast, defense per capita at the lower level of π is given by

$$d(\pi'') = \frac{\pi'' R}{8}.$$ (8.27)

Therefore we have that $d(\pi') > d(\pi'')$ if and only if $\pi'/\pi'' > 2$.

Note that even when $d(\pi') > d(\pi'')$, the peace dividend that is associated with a breakup of countries is given by

$$PD_{\text{break}} = d(\pi') - d(\pi'') = \frac{R}{16}[\pi' - 2\pi'']. \tag{8.28}$$

Such a "peace dividend" is smaller than the peace dividend that would be observed in the absence of country breakup, that is,

$$PD_{\text{nobreak}} = \frac{R}{16}[\pi' - \pi'']. \tag{8.29}$$

*8.4 War, Defense, Borders, and International Law

Even when wars entail no costs ($c = 0$), all expenses in defense are waste from an efficiency perspective. A more efficient solution is for countries to agree in advance (i.e., before the location of R is known) on a partitioning of the world into spheres of influence such that each country has complete control rights (international property rights) over all resources R that fall within its sphere. The first-best partition would be to divide the circle of four independent regions into four equal segments, and spend nothing on defense. However, in the absence of enforcement, each country has an incentive to deviate from this plan, invest in military force, and invade its neighbors' spheres of influence.

While a complete partition can be beyond enforcement, in some world orders a partial partition can be enforced through international law backed by an international enforcement agency and/or by time-honored social norms.

Let us suppose that an existing international law allows for a secure area of size $\xi < \frac{1}{4}$ around each region. Then, only when R falls outside the sphere ("anarchic area") there is actual conflict.

Proposition 8.1 can then be generalized as follows:

PROPOSITION 8.2   For all $0 < h_w \le h_e$, $\pi \ge 0$, $c \ge 0$, $0 \le \rho \le 1$, and $0 \le \xi \le \frac{1}{4}$, in equilibrium, we will have

1. four independent regions ($N = 4$) if and only if

$$\frac{\pi}{4}\left(\frac{1}{4} - \xi\right)\left(\frac{R}{4} + \rho c\right) < h_w, \tag{8.30}$$

2. a unified west and two independent countries in the east ($N = 3$) if and only if

$$h_{\mathrm{w}} < \frac{\pi}{4} \left(\frac{1}{4} - \xi \right) \left(\frac{R}{4} + \rho c \right) \le h_{\mathrm{e}}, \tag{8.31}$$

3. a unified west and a unified east ($N = 2$) if and only if

$$\frac{\pi}{4} \left(\frac{1}{4} - \xi \right) \left(\frac{R}{4} + \rho c \right) > h_{\mathrm{e}}. \tag{8.32}$$

Therefore an expansion of international control rights reduces the importance of national defense and brings about the formation of smaller countries in equilibrium.

However, it is immediate to see that for the same reasons that a reduction in the probability of conflict may lead to local wars, an expansion in the extent of international property rights, while reducing the level of international "anarchy" and the importance of defense, could bring about more conflicts and wars. Formally, we have that the probability of an international conflict is now

$$\chi = \pi \left(\tfrac{1}{4} - \xi \right) N. \tag{8.33}$$

By proposition 8.2, we can immediately derive the following corollary:

COROLLARY 8.3 For any $h_{\mathrm{w}} \le h_{\mathrm{e}}$ such that $\xi' < (1/4) - 4h_{\mathrm{e}}/(R + 4\rho c)\pi$, consider a higher $\xi'' > (1/4) - 4h_{\mathrm{w}}/(R + 4\rho c)\pi$. Let $\chi(\xi')$ denote the probability of an international conflict associated with $\{\pi, R, h_{\mathrm{e}}, h_{\mathrm{w}}, \rho, c, \xi'\}$, and let $\chi(\xi'')$ denote the probability of an international conflict associated with $\{\pi, R, h_{\mathrm{e}}, h_{\mathrm{w}}, \rho, c, \xi''\}$. Then $\chi(\xi') > \chi(\xi'')$ if and only if $\xi'' > (\xi'/2) + (1/8)$.

In other words, an increase in the enforcement of international law that brings about a breakup of countries will also reduce conflict if and only if it is large enough. Otherwise, a more extensive enforcement of international law will, on balance, increase conflict and wars. For example, even a doubling of the "internationally enforced" sphere from $1/16$ to $1/8$—if associated with a breakup of two countries into four countries—would be associated with higher conflict, since the conflict would go from $3\pi/8$ with two countries to $\pi/2 > 3\pi/8$ after the countries become four.

This result shows that when borders are endogenous, so-called improvements in international law may increase conflict. This is a second-best result. While a first-best world would emerge from *perfectly* defined international control rights, quite a different outcome may result when one considers extensions of international property rights that do not completely eliminate areas of anarchy and indeterminacy. The post–cold-war world has seen both an increase in the coordinated attempts to enforce international agreements and control rights, and an explosion of local conflicts and separatism. Our analysis suggests a possible explanation for the coexistence of the two phenomena.

8.5 Conflict, Trade, and the Size of Nations

In chapter 6 we studied the relationship between international trade and the determination of political borders. Then we implicitly assumed complete security of international exchanges and lack of conflict among countries. But there is no doubt that conflict is an important part of international relations and plays a key role in the determination of political borders. In this section we will briefly discuss international trade and openness when the possibility of conflict between countries is explicitly taken into account.

In chapter 6 we stressed an inverse relationship between the degree of international economic integration and the incentives to form larger political units. More openness, we found, makes smaller countries more viable. In chapter 7 and in this chapter we have argued that international conflict, by contrast, makes smaller countries less viable and encourages the formation of larger political units.

The two effects are not unrelated once we consider the existence of a connection between conflict and trade. An important empirical literature, pioneered by Polachek (1980, 1992), has provided evidence of "a strong and robust negative association between conflict and trade" (Polachek 1992, p. 113). Conflict reduces trade among countries. Consequently a cost of conflict are the lost gains from trade. Country pairs engaged in the most trade have the least conflict (see Polachek 1992 and Polachek et al. 1999). The causal direction can go both ways: more trade means bigger losses from hostility, and therefore less hostility. Conversely, less conflict means less barriers to trade, and therefore more trade.[21]

Hence we should expect that the effects identified in chapters 6 and 7 will reinforce each other: less conflict will induce the formation of smaller political units both directly and via increasing openness. But that is not the end of the story. As shown in Spolaore (2001), when conflict interacts with trade, multiple equilibria in conflict, openness, and size of political units are possible. In one equilibrium, countries will be small, and consequently more open and less engaged in conflict. In such a world of high openness and low conflict, political size will matter less, therefore justifying small units as the equilibrium outcome. In another equilibrium, the world will be formed by larger countries, with less economic integration and more conflict. In such a world there will be larger benefits from the extent of the domestic market and the economies of scale in security, and consequently people will want to belong to larger countries in equilibrium.

In Spolaore's (2001) model the existence of multiple equilibria depends crucially on the heterogeneity costs associated with forming larger political units. If heterogeneity costs are very high, only small countries will be formed in equilibrium. If the heterogeneity costs are small enough, large unions will be the only equilibrium outcome. But for intermediate values of the heterogeneity costs, both a world of small countries and a world of large countries are possible in equilibrium. The key condition is that the costs of breaking up a union in a world of large countries must be larger than the benefits of forming a union in a world of smaller countries. The costs from breaking up an existing union include the reduced access to the market of each former union member. Such access is relatively valuable (i.e., has a higher impact on output) when markets in the rest of the world are close (because the other regions belong to a high-conflict union). By contrast, forming a union in a world of small countries and low conflict brings about relatively lower gains, as most of the benefits from trade can be obtained by an independent region through international exchanges with its neighbors. Therefore the same level of heterogeneity costs may prevent the formation of a union in a world of small countries (where the benefits from forming a union are relatively small) but may be offset by the higher costs from breaking a union in a world of large countries.

Within such model, is a world of small countries, less conflict, and high economic integration preferable to a world of large countries, high conflict, and low economic integration? Somewhat surprisingly, the answer is: not necessarily.

Obviously, for given borders low conflict is always better than high conflict. That is, in a world of large countries everyone will be better off if each government can credibly commit to choose low conflict over high conflict. However, in principle that does not mean that a world of small countries and low conflict would be preferable to a world of large countries and high conflict. Why? We can cite two reasons:

1. In a world of small countries, a given level of conflict is more expensive on a per capita basis. As we have stressed in our analysis, investment

in conflict is a public good from a country's perspective. Whether the costs of conflict per capita are actually lower in a small-country world than in a large-country world depends on whether the reduction in the absolute level of conflict is high enough to compensate for the fact that in each small country those costs have to be spread over a small population.

2. In a world of small countries, barriers to international trade are lower than in a world of large countries. However, trade that would occur within political boundaries (and therefore freely) in a world of large countries becomes trade across costly political borders in a world of small countries. Whether output per capita is actually higher in a world of small countries than in a world of large countries depends on whether the benefits from having *low* barriers between regions are high enough to compensate for the costs of having *more* barriers between regions.

However, there is an asymmetry between the large countries' equilibrium and the small countries' equilibrium. While it is true that either world may provide the higher level of utility in equilibrium, Spolaore (2001) shows that the conditions are less "stringent" for a world of small countries. The reason is, again, higher heterogeneity costs in larger countries. In other words, because of the heterogeneity costs, the welfare comparison between equilibria tends to "favor" a world of small countries, all other things being equal.

In summary, whether utility is higher in a world of small countries than in a world of large countries depends on whether the benefits from lower conflict compensate for the smaller base on which those costs must be spread, and on whether the benefits from lower barriers compensate for the losses due to more barriers between regions. Since heterogeneity costs are always lower in a world of small countries than in a world of large countries, the conditions for optimality are less stringent for the small countries' equilibrium than they are for the large countries' equilibrium.

8.6   Conclusions

In this chapter we extended our discussion of the relationship between conflict and size in order to account for an explicit "war game" in which both peaceful bargaining and violent confrontations are possible, the role of international law, and the relationship between conflict and trade. We argued that defense spending is important in both peaceful bargaining and wars, and that a higher probability of conflict and war is associated with incentives to form larger countries. While strengthening

international law may reduce conflict between two countries, it also reduces the incentives to form larger political unions, and may therefore
produce a breakup of countries and an increase in the overall level of
conflict. Finally, if conflict reduces trade, we should observe less conflict
and more trade in a world of smaller countries and more conflict and
less trade in a world of larger countries.

8.7 Appendix A: Ideological Conflict

While we have modeled conflict as distributional (over an economically
valuable pie), our model of international conflict between two sovereign
countries can be reinterpreted in terms of ideological conflict. For instance, consider two countries with different preferences over a unidimensional ideological issue. As long as each country is able to decide its
own policies independently and without affecting its neighbor, no conflict needs to arise. However, it is possible that decisions in one country
affect individuals in the other country. For instance, decisions may regard variables that affect the relationship between the two countries
(i.e., regulation of pollution with crossborder spillovers), and/or policies that each country sees as of direct concern to its citizens, even when
taking place within the other country's borders (human rights, religious
policies, etc.). While each country would like to impose its own most
preferred type, the equilibrium type will depend on the relative strength
of the two countries. To fix ideas, suppose that there exists a continuum
of types for some socioeconomic, cultural, religious, or otherwise defined variable that affects both countries simultaneously. Say the types
are defined over the segment $[a, b]$. Country j prefers type a, and obtains
a payoff equal to $(b - x)G$ whenever the "type" actually implemented
is x such that $a \leq x \leq b$. Analogously, country j' prefers type b, and obtains a payoff equal to $(x - a)G$ for $a \leq x \leq b$. When conflict is resolved
through the use of the two countries' relative strength (i.e., by using d_j
and $d_{j'}$), we have

$$x^* = \frac{d_j}{d_j + d_{j'}}a + \frac{d_{j'}}{d_j + d_{j'}}b, \tag{A8.1}$$

and the two countries' payoffs are given, respectively, by

$$\frac{d_j}{d_j + d_{j'}}(b - a)G \quad \text{and} \quad \frac{d_{j'}}{d_j + d_{j'}}(b - a)G,$$

which is formally equivalent to the specification above for $(b - a)G = R$.

Therefore, within a preference/ideological context, R can be interpreted as a measure of the ideological distance between the two countries: $(b - a)$ times the relevance of the issue, G.

While we do not pursue this specification explicitly within our framework of endogenous country formation, it is worth noting that our model of conflict can be given this alternative interpretation.[22]

8.8 Appendix B: Derivations

8.8.1 Derivation of Lemma 8.1
To derive lemma 8.1, we need to derive the equilibrium defense spending levels for each configuration of countries.

Two Countries
Denote with d_1^* (d_2^*) equilibrium defense spending in country 1 (2) when there are only two countries. The probability of a conflict between the two countries is $\pi/2$. Therefore the expected total payoff in country 1 as a function of defense spending is given by

$$\frac{\pi}{2} \frac{d_1}{d_1 + d_2} R - d_1. \tag{A8.2}$$

Analogously, country 2's expected payoff per capita is

$$\frac{\pi}{2} \frac{d_2}{d_1 + d_2} R - d_2. \tag{A8.3}$$

The Nash equilibrium levels of defense d_1^* and d_2^* are defined as

$$d_1^* = \arg\max \frac{\pi}{2} \frac{R d_1}{d_1 + d_2^*} - d_1, \tag{A8.4}$$

$$d_2^* = \arg\max \frac{\pi}{2} \frac{R d_2}{d_1^* + d_2} - d_2, \tag{A8.5}$$

which imply the first-order conditions

$$\frac{d_2^*}{(d_1^* + d_2^*)^2} = \frac{d_1^*}{(d_1^* + d_2^*)^2} = \frac{2}{\pi R}. \tag{A8.6}$$

The solution to (A8.6) is

$$d_1^* = d_2^* = \frac{\pi R}{8}. \tag{A8.7}$$

As each country has a total population of size equal to 2, defense spending per capita in each country is

$$\frac{d_1^*}{2} = \frac{d_2^*}{2} = \frac{\pi R}{16}. \tag{A8.8}$$

In a two-player game a unique Nash equilibrium is also coalition-proof.

Three Countries
When a country formed by two regions (e.g., country 1) coexists with two independent regions (e.g., country 2 and country 3), the Nash-equilibrium levels of defense equilibrium defense d_1^*, d_2^*, and d_3^* are given by

$$d_1^* = \arg\max_{d_1} \frac{\pi R}{4} \left[\frac{d_1}{d_1 + d_2^*} + \frac{d_1}{d_1 + d_3^*} \right] - d_1, \tag{A8.9}$$

$$d_2^* = \arg\max_{d_2} \frac{\pi R}{4} \left[\frac{d_2}{d_1^* + d_2} + \frac{d_2}{d_2 + d_3^*} \right] - d_2, \tag{A8.10}$$

$$d_3^* = \arg\max_{d_3} \frac{\pi R}{4} \left[\frac{d_3}{d_1^* + d_3} + \frac{d_3}{d_2^* + d_3} \right] - d_3. \tag{A8.11}$$

The solution is

$$d_1^* = d_2^* = d_3^* = \frac{\pi R}{8}. \tag{A8.12}$$

As country 1 has a population of size equal to 2, while countries 2 and 3 have population of sizes 2 and 3 each, we have level of defense per capita equal to $\pi R/16$ in country 1, and equal to $\pi R/8$ in countries 2 and 3.

We also need to show that the above Nash equilibrium (A8.12) is also coalition-proof. In fact, given any set of defense spending by any proper subset of countries, the game induced on the remaining countries has a unique Nash equilibrium.

First, given the level of defense spending in country 1 (d_1), the game induced on countries 2 and 3 has a unique Nash equilibrium, given by

$$d_2^*(d_1) = \arg\max_{d_2} \frac{\pi R}{4} \left[\frac{d_2}{d_1 + d_2} + \frac{d_2}{d_2 + d_3^*(d_1)} \right] - d_2, \tag{A8.13}$$

$$d_3^*(d_1) = \arg\max_{d_3} \frac{\pi R}{4} \left[\frac{d_3}{d_1 + d_3} + \frac{d_3}{d_2^*(d_1) + d_3} \right] - d_3. \tag{A8.14}$$

Second, given the level of defense spending in country 2 (d_2), the game induced on countries 1 and 3 has a unique Nash equilibrium characterized by the solution of the following two first-order conditions:

$$d_1^*(d_2) = \arg\max_{d_1} \frac{\pi R}{4} \left[\frac{d_1}{d_1 + d_2} + \frac{d_1}{d_1 + d_3^*(d_2)} \right] - d_1, \qquad (A8.15)$$

$$d_3^*(d_2) = \arg\max_{d_3} \frac{\pi R}{4} \left[\frac{d_3}{d_1^*(d_2) + d_3} + \frac{d_3}{d_2 + d_3} \right] - d_3. \qquad (A8.16)$$

Analogously, there exists a unique Nash equilibrium for the game induced on countries 1 and 2, given the actions of country 3.

Since the game induced on the remaining countries has a unique Nash equilibrium for any set of choices of defense spending by any proper subset of countries, we have, by definition, that the set of coalition-proof equilibria coincide with the Pareto efficient frontier of the set of Nash equilibria,[23] which in our case is given by the unique Nash equilibrium as characterized in equation (A8.12).

Four Countries
When four independent countries (e.g., countries 1, 2, 3, and 4, each of size equal to 1) coexist, the Nash equilibrium is given by

$$d_1^* = \arg\max_{d_1} \left\{ \frac{\pi R}{4} \left[\frac{d_1}{d_1 + d_2^*} + \frac{d_1}{d_1 + d_4^*} \right] - d_1 \right\}, \qquad (A8.17)$$

$$d_2^* = \arg\max_{d_2} \left\{ \frac{\pi R}{4} \left[\frac{d_2}{d_1^* + d_2} + \frac{d_2}{d_2 + d_3^*} \right] - d_2 \right\}, \qquad (A8.18)$$

$$d_3^* = \arg\max_{d_3} \left\{ \frac{\pi R}{4} \left[\frac{d_3}{d_2^* + d_3} + \frac{d_3}{d_3 + d_4^*} \right] - d_3 \right\}, \qquad (A8.19)$$

$$d_4^* = \arg\max_{d_4} \left\{ \frac{\pi R}{4} \left[\frac{d_4}{d_1^* + d_4} + \frac{d_4}{d_3^* + d_4} \right] - d_4 \right\}. \qquad (A8.20)$$

The solution is

$$d_1^* = d_2^* = d_3^* = d_4^* = \frac{\pi R}{8}, \qquad (A8.21)$$

which implies that defense spending per capita equal to $\pi R / 8$ in each country.

As in the case of three countries, it is straightforward to show that given any set of defense spending by any proper subset of countries, the game induced on the remaining countries has a unique Nash equilibrium. Therefore the levels of defense derived in equation (A8.21) characterize the unique coalition-proof equilibrium defense levels.

The analysis above shows that for any possible configuration of countries, in equilibrium we have that a country formed by two regions has defense per capita equal to $\pi R/16$, while a country formed by one region has defense per capita equal to $\pi R/8$.   ∎

8.8.2   Derivation of Lemma 8.2

The expected returns from conflict (including potential conflict that is resolved within a country's borders) can be calculated as follows:

With two countries, individuals in country 1 expect

$$\frac{1}{2}\left[\frac{\pi R}{4} + \frac{\pi R}{2}\frac{d_1^*}{d_1^* + d_2^*}\right] = \frac{\pi R}{4}. \tag{A8.22}$$

The same returns are expected by individuals in country 2.

With three countries, individuals in the larger country (e.g., country 1) expect

$$\frac{1}{2}\left[\frac{\pi R}{4} + \frac{\pi R}{4}\frac{d_1^*}{d_1^* + d_2^*} + \frac{\pi R}{4}\frac{d_1^*}{d_1^* + d_3^*}\right] = \frac{\pi R}{4}. \tag{A8.23}$$

With two small countries (e.g., countries 2 and 3), individuals expect

$$\frac{\pi R}{4}\frac{d_2^*}{d_1^* + d_2^*} + \frac{\pi R}{4}\frac{d_2^*}{d_2^* + d_3^*} = \frac{\pi R}{4}\frac{d_3^*}{d_1^* + d_3^*} + \frac{\pi R}{4}\frac{d_3^*}{d_2^* + d_3^*} = \frac{\pi R}{4}. \tag{A8.24}$$

Analogous calculations show that with four countries, each will expect $\pi R/4$.

The war costs are given by $(\pi/2)(\rho c/2)$ in a country formed by two regions (i.e., $s_i = 2$) and $\pi \rho c/2$ in a country formed by one region (i.e., $s_i = 1$). Therefore lemma 8.2 holds.

8.8.3   Derivation of Lemma 8.3

As shown above, the absolute level of defense in equilibrium is always $\pi R/8$. Therefore the expected probability of winning a conflict is $\frac{1}{2}$ for each country. In a country formed by two regions, expected conflict returns per capita net of expected war costs are given by

$$\frac{\pi R}{4}\frac{1}{2} + \frac{\pi}{2}\left[\frac{R}{2} - \rho\frac{c}{2}\right] = \frac{\pi(R - \rho c)}{4}, \tag{A8.25}$$

where the first term indicates the peaceful division of R within the country, the second term indicates the expected payoff from conflict resolution, and the third term refers to the costs of war.

By contrast, net payoff in a country formed by one region is

$$\frac{\pi}{2}\left[\frac{1}{2}R - \rho c\right] = \frac{\pi(R - 2\rho c)}{4}. \tag{A8.26}$$

Individual utility in a country formed by two regions is

$$U_{\text{uni}} = y - \frac{\pi R}{16} + \frac{\pi(R - \rho c)}{4} - h_k, \tag{A8.27}$$

while in a country formed by one region individual utility is given by

$$U_{\text{ind}} = y - \frac{\pi R}{8} + \frac{\pi(R - 2\rho c)}{4}. \tag{A8.28}$$

Therefore unification is (strictly) preferred to independence if and only if

$$\frac{\pi}{4}\left(\frac{R}{4} + \rho c\right) > h_k. \tag{A8.29}$$

∎

8.8.4 Derivation of Proposition 8.1

Proposition 8.1 is an immediate implication of lemma 8.3. It is immediate to see that proposition 8.1 characterizes a Nash equilibrium. Moreover for any other Nash equilibrium there will be a group of individuals who will be strictly better off by deviating and moving to the equilibrium characterized in proposition 8.1.

First, consider the case $\pi[(R/4) + \rho c]/4 < h_w$. In this case, voting for independence is a dominant strategy for each individual. For any equilibrium in which a majority has voted for unification, there exists a coalition of individuals (in fact, everyone) who would be better off by switching to independence. Hence independence for all regions is the only outcome that can be sustained as a coalition-proof Nash equilibrium.

When $h_w < \pi[(R/4) + \rho c]/4 < h_e$, any outcome in which the east is unified would be upset by a majority (in fact, all) eastern individuals, who are better off when the two eastern regions are independent. On the other hand, voting for unification is the dominant strategy in the west.

When $\pi[(R/4) + \rho c]/4 > h_e$, voting for unification is the dominant strategy everywhere.   ∎

9

Federalism and Decentralization

9.1 Introduction

National governments normally do not provide all the public goods and are not responsible for every policy. On the contrary, many policy prerogatives are attributed to subnational jurisdictions. Even though the degree of decentralization varies across countries, subnational levels of governments often have important policy functions and increasingly so.

In policy circles the discussion about fiscal federalism and decentralization often assumes a central role and, by and large, decentralization is looked at favorably.[1] As Oates (1999) puts it, "decentralization is in vogue." Our goal here is not to provide an overview of this field.[2] The more modest purpose of this chapter is to link our discussion of the optimal size of nations with that on the optimal amount of decentralization. In particular, we will discuss how the possibility of decentralizing government functions influences the size of countries in equilibrium.

Recall that in chapter 2 we asked the question, Why countries? That is, we investigated why it is not feasible to organize governments in a complex maze of overlapping jurisdictions. We argued that a single unified government economizes on the transactions costs and internalizes economies of scope lost in the "maze." In this chapter we view decentralization as an intermediate organization form in between the maze of overlapping jurisdictions on the one extreme and the one-level-of-government-does-it-all on the opposite extreme.

As we will see, the question of how much to decentralize is also closely linked to politicoeconomic considerations. The ideal level of decentralization will not be the same in a democracy and in a dictatorship.

9.2   Federalism

In the literature and in policy discussions the word "federalism" is used in two different ways. In the US tradition, more federalism implies giving more prerogatives to the federal government. In Europe and elsewhere, federalism is synonymous of decentralization. This difference reflects different initial conditions: in the United States, a federal system consolidated from territories that were originally loosely associated. In Europe (e.g., France, Spain, Italy, Belgium, and United Kingdom), more federalism implies moving away from centralized forms of government.

The literature on federalism typically focuses on three broad topics. One is the formation of federations, the classic modern contribution being Riker (1964). The second one is the attribution of responsibilities and prerogatives between different levels of governments, national and local. The third is the web of fiscal and budgetary relationships between national and local levels of government, and the related question of which level of government should use which type of taxes.

The analysis of this book has much to say about the first two points, and relatively little, if anything at all, about the third one. In what follows we briefly highlight how our arguments relate to parts of the literature on "federalism."

9.2.1   Formation of Federations

The discussion of what determines the size of a country is, of course, quite related to the question of why and how federations of previously independent regions form and stay together.

Let us go back for a moment to the discussion of chapter 2, where we argued that in the absence of transaction costs or economies of scale, one would not need "countries"—even federal ones. The world could be organized in a complex web of overlapping single-purpose jurisdictions. Suppose, for simplicity, a world in which that there exist only two public goods, A and B, and six million people. Suppose that the optimal unconstrained solution is to divide the world in three equal-size jurisdictions—each with two million people providing good A and two equal-size jurisdictions and each with three million people providing good B. That must mean that in each of the two B jurisdictions some citizens obtain and pay for good A from one of the A jurisdictions, while some other citizens get their A public good from a different A jurisdiction, which also provides public goods to citizens of the *other* B jurisdiction. Is that feasible?

For certain types of goods this situation would be impossible. The prime example is external defense and the ultimate monopoly of coercion: it would be hard to imagine individuals sharing, say, a school district but being subject to two different military jurisdictions, potentially at war with each other. Or, to think of an even more extreme example, citizens sharing a common local police force but not a common legal and judicial system or a national army. These arrangements are hard to imagine because there exists a fundamental bundle of public goods having to do with the ultimate ability to enforce laws and use force. These public goods must be shared by all individuals as a precondition for the common provision of other public goods. We call this view the "hierarchical hypothesis."

An extreme case that satisfies the hierarchical hypothesis is the one of centralized governments that provide all public goods, as should be familiar from chapter 3. But the hierarchical hypothesis per se does not require that *all* public goods be centralized. Only that the borders of jurisdictions that provide subordinate public goods should not cross the borders of those jurisdictions that provide the hierarchical public goods. In other words, different jurisdictions can be organized federally.

Therefore a federation is somewhere in between the maze of overlapping jurisdictions, and the simplified case of a single national government doing everything. A federal government delegates prerogative to state and local governments, but state and local borders do not cross federal borders.

The one policy prerogative that federal government cannot delegate downward is the military and the monopoly of coercion. In fact Riker's (1964) view about the creation of federations is precisely an argument about defense for security reasons against foreign threats. The fundamental reason he gives for why independent entities form a federation is to join military power. According to Riker, all federations are formed in response to a foreign threat, and by our terminology, a way of taking advantage of economies of scale in defense. Whether or not this is the *only* motivation for forming federation is debatable. For example, as discussed in chapter 6, the desire to form of a larger domestic market in a world of international trade barriers may play an important role. If this is the case, defense and protection of internal trade and common external trade policies should be two key components of the attributions of a federal government. But beyond those prerogatives, what else should the central government do? This is the question that we address in the next section.

Another related reason that leads to the formation of federations is the question of externalities. Certain policies followed independently by a region may have negative consequences if not coordinated with the policies of other regions. The formation of a federation allows for this coordination. A standard textbook example is pollution. Alternatively, there may exist positive externalities that could be lost if policies are chosen independently. If regions join a federation, these externalities can be "internalized"—that is, the federation can chose policies that fully take into account the cross effects among regions. We will return in greater detail to these issue in our discussion of the European Union in chapter 12.

9.2.2   The Attribution of Responsibilities between Different Levels of Government

Our discussion in the previous chapters can be used to address the question of the optimal attribution of responsibilities within different levels of governments. We can apply the basic trade-off between economies of scale and heterogeneity of preferences. In fact a classic argument for decentralization in the local public finance literature is that local governments are better suited at targeting local preferences. Obviously this argument is relevant to the extent that there are heterogeneous preferences: if every citizen of a country had identical preferences, the purpose of decentralization would vanish. Therefore, according to our analysis, lower levels of governments should provide those functions and goods for which economies of scale are less important and heterogeneity of preferences is higher. Higher levels of governments should provide public goods and policies for which economies of scale are large and heterogeneity of preferences low. For instance, defense and foreign policy clearly "belong" to the national government, while education and school policy seem to have a more local nature.

In practice, a distinction between government functions along a neatly organized trade-off may be far from clear-cut. Certainly from a practical perspective the problem of attribution of responsibilities is complex, and the answer may be different in different countries. In chapter 12 we address in some detail a specific case, the European Union, which can be thought of as a sort of federation, or at least as a union of countries.

In thinking about the formation of countries and the relationship between national governments, one can push the analogy with local governments within a state only up to a point. First of all, much of the literature on local governments focuses on mobility of individuals across jurisdictions, following the seminal contribution of Tiebout (1956). In an international context mobility is likely to be much lower. Moreover national governments normally engage in a vast array of redistributive policies across localities. This observation leads us directly into the issue of fiscal relationships between central and local governments.

9.2.3   The Fiscal Relationships between Central and Local Governments

A fundamental question in the fiscal federalism literature is the degree of correspondence between tax collection and provision of public goods. At one extreme we find systems where each jurisdiction has to raise enough taxes to pay for its expenditure. At the other extreme, taxes are collected nationally and transferred with some system to subnational levels of government. The choice between these two systems or something in between is very important.

Consider first the case of taxes collected nationally and spending programs decoded locally. This system often leads to fiscal imbalances, because subnational levels of governments do not internalize the fiscal costs of spending programs since taxes are collected nationally and spending programs are chosen locally.[3] Thus, purely from the point of view of economic incentives, one should enforce a complete correspondence between taxation and spending. Each level of government should collect the taxes needed to provide the public goods for which it is responsible. Much of the literature on fiscal federalism studies how to create intergovernmental fiscal relationship that minimize these perverse incentive problems.

The alternative type of decentralization structure requires a complete correspondence of taxation and expenditure for each level of government. This system avoids the incentive problems highlighted above but does not allow for direct redistributions across different regions of the same countries. These redistributions may be especially desirable in the case of large income disparities between regions, as discussed earlier in chapter 4. A progressive income tax would automatically redistribute from wealthier to poorer individuals, and therefore from richer to poorer regions. However, direct regional transfers have different redistributional implications that are not always desirable. For instance, if the poorer regions have a high degree of income inequality, the very rich resident of poor regions may end up gaining from a system of interregional transfers. On the other hand, for reasons discussed in chapter 4 as well, a national government may indeed choose to redistribute in favor of a certain region per se, and not only from rich to poor individuals nationwide.

In his classic work on constitutions Hayek (1959) opposes centralization because he sees it as a means for infringing on the so-called liberty of the wealthier regions, which would be subjected to expropriation from the poorer ones. He notes that "it is usually the authoritarian planner who, in the interest of uniformity, governmental efficiency, and administrative convenience supports the centralist tendencies and in this receives the strong support of poorer majorities, who wish to be able to tap the resources of the weather regions." Thus Hayek emphasizes two important connections, one between centralization and redistribution, and one between centralization and authoritarianism. An authoritarian government for Hayek can also be one supported by a majority, to the extent that this majority does not respect the rule of law and individual liberty.

A different argument concerning the interaction between political institutions and fiscal federalism is put forward by the literature on transition economies, and in particular, by Pian and Roland (1998).[4] According to this model decentralization in transition improves efficiency because it hardens the soft budget constraint. This effect is due to a competition between localities in providing productivity enhancing public infrastructure in a world of capital mobility.[5]

In practice, the discussion of what form of decentralization to adopt is also related to the level of development. Countries at a low level of development may simply not be able to leave to localities independent handling of public finance. Especially in poor and rural regions of developing countries, central government intervention may be unavoidable for reason of technical competence. Underestimating this problem may lead to serious problems from poor institutional design.

9.2.4 Decentralization, Dictators, and Democratization

As was mentioned earlier, an important question widely emphasized by the local public goods literature (in a literature started by Tiebout 1956) is that of mobility of individuals across jurisdictions.

The traditional view (see Musgrave 1959 and Oates 1972) is that tax competition among localities would lead to a race toward the bottom in terms of provision of public goods, implying an inefficiently small size of government. In other words, if we allowed for mobility of individuals, the optimal organization of subnational jurisdictions sketched above would lead to an undersupply of public goods. We labeled this view "traditional" because it does not take into account politicoeconomic considerations that would lead to a departure from optimal policies in the first place. In particular, if public policies are geared toward an excess of public spending, then decentralization would work against this distortion. Nondemocratic rulers that are not constrained by population heterogeneity would prefer more centralization in order to reduce the costs related to the provision of decentralized public goods and extracts more rents form the population. So for a Leviathan, a tightly controlled centralized government ensures high taxes and a use of the tax revenues favorable to the Leviathan and his elite.

Decentralization is, in this sense, a way of constraining Leviathans, particularly when geographical mobility is high. As Brennan and Buchanan (1980) argue, due to the tax competition between localities, "inter-jurisdictional mobility of persons in pursuit of fiscal gains can offer a partial or possibly complete substitute for explicit fiscal constraints on the taxing power" (p. 185). Hayek (1959) emphasized another advantage of decentralization not only as a way of achieving limited government intervention but also as a way of promoting competition. He stresses that "competition between local authorities... where there is freedom of movement provides ... that opportunity for experimentation with alternative methods which will secure most of the advantages of free growth." In other words, decentralization is the next best thing when certain services cannot be freely provided by the market.

A related point is raised by the theories of "market preserving federalism" as in Weingast (1995) and McKinnon (1997). According to the former author, for instance, a federalist arrangement solves the problem of enforcing property rights, by posing limits to the central ruler to expropriate too much.

Note the parallel between Brennan and Buchanan (1980) and what we labeled the traditional view of Musgrave (1959) and Oates (1972). Both agree that decentralization with mobility leads to lower taxes. While this is desirable for Brennan and Buchanan who view the government as a Leviathan, it is undesirable for Musgrave who views the government as benevolent.

However, it is not clear in Brennan and Buchanan *why* a Leviathan would choose to be constrained by a decentralized system of government. Our answer is that the Leviathan will need to either reduce taxes directly or decentralize in order to satisfy a sufficiently large fraction of the population to avoid insurrections. This constant will be particularly binding if the degree of heterogeneity of the population is high. In fact one of the major problems of dictators throughout history from the Roman emperors to the secretary generals of the communist party of the Soviet Union has been to keep ethnic or linguistic minorities under control. The delicate balance between expansion and increasing heterogeneity of the population is what decides the fate of empires.

As we argued in chapter 5, democratization should lead to the breakup of large political jurisdictions into smaller ones. Here we generalize our argument: when dictators fall, even if the nation does not break up, at least it becomes more decentralized. In other words, democratization may lead to decentralization, instead of, or in addition to, separatism. Empirical work by Ades and Glaeser (1995) and Panizza (1999) are consistent with this discussion. For instance, Panizza (1999) studies a vast sample of countries and finds that after controlling, among other things, for country size and ethnic fractionalization, measures of the degree of democratization are strongly and positively correlated with the degree of fiscal decentralization.

*9.3   A Formal Model of Decentralization

9.3.1   The Optimal Organization of Decentralized Jurisdictions

We explore how jurisdictions would be organized when there exists a hierarchy of public goods. To fix ideas, consider two public goods: A and B, with the relevant heterogeneity costs and economies of scale parameters denoted, as usual, by a_A, a_B, k_A, and k_B, as in chapter 2. Utility, as usual, is given by[6]

$$u_i = y - t_i + g - a_A l_{Ai} - a_B l_{Bi}. \tag{9.1}$$

If the two goods can be provided separately, namely by distinct governments within distinctly identified borders, average utility will be maximized as long as good A is provided by N_A governments and good B is provided by N_B governments, where N_A is the positive integer closer to $\sqrt{a_A/4k_A}$ and N_B is the positive integer closer to $\sqrt{a_B/4k_B}$.

As in the example discussed before, suppose, for instance, that $N_A = 2$ and $N_B = 3$. This would mean that half of the citizens of the central B-jurisdiction would obtain good A from the left A-jurisdiction, while the other half would obtain it from the right A-jurisdiction.[7]

Now assume that a government can provide good B only if all his residents share the same good A. In other words, we assume the following hierarchical hypothesis:

Two citizens who share the same good B must also share the same good A while the inverse does not hold; two citizens who share the same A can belong to different B-jurisdictions.

How does this assumption affect the optimal size of jurisdictions? Let N_A^h and N_B^h denote the optimal number of A-jurisdictions and B-jurisdictions when the hierarchical hypothesis is introduced. We will continue to use N_A and N_B to denote the optimal number of A-jurisdictions and B-jurisdictions that would be chosen if hierarchical considerations could be ignored.

The following result characterizes the optimal size of jurisdictions under the hypothesis of hierarchical public goods:

PROPOSITION 9.1   If $N_A > N_B$, that is, if heterogeneity costs relative to economies of scale are higher for public good A than for public good B, the optimal solution is to have $N_A^h = N_B^h = N_{AB}^h$, where N_{AB}^h is the integer closer to

$$\sqrt{\frac{a_A + a_B}{4(k_A + k_B)}}. \tag{9.2}$$

The proof is in the appendix.

In other words, if the primary good implies relatively smaller jurisdictions than the secondary good, the optimal solution is to provide unified jurisdictions that supply both goods in a centralized way. Therefore this is another case in which we have a centralized jurisdiction that does everything.

Note that, since $a_A/k_A > a_B/k_B$, we have

$$\sqrt{\frac{a_A}{4k_A}} > \sqrt{\frac{a_A + a_B}{4(k_A + k_B)}} > \sqrt{\frac{a_B}{4k_B}}, \tag{9.3}$$

which implies that, in general, the optimal number of jurisdictions N_{AB}^h will be smaller than N_A and larger than N_B.

For example, A is a defense system and B is a system of earthquake and hurricane insurance. Everybody would like large jurisdictions that provide wider insurance against natural disasters, but it may not be feasible to share such a civil system if different regions have different military/legal systems. When the hurricane strikes, the other regions may refuse to provide help in the absence of potential coercion. This is why it is difficult to find confederations in which countries maintain complete independence for defense but share broad insurance institutions for natural disasters, and so on. More generally, the model sheds light on why many small states have exclusive control over functions that they would be better off sharing with their neighbors. The reason lies in their desire to maintain full control over other essential functions with much higher heterogeneity costs. Therefore the existence of "essential" goods with high heterogeneity costs provides an additional force toward unification of public services, beyond the centralizing forces due to direct economies of scope in production.

However, in general, it seems likely that the heterogeneity costs to economies of scale ratio would be lower for the essential good A than for good B (again, think of defense/law and order vs. school districts or water supply). In that case, a pyramidal system is the natural solution. Formally,[8]

PROPOSITION 9.2   If $N_A < N_B$, that is, if the heterogeneity costs to economies of scale ratio is higher for public good A than for public good B, the optimal solution is a world with N_A^h A-jurisdictions and N_B^h B-jurisdictions, where N_A^h and N_B^h are the integers closer, respectively, to $\sqrt{a_A/4k_A}$ and $\sqrt{a_B/4k_B}$ such that

1. the ratio N_B^h/N_A^h is also an integer, and

2. for any other pairs of integers N' and N'' such that N''/N' is also an integer,

$$\frac{a_A}{4N_A^h} + k_A N_A^h + \frac{a_B}{4N_B^h} + k_B N_B^h \le \frac{a_A}{4N'} + k_A N' + \frac{a_B}{4N'} + k_B N''. \qquad (9.4)$$

The proof is in the appendix.

The following numerical example will illustrate our results.

Suppose that $a_A = 16$, $a_B = 324$, and $k_1 = k_2 = 1$. Then the unconstrained solution would be 2 jurisdictions for A and 9 for B. But this would mean that a B jurisdiction (the central one) would cross the borders of the two A jurisdictions. That is, half of the citizens of the central B-jurisdiction would belong to the left A-jurisdiction, while the other half would belong to the right A-jurisdiction (figure 9.1). This example violates the constraint that citizens who share good B must also share the same good A.

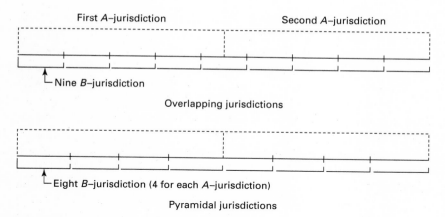

Figure 9.1
Overlapping jurisdictions and pyramidal jurisdictions

One can show that for our choice of parameters, the constrained solution is $N_A^h = 2$ and $N_B^h = 8$. That is, the number of B-jurisdictions is reduced to allow for a pyramidal structure in which citizens who belong to a given A-jurisdiction are divided into four B-jurisdictions, with no overlap. The fact that our example implies an "adjustment" of the number of smaller jurisdictions does not mean that this must always be the case. Which type of jurisdiction will "adapt" to fit into a pyramidal system does not depend on jurisdictions' size but *on the relative importance of each type of public good in individuals' utility function.* For example, consider the following different numerical example: $a_A = 16$, $a_B = 3240$, $k_A = 1$, and $k_B = 10$. The unconstrained solutions are unchanged: two A-jurisdictions and nine B-jurisdictions. However, now the heterogeneity costs and the economies of scale parameters for good B are ten times higher than in the previous example. Such increase in the "importance" of good B leads to a different "constrained" solution. Now utility is maximized with three A-jurisdictions and nine B-jurisdictions: the "less important" good (in utility terms) has to "adapt." This example is instructive because it points to the fact that "smaller" does not mean "less important:" jurisdictions may be smaller because they entail very high heterogeneity costs, which offset large economies of scale.

9.3.2   Decentralization with Leviathans
Let's return to the model of a Leviathan who is interested in maximizing fiscal rent but subject to the constraint that a fraction δ of the population

has to be kept above a certain minimum level of utility. Suppose that this Leviathan must provide two public goods (e.g., A and B), costing k_A and k_B. If rulers could completely ignore individuals' utility (except in the limited sense that they must provide the two public goods), they could maximize their net rents by supplying both goods in a completely centralized fashion (i.e., by forming just one centralized Leviathan). However, as the no insurrection constraint δ rises, the Leviathan faces the problem of increasing heterogeneity costs in the larger jurisdiction. As we saw in chapter 5, smaller jurisdictions provide a way to deal with that constraint. Decentralization provides an alternative way of reducing those costs. How much would a Leviathan decentralize? Would he decentralize more or less than what would be socially optimal?

In this section we briefly consider this issue in a simple model of decentralization. Suppose that A (defense) is an essential good that must be shared by all subjects who also share good B. Suppose that borders are decided according to a two-stage process. First, the borders of A-jurisdictions are determined in order to maximize the joint rents of the Leviathan. Once A-borders are determined, the Leviathan decides how many B-jurisdictions to provide within his borders.[9]

Since we are interested in political decentralization and not in purely administrative subdivisions, we will assume, quite naturally, that if the Leviathan decides to decentralize and create B-jurisdictions, he will not be able to influence the choice over the location (i.e., the type) of public good B, which will be determined by the citizens of each autonomous B-jurisdiction. Consistent with our previous analysis, such citizens will then pick the median location within their jurisdictions.[10]

We will make the following simplifying assumptions:

1. $k_A > k_B$
2. $a_A = a_B = a$

Since we are interested in the Leviathan's choices over decentralization, we will focus on the second-stage problem (i.e., the choice of borders for public good B, taking the borders for public good A as given).

Suppose that the Leviathan controls a country of size s, whereby s is the size of the A-jurisdiction. One public good located in the middle of the country is provided to all inhabitants of the jurisdiction at a total cost k_A. To fix ideas, suppose that a social planner who could decide the number of B-jurisdictions (given A-borders) would choose to provide two jurisdictions. It is immediate to verify that social welfare is higher with two B-jurisdictions than with just one if and only if[11]

$$k_B \leq \frac{as^2}{8}. \tag{9.5}$$

How many B-jurisdictions will the Leviathan provide? As we have already mentioned, a Leviathan who faces no democratic constraint ($\delta = 0$) would never decentralize (i.e., he would never provide two separate B-jurisdictions), since that would just reduce his rents by k_B. He would provide the minimum amount of public good B (one), located at the center of the country, exactly like public good A. How about a Leviathan who faces a democratic constraint (e.g., $0 < \delta < \frac{1}{2}$)? If such a Leviathan chooses complete centralization, he will be able to charge the following tax to each individual:[12]

$$t = y - u_0 - a\delta s. \tag{9.6}$$

Therefore he will be able to extract the following total rent per person:

$$R_1 = (y - u_0 - a\delta s)s - k_A - k_B. \tag{9.7}$$

By contrast, if the Leviathan provides two B-jurisdictions, he will be able to charge the following tax per person:[13]

$$t = y - u_0 - \frac{as}{4}. \tag{9.8}$$

Equation (9.7) derives from the geometry of utilities. Figure 9.2 illustrates individual utilities from public goods when public good A is located in the middle of the country (i.e., at a distance $s/2$ from the left border) and two public goods B are located at distances $s/4$ and $3s/4$ from the left border.

Clearly, since individuals are uniformly distributed, half of the population is located between points $s/4$ and $3s/4$. For each individual located between $s/4$ and $3s/4$ the sum of the distances from the two public goods (i.e., the distance from A plus the distance from the nearest B) is equal to $s/4$. Hence the utility from the two public goods is equal to $-as/4$. Consequently a Leviathan who has to give a total utility at least as large as u_0 to at least $\delta \leq \frac{1}{2}$ of the population will have to set taxes such that $u_0 = y - t - a(s/4) = y - t - as/4$, which can be rewritten as equation (9.7).

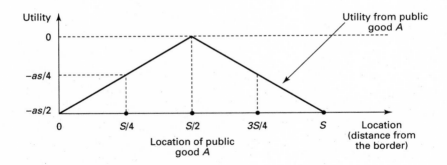

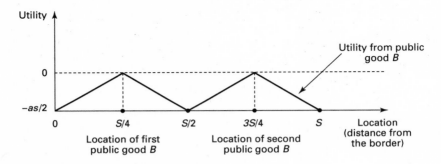

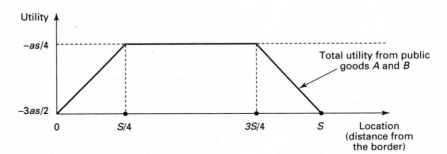

Figure 9.2
Utility from public goods A and B

Hence in the case of decentralization the Leviathan will be able to achieve the following rent:

$$R_2 = \left(y - u_0 - \frac{as}{4} \right) s - k_A - 2k_B. \tag{9.9}$$

By comparing (9.6) and (9.8), we can immediately obtain the following:

PROPOSITION 9.3   The Leviathan will choose to decentralize—that is, $R_2 \geq R_1$—if and only if the "democratic constraint" δ is high enough, namely if and only if the following condition is satisfied:

$$\delta \geq \frac{1}{4} + \frac{k_B}{as^2}. \tag{9.10}$$

The proposition above is instructive:

1. All other things equal, decentralization is more likely the higher is δ.

2. At low levels of $\delta (\delta \leq \frac{1}{4})$, the Leviathan would *never* decentralize, no matter how small is k_B (the cost of the B public good). Of course, that is inefficient for any $k_B \leq as^2/8$.

3. For higher levels of δ, the Leviathan may or may not decentralize. For all $\frac{1}{4} < \delta \leq \frac{3}{8}$, he will *not* decentralize, although decentralization would be efficient, as long as $as^2(\delta - \frac{1}{4}) \leq k_B \leq as^2/8$. On the other hand, if $k_B < as^2(\delta - \frac{1}{4}) \leq as^2/8$, the Leviathan will (efficiently) decentralize.

4. When $\frac{3}{8} < \delta < \frac{1}{2}$, we have efficient decentralization if $k_B < as^2/8 < as^2 (\delta - \frac{1}{4})$ but inefficient decentralization if $as^2/8 < k_B < as^2(\delta - \frac{1}{4})$.

In other words, very dictatorial Leviathans will never decentralize, even when it is efficient. Semidictatorial Leviathans will sometime decentralize but not as often as they should. On the other hand, almost-democratic Leviathans may sometime decentralize too much to reduce the heterogeneity costs in their jurisdiction.

Our analysis so far is based on the reasonable assumption that within decentralized jurisdictions the location of the public good is chosen by the local median voter (political decentralization). However, an alternative assumption is that the Leviathan can also influence the location of good B (the local capital) within each jurisdiction. In this case the Leviathan would have an additional tool to maximize his rents when faced with heterogeneity costs. For example, within our example of two B-jurisdictions, a rent-maximizing Leviathan may have an incentive to place the local capital of each B-jurisdiction farther away from the *local* median and closer to the *national* median. Why? A Leviathan who does not need to please a majority of the population but needs to please a minority (i.e., a privileged elite) can extract higher rents if he can increase the utility of the higher-utility individuals (the elite) who are located near the country's capital by reducing the distance between them and their favored good B. Of course, this would take place at the expense of the people located far from the center. Under this alternative specification, one would have a further bias against decentralization in a nondemocratic world. In a nondemocratic country, even when separate jurisdictions are indeed created, the actual choice of *local* policies would be closer to national preferences (and more distant from local preferences) than if local policies were chosen democratically.

9.4   Conclusions

In this chapter we examined the question of decentralization as an organization of governments that is intermediate between a maze of overlapping jurisdictions and the case of a unique central government that does it all. In this context, the trade-off between economies of scale and heterogeneity of preferences provides a critical point of view to address the question of attribution of responsibilities between different levels of government.

We have also examined how different levels of centralization would be chosen by a Leviathan and how the latter's policies would be influenced by arrangements concerning fiscal decentralization. Specifically, we have argued that a relatively unconstrained Leviathan would choose a centralized system; as a democratic constraint, or a no insurrection constraint, becomes more binding, even a Leviathan is forced to decentralize. Thus we predict a positive correlation between decentralization and democratization.

9.5   Appendix: Derivation of Propositions 9.1

Since no two individuals can belong to the same B-jurisdiction but to two different A-jurisdictions, A-jurisdictions and B-jurisdictions must have the same size. But suppose not. Then the A-jurisdiction would have to be larger, and utility could be improved by (1) reducing the size of the A-jurisdiction to the size of the B-jurisdiction and/or (2) enlarging the size of the B-jurisdiction to make it equal to the size of the A-jurisdiction. Since the two types of jurisdictions must have equal size (call it $1/N_{AB}$) at an optimum, their optimal common size will be determined by the maximization of

$$g - \frac{a_A + a_B}{4 N_{AB}} + y - (k_A + k_B) N_{AB},$$

which implies equation (9.1) of proposition 9.1.

10   Size and Economic Performance

10.1   Introduction

In this chapter we explore the empirical evidence concerning two important implications of our models:

• The size of government is inversely related to country size, that is, the ratio of government spending over GDP should be larger in smaller countries.

• The relationship between country size and economic success, measured by achievements in terms of growth and per capita income depends on the trade regime. Small countries can prosper in a world of free trade if they adopt open policies; while in a world of trade restrictions, larger countries have an advantage, since they have larger markets.

An empirical examination of these two proposition leads us straight into two major areas of empirical research, namely what explains the size of government, and the determinants of economic growth. We do not plan to even begin to review the results of these two vast areas of research; this task would require not one but two volumes.[1] Nevertheless, the existing empirical evidence on these two topics will help us choose what variables to hold constant when we examine the relationship of country size to government size, trade, and growth.

We begin, in section 10.2, by exploring the correlation between country size and government size. This section heavily draws upon Alesina and Wacziarg (1998). In section 10.3 we explore the relationship of country size to trade and growth. This section is vastly based upon Alesina, Spolaore, and Wacziarg (2000).

10.2 Small Countries and Large Governments

10.2.1 Basic Correlations

We begin in table 10.1 with some basic correlations linking various measures of government size and its components to the size of countries measured by their population. Government spending shares are measured for the five-year period, from 1986 to 1990, which is the most recent period for which all the categories of outlays were available on a comparable basis for most countries when the empirical work was performed. Since the emphasis of this evidence is on cross-country comparisons, the fact that the data are not very recent is not a major problem.

Country size is negatively related to the share of government consumption, the share of total government current expenditures (including transfers and payments) the share of consumption spending excluding education and defense, and the share of education related expenditures. Country size appears unrelated to defense spending and to public investment. As for the former, an important determinant of defense spending is, of course, the structure of international military alliances. So, while a small country in isolation may have to spend a lot per capital on defense to achieve a given level of military security, it may also opt to free ride in an alliance with larger countries.[2] As for public investment one has to keep in mind that this variable is very poorly measured, especially in developing countries. Therefore one cannot draw especially strong conclusions.

Broadly speaking, these simple correlations suggest that larger countries can afford to have a smaller government and therefore lower per capita taxes. This is one of the crucial implications of our models. However, many other factors in addition to the size of the country influence the size of government.

10.2.2 Multivariate Regressions

We now look at multivariate regression for government consumption. Table 10.2 presents estimates for the log of population when several controls are included sequentially. We do this for the 1985 to 1992 time period, which is the most recent period for which these data are available.

The coefficient estimates are negative and significant at standard confidence levels in every specification, indicating the existence of increasing returns to the provision of public goods. It is noteworthy that the coefficient of size remains significant even after controlling for population density, and an exhaustive set of regional dummies. As expected, density enters negatively but does not eliminate the effect of size.[3]

Table 10.1
Univariate regressions for openness and government size, 1986–1990 averages

Dependent variable	Government consumption	Government current expenditure	Government consumption net of defense/education	Defense spending	Education spending	Public investment
Constant	28.253	35.689	24.174	4.276	6.546	6.858
	(6.753)	(7.873)	(5.186)	(2.110)	(5.769)	(1.101)
	−0.865	−1.322	−0.719	−0.120	−0.301	0.018
Log population 1985	(−1.877)	(−2.653)	(−1.347)	(−0.616)	(−2.508)	(0.029)
R-squared	0.031	0.047	0.017	0.003	0.080	0.000
Number of observations	132	101	69	81	103	48

Source: For the original sources of these data, see table 1 of Alesina and Wacziarg (1998).
Note: Country size measured by the log of population. *t*-statistics are based on heteroskedastic-consistent (White-robust) standard errors, and are in parentheses.

Table 10.2
OLS regressions for the ratio of government consumption to GDP, 1985–1992

Dependent variable	(1)	(2)	(3)	(4)	(5)	(6)
Constant	27.393	46.931	47.230	30.899	54.951	53.823
	(7.725)	(7.075)	(7.003)	(8.832)	(5.015)	(4.849)
Log population 1985	−0.777	−0.830	−8.54	−0.775	−1.102	−1.90
	(−1.949)	(−2.403)	(−2.412)	(−2.324)	(−3.479)	(−3.425)
Log per capita income 1985	—	−1.686	−1.742	—	−2.015	−1.945
		(−1.823)	(−1.8550)		(−1.561)	(−1.501)
Urbanization rate 1990	—	−0.115	−0.104	—	−0.090	−0.075
		(−2.513)	(−2.140)		(−2.147)	(−1.659)
Population density 1985	—	—	−1.628	—	—	−1.755
			(−2.529)			(−1.948)
Latin America Dummy	—	—	—	−6.915	−6.865	−7.089
				(−2.907)	(−3.045)	(−3.139)
Sub-Saharan Africa Dummy	—	—	—	0.910	−4.036	−3.812
				(0.411)	(−1.415)	(−1.313)
South East Asia Dummy	—	—	—	−6.075	−7.151	−6.121
				(−2.165)	(−3.149)	(−2.514)
OECD Dummy	—	—	—	−9.658	−5.298	−5.807
				(−4.598)	(−2.303)	(−2.468)
SSR	9931.38	7152.74	7061.57	7442.67	6395.25	6306.73
Adjusted R-squared	0.022	0.275	0.279	0.245	0.331	0.335
Number of observations	136	133	133	136	133	136

Source: See table 10.1.
Note: t-statistics based on heteroskedastic-consistent (White-robust) standard errors, and are in parentheses.

Table 10.3
OLS regressions for the ratio of government consumption to GDP for different time periods

Dependent variable	1960–90	1960–92	1985–92	1990–92
Log population	−0.711	−0.705	−1.090	−1.033
	(−1.980)	(−1.982)	(−3.425)	(−3.015)
Adjusted R-squared	0.326	0.334	0.335	0.334
Number of observations	117	117	133	107

Source: See table 10.1.
Note: t-statistics based on heteroskedastic-consistent (White-robust) standard errors, and are in parentheses. Other controls (not shown) are the same as column 6 of table 10.2.

Many of the countries in the sample obtained independence relatively recently. Since it may take several years, or decades, for a decolonized country to adjust its public sector to its needs, one may expect that multivariate regressions on the determinants of government size should be more meaningful in more recent years. In technical terms, in more recent years the size of government may be closer to its steady state after the postdecolonization adjustment.

The results described in table 10.3 are broadly consistent with this interpretation. This table shows the coefficient on population size for each of the five-year periods; the specification is the same as that of column 6 of table 10.2, even though all the other coefficients are not shown. The results suggest that the effect of country size is more visible, both in terms of magnitude and in terms of statistical significance in more recent periods. One possible interpretation for this finding is that many newly decolonized countries in the 1960s had yet to build up their public sectors. As their governments converged to their equilibrium size, the effect of the fundamental determinants of government size started to play a larger role. A different interpretation of these results may simply be that measurement problems are larger in earlier periods.

According to our theory, larger countries should have smaller governments because of economies of scale in the provision of public goods. Thus we should expect expenditures related to nonrival public goods such as roads, parks, and general administration to bear a negative relationship to country size. The same cannot be expected, however, for transfers and interest payments on the public debt.

Table 10.4 is broadly consistent with this interpretation. The right-hand side variables used for each of the government spending components are not identical, since different items of government outlays are

Table 10.4
OLS regressions for various categories of public spending, 1985–1992

Dependent variable	Public consumption (1)	Public expenditures net of defense/education (2)	Expenditures including transfers/interest (3)	Public expenditure on defense (4)	Public expenditure on education (5)	Public investment (6)
Constant	57.802 (4.876)	39.544 (1.662)	10.323 (0.534)	-2.521 (-0.376)	-0.322 (-0.105)	54.413 (2.085)
Log population 1985	-1.260 (-3.445)	-2.061 (-2.651)	-1.560 (-2.071)	-0.008 (-0.027)	-0.253 (-1.874)	0.430 (0.880)
Log per capita income 1986	-2.187 (-1.596)	0.892 (0.328)	3.899 (2.304)	1.211 (1.981)	0.879 (2.805)	-3.232 (-1.550)
Population density 1986	-1.615 (-1.838)	—	0.108 (0.041)	—	-0.558 (-3.120)	-4.989 (-2.195)
Democracy index 1985–1989	—	-0.702 (-0.209)	—	-4.177 (-1.994)	-0.783 (-0.913)	-1.659 (0.552)
Dependency ratio 1985	—	—	9.185 (0.810)	—	—	-16.503 (-2.037)
Urbanization rate 1990	-0.081 (-1.649)	-0.009 (-0.135)	—	—	—	—
Ethnolinguistic fractionalization	—	-0.074 (-1.255)	-0.081 (-1.522)	-0.24 (-2.382)	—	—
War dummy (1960–1985)	—	—	—	0.087 (0.415)	—	—

Revolutions 1985–1989	—	—	—	3.183 (1.462)	—	—
Latin America Dummy	-6.766 (-2.784)	-10.215 (-4.279)	-10.742 (-3.285)	-1.657 (-0.897)	-0.125 (0.171)	-4.888 (-3.140)
Sub-Saharan Africa Dummy	-4.574 (-1.606)	-3.811 (-0.954)	-1.570 (0.410)	-0.988 (-0.792)	0.029 (0.048)	-2.824 (-1.762)
South East Asia Dummy	-6.232 (2.568)	-5.660 (-1.720)	-5.002 (-1.511)	-2.023 (-1.627)	-0.428 (-0.831)	-5.518 (-3.394)
OECD Dummy	-5.561 (-2.290)	4.214 (1.096)	1.156 (0.242)	-1.876 (-0.882)	0.016 (0.0240)	6.262 (-2.197)
Adjusted R-squared	0.341	0.437	0.349	0.187	0.189	0.389
Number of observations	130	61	87	71	103	48

Source: See table 10.1.

Note: t-statistics based on heteroskedastic-consistent (White-robust) standard errors, and are in parentheses. All dependent variables enter as percentage points of GDP. All regressions are for the 1980 to 1984 period.

especially influenced by special factors. For example, defense spending may be especially sensitive to political instability and wars, while other components of government spending are sensitive to other variables. Government consumption net of spending on defense and education is significantly negatively related to size, and this is not sensitive to the inclusion of any of the controls appearing in column 2. Similarly this result is robust with respect to different time periods.[4] However, as we move to the broadest measure of government expenditure, which includes transfers and interest payments (column 3), which should not be related to country size, the effect of the log of population, while still negative, loses some of its statistical significance, relative to column 1. The magnitudes of these effects, for columns 1 through 3, are roughly equal, in line with our theoretical predictions. Adding transfers and interest payments to government consumption should not modify the estimated effect of country size if the added categories are unrelated to it.

Columns 4 and 5 contain estimates for government spending on defense and education (as a share of GDP) respectively. While defense spending seems unrelated to country size, a result that we pointed out above, the results for education related expenditures are somewhat more surprising. We indeed find (weak) evidence that larger countries tend to spend less on education. This may come as a surprise because education is not generally considered to be a nonrival good, so that its cost should rise roughly proportionately with population (for a fixed desired level of educational services). However, the magnitude of the effects is much smaller than for columns 1 through 3, and the coefficient is only borderline significant at standard confidence levels.

Last, column 6 examines the relationship between country size and the ratio of public investment to GDP. Although the coefficient on the log of population is negative, it is statistically insignificant and much smaller in magnitude than the corresponding estimate for broad categories of government outlays (columns 1–3). This is also true when any of the control variables appearing in the public investment equation are excluded. However, one should note that the cross-country data for public investment are probably characterized by significant measurement error, to put it mildly.

10.2.3   Openness and the Size of Government

The previous discussion implies a positive correlation between size of government and openness. Small countries have a larger government in per capita terms and are more open. So more open economies have a larger government, since they are relatively small.

Rodrik (1998) has put forward a different argument (originally suggested by Cameron 1978) linking openness and government size. This author argues that more open countries have larger governments (in per capita terms) because since they are more open to international shocks, they need a larger stabilizing role of government. Therefore this theory should apply, especially or exclusively, to government transfers. He finds that for OECD countries openness is strongly correlated with the size of transfers over GDP. This holds both when openness is simply measured by the share of trade over GDP, or by the product of a terms of trade share over GDP. Instead, openness is unrelated to the size of government consumption: there is no correlation between government consumption and openness within the OECD country group. The sample of OECD countries is relatively small, and it is not clear how robust Rodrik's results are to the inclusion of other possible determinants of the size of government transfers. For example, within the OECD country small and open economies tend to have more proportional electoral systems. Milesi-Ferretti, Perotti, and Rostagno (2002), show that the effect of these measures of openness on the size of government transfers disappears when one controls for the degree of proportionality of the electoral system in OECD countries.[5] Although it is hard to disentangle the effects of these variables on the size of transfers, given the small sample size, the effect of the electoral system is much stronger than the effect of openness.

As for developing countries, Rodrik does not find any relationship between openness and the size of government transfers, which he attributes to the poor quality of the data on transfer for developing countries. Therefore he uses government consumption to establish a relationship between size of government and openness. That is, Rodrik finds a relationship between government consumption and openness, and not between transfer and openness, which is what his argument would imply. Whether data on government consumption in developing countries are of better quality than data on government consumption is highly debatable. Rodrik's results, instead, hinge crucially on the difference in the quality of these data.

In summary, Rodrik's view implies a direct correlation between size of government and openness because of the stabilizing role of government. The argument set forth in this book is that this correlation is "mediated" by the size of countries: small countries should have larger governments and be more open. In principle, these two views are not incompatible. Rodrik's point should apply especially to government transfers.

However, the evidence on transfers, consistent with Rodrik's point, is lacking for developing countries and inconclusive for OECD countries. The argument put forward in this book should apply more directly to government consumption, and in this chapter we have presented supporting evidence on this point.

10.3 Openness, Growth, and Size of Countries

This section, which is based upon section 3 of Alesina, Spolaore, and Wacziarg (2000), tests the predictions that both the level of per capita income and the rate of growth of the economy should be

1. positively related to trade openness,

2. positively related to country size, and

3. negatively related to country size multiplied by openness.

Smaller countries benefit more from being open to trade than large countries, or, to put this another way, more open countries benefit less from size than countries that are more closed to trade.

Previous research has provided some support for this hypothesis: Ades and Glaeser (1999), in a sample of poor countries, show that the interaction between openness and country size bears a significantly negative estimated coefficient. However, they use per capita income as a measure of market size, whereas we use total income or population. Wacziarg (1998) extends the Ades and Glaeser results to a wider sample of countries. Vamvakidis (1997) presents similar regressions, but uses policy measures for openness, rather than trade volumes. He also obtains a significantly negative estimate for the interaction between openness and market size.

10.3.1 Some Simple Statistics
We begin in table 10.5 with some simple correlations for openness, country size, and growth. We measure openness as the ratio of import plus exports over GDP, which is available for most countries. Openness is positively correlated with growth but negatively correlated with both of our measures of country size, which is consistent with our discussion of the relationship between a country's size and its degree of openness to trade.

More interesting as a test of our theory is table 10.6, which presents conditional correlations. First, the correlation between openness and the

Table 10.5
Simple correlations for growth, per capita income, openness, and country size

	Growth	Log GDP	Log per capita GDP 1960	Log population	Openness
Average annual growth	1.000				
Log total GDP	0.228	1.000			
Log per capita GDP 1960	0.197	0.521	1.000		
Log population	0.042	0.872	0.053	1.000	
Openness ratio	0.368	−0.418	0.111	−0.602	1.000
Number of observations 119					

Sources: From Alesina, Spolaore, and Wacziarg (2000), based on data from Summers and Heston (xxxx).
Note: All variables except log income per capita 1960 are averaged over the 1960 to 1989 period.

Table 10.6
Conditional correlations

Variable	Conditioning statement[a]	Correlation with growth[b]	Number of observations
Openness	Log population > median = 8.629	0.150	58
Openness	Log population ≤ median = 8.629	0.641	61
Openness	Log GDP > median = 16.049	0.353	59
Openness	Log GDP ≤ median = 16.049	0.637	60
Log population	Openness > median = 52.559	−0.116	59
Log population	Openness ≤ median = 52.559	0.454	60
Log GDP	Openness > median = 52.559	0.089	59
Log GDP	Openness ≤ median = 52.559	0.547	60

Sources: From Alesina, Spolaore, and Wacziarg (2000), based on data from Summers and Heston (xxxx).
a. Medians are computed from individual samples, while correlations are common sample correlations.
b. Average annual growth rate of per capita GDP, 1960 to 1989.

growth of per capita income is equal to 0.64 for small countries (where "small" is defined by restricting the sample to countries with the log of population below the full sample median), while it is only 0.15 for large countries (large countries are all those that are not small). Second, the correlation between the log of population and growth is 0.45 conditional on openness being below the full sample median, while it is slightly negative (-0.12) for open countries. The same holds when considering the correlation of the log of GDP with growth. Thus country size is correlated less or not at all with growth for countries that are more open to trade.

10.3.2 Regression Analysis

Table 10.7 presents regressions for averaged variables over the period 1960 to 1989. For each measure of country size, we show three specifications. First, we give a regression of growth on a constant, openness, country size and their interaction. Second, we add the logarithm of per capita income, measured in 1960. Last, other determinants of growth commonly identified in the literature are included in regression. These are the ratio of government consumption to GDP, the fertility rate, male and female human capital, and the investment rate. Throughout, the size of the sample was determined solely by the availability of data. That is, the sample size decreases as more variables are included in the regressions, as some newly included variables are available for fewer countries.

The signs of the coefficients are consistent with the theory: the interaction term bears a negative coefficient, while both country size and openness have positive coefficients. In words, this implies that the effect of openness on growth is decreasing with the size of countries. While the estimated coefficients on the latter are also consistently significant, the coefficient on the interaction term is at worst only significant at the 13 percent level. In three of the six regressions, however, it is statistically significant at the 5 percent level. These coefficients indicate effects that are large, in addition to being statistically significant.

For instance, for a very small country (i.e., with a log of total GDP equal to zero), the effect of a ten percentage point increase in openness on annual growth is between 0.60 and 0.95 percentage points, depending on the specification. This effect falls in the range 0.12 to 0.30 when the log of total GDP is the sample median (equal to 16.049). Similarly the effect of one standard deviation increase in the log of total GDP (equal to 1.99) on annual growth rates, for a hypothetical closed country (zero openness), varies between 0.61 and 1.48. At the median of openness

Table 10.7
Determinants of growth rates: OLS estimates

Growth of per capita GDP 1960–1989	Size (1)	Log of (2)	GDP (3)	Size (4)	Log of (5)	Population (6)
Intercept	−9.956 (2.231)	−9.247 (2.260)	6.299 (2.828)	−4.900 (1.375)	−6.330 (1.773)	7.884 (2.495)
Size openness	−0.004 (0.002)	−0.004 (0.002)	−0.003 (0.002)	−0.004 (0.0025)	−0.004 (0.0026)	−0.004 (0.002)
Country size	0.646 (0.133)	0.742 (0.139)	0.306 (0.102)	0.624 (0.143)	0.606 (0.142)	0.278 (0.119)
Openness	0.094 (0.035)	0.095 (0.035)	0.060 (0.030)	0.057 (0.020)	0.057 (0.021)	0.044 (0.017)
Log of per capita income 1960	—	−0.339 (0.189)	−1.277 (0.216)	—	0.229 (0.137)	−1.144 (0.198)
Fertility rate	—	—	−0.322 (0.126)	—	—	−0.306 (0.127)
Male human capital	—	—	1.684 (0.440)	—	—	1.817 (0.454)
Female human capital	—	—	−1.465 (0.441)	—	—	−1.587 (0.448)
Government consumption (% GDP)	—	—	−0.043 (0.020)	—	—	−0.044 (0.020)
Investment rate (% GDP)	—	—	0.076 (0.024)	—	—	0.084 (0.024)
Adjusted R-squared	0.321	0.333	0.652	0.244	0.249	0.647
Regression standard error	1.437	1.424	1.013	1.512	1.511	1.020
Number of observations	119	119	97	120	119	97

Sources: From Alesina, Spolaore, and Wacziarg (2000), based on data from Summers and Heston and the Barro and Lee data set available online.
Note: Heteroskedastic-consistent (White-robust) standard errors are in parentheses. All of the variables are averaged over the 1960 to 1989 period, except initial income in 1960.

(equal to 52.56), the effect is between 0.30 and 1.06. The same pattern holds when size is measured by the log of population. Thus the estimated effects are large and their signs are consistent with our theory.

These results may also shed some light on a recent heated debate in the literature. Rodriguez and Rodrik (2001) have argued that there is no robust empirical correlation between trade and growth, contrary to what other researchers have found, including Frankel and Romer (1999), Frankel and Rose (2002), and Alcala and Ciccone (2001). Our results suggest that the effect of trade on growth is mediated by the size of countries.

10.3.3   Results for the Level of Income

Table 10.8 presents regressions using the level of per capita income in 1989 as a dependent variable (without including lagged per capita income on the right-hand side). Explaining income levels, as opposed to rate of growth of income, is much more demanding. As stressed by Hall and Jones (1999), levels regressions require a broader set of controls than growth regressions, since the source of variation captured by initial income in growth regression now has to be accounted for otherwise. Another important issue that arises with level regressions is endogeneity with respect to trade and the interaction term between trade and country size. This issue is addressed here by using end-of-period income as a dependent variable and by instrumenting for the trade and the interaction between trade and size using several instruments.

Overall, table 10.8 provides further evidence in line with the theory, although the coefficients fall relative to the regressions for growth discussed above. Focusing on the regressions, which include the greatest set of controls (columns 3 and 6), both the interaction term between openness and size and the openness term appear with a significant coefficient; the coefficient on size is now insignificant, although again of the sign consistent with the theory. The long list of variables included in the regression are listed at the bottom of the table. In the next section (which can be skipped by the nontechnically inclined reader) we discuss several statistical issues concerning our results.

*10.4   Extensions

10.4.1   A Panel Data Approach

The regression results on growth presented above use an average of the data from 1960 to 1989 as a dependent variable.

The efficiency of the estimates can potentially be improved by exploiting the within-country variation in growth, openness, and country size. To do this, we use a seemingly unrelated regression (SUR) estimator, which is widely used in the cross-country growth literature. Specifically, we employ five-year averages of the variables between 1960 and 1989, and estimate a system consisting of one growth equation per time period.[6]

The results are presented in table 10.9. The signs of the coefficients are unchanged relative to the OLS regressions. As with OLS estimates, the

Table 10.8
Determinants of income levels: Estimates of instrumental variables

Log of per capita income 1989	Size (1)	Log of (2)	GDP (3)	Size (4)	Log of (5)	Population (6)
Intercept	-4.736	0.906	8.010	1.725	6.444	8.820
	(2.233)	(5.253)	(2.148)	(1.929)	(1.873)	(1.002)
Size openness	-0.001	-0.008	-0.004	-0.0002	-0.010	-0.006
	(0.002)	(0.003)	(0.002)	(0.002)	(0.003)	(0.002)
Country size	0.636	0.442	0.068	0.494	0.243	0.004
	(0.131)	(0.314)	(0.143)	(0.184)	(0.206)	(0.121)
Openness	0.049	0.141	0.063	0.032	0.079	0.040
	(0.038)	(0.064)	(0.029)	(0.020)	(0.027)	(0.016)
Number of observations	114	80	71	115	81	72
Adjusted R-squared	0.12	0.80	0.93	0.13	0.86	0.92
Regression standard error	1.052	0.566	0.361	1.1769	0.469	0.368

Source: From Alesina, Spolaore, and Wacziarg (2000). For original sources, see table 10.7.
Note: Heteroskedastic-consistent (White-Robust) standard errors are in parentheses.

Included controls:
Columns (1) and (4): No controls
Columns (2) and (5): Ethnolinguistic fractionalization, urbanization rate in 1970, distance from major trading partners, average number of revolutions and coups per year, and a set of dummies for whether there was a war between 1960 and 1985, whether the country was ever a colony (since 1776), postwar independence, oil-exporting countries, Muslim majority, Catholic majority, Protestant majority, Confucian majority, Hindu majority, socialist country, Latin America, South East Asia, OECD, Sub-Saharan Africa.
Columns (3) and (6): Same as columns (2) and (5) plus fertility rate, male human capital, female human capital, government consumption as a share of GDP, investment rate.

Instruments used: Log of population, dummies for small country, small island, island, landlocked country, and each of the interactions of these dummies with the log of population.

Table 10.9
Determinants of growth rates: IV Estimates

Growth of per capita GDP 1960–1989	Size (1)	Log of (2)	GDP (3)	Size (4)	Log of (5)	Population (6)
Intercept	−13.793	−14.299	−1.271	−9.955	−10.365	3.083
	(3.869)	(3.825)	(3.713)	(3.233)	(3.293)	(3.032)
Size openness	**−0.006**	**−0.008**	**−0.007**	**−0.007**	**−0.007**	**−0.007**
	(0.004)	**(0.0037)**	**(0.002)**	**(0.005)**	**(0.005)**	**(0.003)**
Country size	**0.833**	**1.133**	**0.701**	**1.066**	**1.035**	**0.603**
	(0.226)	**(0.255)**	**(0.201)**	**(0.307)**	**(0.315)**	**(0.204)**
Openness	**0.131**	**0.163**	**0.136**	**0.102**	**0.101**	**0.077**
	(0.061)	**(0.058)**	**(0.038)**	**(0.039)**	**(0.039)**	**(0.023)**
Log of per capita income 1960	—	−0.662	−1.229	—	0.118	−0.980
		(0.329)	(0.228)		(0.179)	(0.200)
Fertility rate	—	—	−0.253	—	—	−0.243
			(0.132)			(0.133)
Male human capital	—	—	1.501	—	—	1.561
			(0.459)			(0.471)
Female human capital	—	—	−1.319	—	—	−1.346
			(0.477)			(0.472)
Government consumption (% GDP)	—	—	−0.043	—	—	−0.043
			(0.023)			(0.022)
Investment rate (% GDP)	—	—	0.055	—	—	0.072
			(0.029)			(0.027)
R-squared	0.271	0.246	0.617	0.116	0.149	0.629
Regression standard error	1.508	1.541	1.115	1.656	1.636	1.099
Number of observations	119	119	97	120	119	97
Hausman χ^2	0.87	0.68	0.39	1.48	1.19	0.00
p-value	0.832	0.953	~1.00	0.686	0.880	~1.00

Source: From Alesina, Spolaore, and Wacziarg (2000). For original sources, see table 10.7.
Note: Heteroskedastic-consistent (White-robust) standard errors are in parentheses. Instruments used: small country dummy, island dummy, small island dummy, landlocked country dummy, and the interaction of each of these variables with the log of population.

magnitude and precision of the parameter estimates are reduced when we include other controls in the regression, although the sign patterns are preserved.

10.4.2 Endogeneity of Openness

Growth may affect openness, rather than the other way around. This problem potentially extends to the endogeneity of the interaction term between openness and country size. Therefore the estimates presented above may have an endogeneity problem.

In order to address this issue, Frankel and Romer (1999) used instruments for openness using exogenous gravity variables, and they show that the estimated coefficient on the trade to GDP ratio in a cross-country income level regression is actually increased when endogeneity issues are properly accounted for. As gravity variables (i.e., as potential instruments for openness and for the interaction term between openness and country size) they use mostly geographic variables that are likely to be strongly associated with the degree of openness, and unlikely to be affected by growth. Using these variables as instruments we can show that the results presented above are robust.

Following Frankel and Romer, we use the following instruments: indicator variables for whether a country is an island, a small island, a small country, or a landlocked country. Then we add the interaction between each of these variables and the log of population to the list of instruments, in order to explicitly account for the potential endogeneity of the interaction term between openness and country size. Since they are pure geography variables, these instruments are unlikely to be influenced by reverse causation with respect to post-1960 economic growth.

The results from the instrumental variables procedures are in line with the previous OLS results, which come out reinforced in terms of statistical significance. The pattern of signs, as predicted by the theory, is maintained. This suggests that the endogeneity issue applied to openness and that the interaction terms is unlikely to be an important source of fragility for our results.[7]

The question concerning the relationship between trade and growth is hotly debated. In their provocative paper Rodriguez and Rodrik (2001) discuss several weak points in the available evidence in favor of a positive correlation between openness and growth, even though they present no evidence of negative correlation. Frankel and Rose (2002) respond to some of these criticisms. Their result concerns the effects of trade on growth in a sample of small countries, those that are part of currency unions. Frankel and Rose's results resonate with ours because we also emphasize how openness is particularly beneficial for small countries. Alcala and Ciccone (2001) find that openness to trade has a very large positive effect on productivity if a more sophisticated measure of openness is used.

10.5 Conclusions

In this chapter we provided evidence in favor of two critical implications of our approach. One is that economies of scale lead to smaller governments (in per capita terms) in larger countries. The second is that the effect of country size on economic success is mediated by the trade regime. Small countries can prosper with free trade, while size matters in a world of trade restrictions.

The first result highlights the cost, in terms of loss of economies of scale, associated with choosing a smaller jurisdiction. From this perspective Alesina, Baqir, and Hoxby (2000) investigate data drawn from US municipalities, special districts, and school districts. One advantage of studying localities within the United States is that their borders change relatively frequently, and this allows for many observations that can be used in statistical analysis.

These authors study how counties in the United States subdivide themselves in school districts, municipalities, and special districts.[8] Like nations, localities in the United States come in all sizes. The largest county in the United States (Los Angeles) has 8,863,164 inhabitants; the smallest (Loving, Texas) has 107. The largest school district (New York City) has 1.4 million school-aged children; the smallest has 2. There are also a lot of localities in the United States: about 3,000 counties. The average number of school districts per county is 5.5, the average number of municipalities is 6.5, and the average number of special districts is 11.[9]

These authors show that Americans are willing to give up substantial benefits of scale in order to belong to more homogeneous communities in terms of race, ethnicity, and income. The borders of counties have remained relatively stable, but the subdivisions into municipalities, school districts, and special districts have not. Over the last thirty years there has been a tendency to consolidate localities, and this has occurred more rapidly in homogeneous counties. Traditionally most of the literature on localities has focused on the fact that individual sort themselves out by income.[10] Alesina, Baqir, and Hoxby (2000) point out that homogeneity by race and (to less extent, by ethnicity) is perceived as important, or even more important than homogeneity by income class. The economic evidence on this point includes a so-called natural experiment associated with the two world wars. During both wars there was large south to north migration of blacks to fill vacancies in the war industries, a phenomenon termed the "Great Migration" that is extensively studied by historians. These authors examine the pattern of formation of local jurisdictions in northern counties affected by the Great Migration, and they show that counties receiving black southern immigrants become much more fragmented in smaller localities. As a result many new municipalities and school districts were created to deal with issues of the racial heterogeneity in each county. After accounting for various other economic and geographical determinants of borders, these authors find evidence of a trade-off between economies of scale and income and racial heterogeneity.

The second result on trade and growth is important for two reasons. First, it confirms an important building block of our model of country size, namely that national states can afford to be small if they are open. Second, it sheds some light in the heated debate on the relationship between international trade and growth. Our results suggest that country size mediates the correlation between trade and growth.

Since country size is important for growth, depending on the trade regime, we could ask how "costly" borders are in terms of growth. This is the question explored by Spolaore and Wacziarg (2002). They developed a model that provides a theoretical foundation to estimate empirically the effects of political borders on growth. In their model they treat economic integration as endogenous, and negatively dependent on country size; that is, smaller countries choose to have lower barriers to trade, all other things being equal. Political integration between two countries results in a positive market size effect and a negative effect through reduced openness vis-à-vis the rest of the world. In their estimates of the growth effects that would result from the hypothetical removal of national borders between pairs of adjacent countries, interestingly, they find that only in 17 out of 132 hypothetical mergers would both countries benefit economically from full integration. Pairs that would benefit economically from a political merger include the United States and Canada, Spain and Portugal, and Germany and France.

11   The Size of Nations: A Historical Overview

11.1   Introduction

In the previous chapter we successfully tested several correlations implied by our theory, concerning size and economic outcomes. We now examine our theoretical results in terms of history and the evolution of the size of states. Our intent is not to provide a history of state formation and breakup. Our goal is more modest, in that we compare historical patterns with the propositions we discussed earlier:

• The size of a country emerges from a trade-off between the benefits of scale and the costs of heterogeneity in the population.

• Heterogeneity costs stem from differences in preferences over public policies. Such differences are related both to noneconomic factors (cultural, religious, and linguistic) and to economic factors, such as income differences in the population; regional differences in per capita income create secessionist tendencies.

• Benefits of scale include the provision of public goods and the size of the market.

• The benefits of market size depend on the trade regime; small countries are viable in a free trade regime; a large size is crucial in a world of trade barriers.

• Size matters for security reasons; in a more peaceful world one should observe an increase in the number of countries; conversely, external threats lead to the creation of larger countries and the centralization of federations.

• Democratization should be associated with an increase in the number of countries; on the contrary, dictators try to consolidate large political jurisdictions.

We are not going to go into a complex historical debate about what is a nation, a state, or a country. As we noted in chapter 1, the definition of "state" is controversial. Some authors, such as Tilly (1990) refer to states as "the world's largest and most powerful organizations for more than five thousand years." Others prefer to limit the definition of "state" to modern national states—as successful monopolists of the legitimate use of force within a given territory, according to Weber's (1958) famous definition, which we also cited in chapter 1. Since our theory has been mainly motivated by modern and contemporary developments, in this chapter we will not consider ancient states and communities, such as Egyptian and Mesopotamic kingdoms or Greek and Phenician city-states—although we do suspect that our analysis would be consistent with those ancient institutions.

Hence we will start our quick historical overview with a subject with which we are relatively more familiar, namely the surge and expansion of city-states during the European Middle Ages. In a sense, the period before the so-called Renaissance offers a natural historical break. In the so-called dark ages (in reality the birth date of the modern Western world) political power was rather diffuse and, in Western Europe, contended between the pope and the emperor. Local lords ruled the countryside and cities were almost nonexistent. In this period it is quite difficult to talk about "states" in a way that is applicable to our theoretical structure.

11.2   European City-States

Europe awoke from the dark ages through a sharp increase in urbanization which started at the end of the twelfth century and continued throughout the thirteenth century. The three centuries that followed were characterized by the economic growth of the city-states: Venice, Lisbon, Genoa, Antwerp, and Amsterdam in chronological order of leadership. This was a period where the core of Europe was extremely fragmented.

The city-state of this period is a clear example of a political entity (i.e., a country in our models) that could prosper economically even if extremely small because its market was unrelated to its political borders. The successful cities at the two poles of Europe (Italy and the Low Countries) reached extraordinary levels of wealth. In the early fourteenth century, Venice's budget was approximately equal to that of the entire kingdom of Spain, and only 20 percent less than that of the kingdom of France.[1] Amsterdam and the United Provinces were very rich, even though, as a French ambassador commented in 1724: "It is a very small country; the amount of wealth and other grains grown here does not suffice to feed a hundredth of its inhabitants."[2] In fact, not only were the United Provinces small, but they were also very decentralized, made up by an assembly of minuscule states. They were the first example of a modern federation.[3] Genoa, a French diplomat noted with astonishment, had "about thirty leagues along the coast ... and seven or eight leagues of plain ... the rest is barren mountain."[4] In the case of Venice, the westward expansion in Italy was only motivated by building infrastructure for trade,[5] the eastward expansion on the Eastern seashore (kept under constant check and balance by the Turks) was motivated by the need to keep trade lines open.

These minuscule city-states could survive because they prospered in a period when capitalism and wealth were based on trade. A contemporary observer described Amsterdam as a place where "commerce [was] absolutely free, absolutely nothing is forbidden to the merchants, they have no rule to follow but their own interest. So when an individual seems to do, in his own commercial interest, something contrary to the state, the state turns a blind eye and pretends not to notice."[6]

The governments of these cities did not provide many of the public goods, infrastructure and administrative services that we think as normally associated with modern government. In Venice, Genoa, and Amsterdam "the state is powerless and poor, although individuals are wealthy."[7] In other words, the city-states could afford to be very small, because economies of scale in the production of public goods were relatively low, and their economies were based on free trade. The combination of free trade and small government was in fact the key ingredient of the growth and success of city-states. These political units were very rich in economic power, but being so small, they were potentially weak in a military sense. Superior political and military organization gave to merchants and other economic agents in small city-states a relative advantage in defense during part of the Middle Ages—a "protection rent," following Frederic C. Lane's (1958) definition. However, such "protection rents" were steadily eroded over time. As pointed out by McNeil (1974) the increasing costs of public goods (including defense itself) played a major role in this trend.

It is quite arduous to speak of "democracy" as the political organization of this time, but the city-states were certainly more open, free, and tolerant than the absolutist regimes that would follow them. Although the city-states were not "democracies" in a contemporary sense of the word, they were "constitutional oligarchies, dominated by the most powerful families who filled the executive bodies, legislative and advisory council and special commissions that governed the city state."[8] Voting rights in Italian city-states were limited to about 5 to 15 percent of the male population, which is not a trivial percentage if compared to what followed in history, until the early twentieth century. For instance, in England at the end of the nineteenth century a similar fraction of the male population had voting rights. In addition "the feature that most distinguished [Italian cities] from that of other regions of Europe, was the extent to which men were able to take part in determining, largely by persuasion, the laws and decision governing their lives."[9] Obviously not everyone had a "voice" in the political arena, but the city-states in northern Italy had remarkably advanced toward relatively modern forms of democracy, where the guilds were the backbone of political participatory arrangements. Putnam (1993) draws a sharp contrast between the relatively open and democratic city-states in northern Italy and the autocratic regime of southern Italy, derived from the Norman occupation. He argues that this difference permeates the history of Italy and has influenced the north–south disparity in development and quality of government to this day. As De Long and Shleifer (1998) put it, in the medieval city-states commerce flourished precisely because it was unrestricted by suffocating political influences.

In summary, from about 1300 to about 1600 European city-states were, for the most part, politicoeconomic entities that had some characteristics of today's small, open, and democratic countries.

11.3 From Small City-States to the Leviathan

Historians often take 1494, the date of the French invasion of Italy as a symbolic date that marks the beginning of the period of absolutism which dominated the scene at least until the French Revolution. These three centuries also witnessed the consolidation of several large states in Europe such as France, England, Spain, and Russia.

Large states emerged from the consolidation of fiefdoms. Europe moved from an organization of independent lords to a system of states because of several reasons. First a growing economy needed institutions that guaranteed property rights and the formation of larger ("national") markets, in addition to the one guaranteed by small city-states. North and Thomas (1973) stress that economies of scale in providing these institutions led to a decline of feudal estates. In a world of trade restrictions among independent political units, the need to reduce the costs of inter-border trade led to the formation of larger political units. As North and Thomas (1973, p. 94) point out, as the benefits from economic exchange among different regions expanded "a need was created for larger political units to define, protect and enforce property rights over greater areas." In other words, one of the goal of state building was to provide the infrastructures needed to develop domestic markets in a world in which trade across political borders would be highly costly and unprotected. This process was facilitated by the alliance of the king and city dwellers, united by their hatred of the lords. In fact the relationship between the increase of economic activities in the cities and the consolidation of centralized states is central in Adam Smith's view, when in *Book III of the Wealth of Nations,* he writes that "commerce and manufacturers gradually introduced order and good government and, with them, the liberty and security of individuals among the inhabitants of the country who had before lived ... in a state of servile dependency upon their superiors."

The second force was the increase in the cost of wars and of public administration. As Tilly (1990) emphasizes, wars made states: technological innovation in warfare is critical. "Armies became professional, and the costs of wars escalated; part time gentlemen soldiers could no longer cope. The emergence of salaried career officers was accompanied by the consolidation of a professional military cost."[10] Changes in military technology made the benefit of scale more valuable so that monarchs could consolidate their grips on local lords and establish more centralized states. After the wars and war preparations consolidated a state system in Europe, the monarchs used their power of coercion to incorporate in their territorially defined states the free capital-rich cities. From year 1500 onward "the diffusion of firearms ... tipped the military advantage toward monarchs who could afford to cast cannon and build the new kinds of fortress that cannon could not easily shatter."[11]

The monarchs established a more centralized control over cities and countryside, keeping in check local lords. "The art of fortification managed to catch up with the severity of bombardment: by the 1520s it necessitated building larger and more expensive castles. This required larger estates to foot the bill, so that the balance of advantage remained with the bigger political units, and, most of all, with the King."[12] For example, Castile's tax revenues rose from less than 900,000 reales in 1474 to 26 million in 1504.[13] Virtually the entire increase in tax revenues needed by monarchs of this period was due to the fact that wars were becoming more expensive and armies were growing exponentially both in terms of men and costs.

In the relationship between military needs and taxation, rulers needed tax revenues to support an army, and an army to guarantee a flow of revenues. As Wilson (1967, p. 498) notes "the cost of dynasticism were rising rapidly. Courts were larger and more luxurious and wars were longer. The yield of crown land and spasmodic war levies did not add up to support the cost."

The tax problem was in fact twofold. One was the mere size of the necessary fiscal revenues; the other was the irregularity of the tax revenues. This created the problem of finding ways to finance public expenditure in periods of shortages of revenues, giving rise to an additional incentive to create more elaborate fiscal infrastructures (Eartman 1997). While until the twelfth or thirteenth century, unpaid armies made up by feudal lords were the norm, two centuries later armies were much larger, paid and expensive. Warfare was the common way of settling disputes and increasing wealth for the kings. In effect, the manner of warfare changed so that states with large populations were at a military advantage because they could draw their large military forces from these populations.[14]

Territorial expansion, and an increase in fiscal pressure was the answer to increased military needs. Some countries continued the practice of patrimonial fiscal structure (France, Spain, Portugal, Papal states, Poland, and Hungary) while others introduced administrative systems more similar to a modern bureaucracy (Britain, Sweden, and Prussia).[15] An interesting question is why certain states adopted one system or another, but for our purposes it suffices to say that both systems were a response to an increase in the costs of running a country.[16] In both systems the administrative and clerical staff dramatically increased. In England, in the eighteenth century there were 10,000 government employees, organized along modern bureaucratic lines.[17] In France, in the middle of the seventeenth century tax rebellions were widespread and often led to internal military confrontations. In the eighteenth century civil servants progressively replaced unpaid clergymen in various administrative roles and the king employed more and more imaginative ways of raising taxes and borrowing. However, frequent default on public debt reduced the king's credibility in public finance to historical lows. The gigantic needs of fiscal revenues due to mostly unsuccessful wars eventually led to the collapse of the *ancient regime*.

City-states could not easily survive in this new military-intensive, taxation-intensive era. Italian cities became the battle ground of Spain and France and lost their independence. Venice, due to its naval commerce, maintained its institutions but lost their predominance. The much debated decline of Venice needs to be seen in relation to the cost of sustaining a formidable land army as well as a reserve fleet of 100 galleys.[19] Venice was too small to afford both.

Only the United Provinces retained their economic strength despite their small size because they took advantage of trade associated with the discoveries of the Indies and America. It was trade and the booming Atlantic economy that allowed the Dutch to retain a large politicoeconomic importance despite the relatively small land size. The Dutch were successful because they promoted free trade and competitive practices.

The participatory democracy of the Italian and northern European city-states was lost in the period of absolutism, although the degree of dictatorial power of different regimes ranged from the absolute and unchecked power of the king of France to the English case where the monarch was balanced by a powerful parliament. Thus we move from small, relatively democratic city-states based on trade to large dictatorships based on rent extraction.

Outside Europe, large kingdoms evolved into empires. The large Ottoman empire quickly turned into a bureaucratic machine geared toward extracting rents from its citizens. While in Amsterdam the merchants ruled, in the Ottoman empire "the largest merchants could not rival a middle level member of the political class such as a junior governor... in terms of wealth, to say nothing of officials higher up in the administrative hierarchy."[20] The Ottoman empire was a "bureaucratic state, holding different regions within a single administrative and fiscal system, in which the most important figures were the tax collectors, whose task was to support the lavish life-style of the ruling class."[21] In fact "policies followed by the late sixteen century Ottoman Empire were quite often minimal to the accumulation of commercial capital."[22] While the city state prospered on being small and open, "the strong point of [the Ottoman Empire]... lay in obtaining economies of scale by uniting... a diversity of people."[23] Needless to say, this diversity of people is the reason for the final collapse of the empire.

Similar arguments apply to India. The ruling class in the sixteenth and seventeenth centuries was exclusively interested in extracting rents. The estimated total tax revenue of the government was close to 20 percent of national income, a value on the high side even for today's developing countries. However, "next to nothing was spent in India on providing infrastructures. Most taxation was devoted to supporting the elite."[24] The Indian population did rebel but received basically more repression. On the lavish spending of the elite, Kennedy (1987, p. 13) writes that their conspicuous consumption surpassed that of the Sun King at Versailles. It is not surprising that an Indian proverb warns to "never stand behind a horse or before an official." This policy of pure rent extraction eventually led to the decline of the Indian empire.

China was another immense empire that could survive, despite its size, because of the relatively high degree of homogeneity of its population. Also with the exception of the Mongols, China had relatively few external rivals. As Tilly (1992, p. 71) points out, "Chinese dynasties collapsed when the empire's administrative reach extended its grasp, when warlords organized in the Empire's intensities and when mobile invaders ... swept into imperial territories." Kennedy (1987, pp. 111–12) notes that "Ming China increasingly suffered from ... being too centralized, despotic and severely orthodox in its attitude toward ... commerce. Without clear directive from above the arteries of the burocray hardened preferring conservatism to change." In other words, a large, overly centralized, anti-trade regime. Garner (2001) provides an interesting contrast between the relative homogeneity and large size of China versus the fragmented Europe in the thirteenth to fifteenth centuries. He argues that the political fragmentation of the latter, by creating competition among rulers generated enough innovation that more than compensated for the economies of scale enjoyed by a much larger China.

Recall that an implication of our model is that dictatorial empires should be larger than the optimal size from the point of view of economic efficiency. The rents of the Leviathans are maximized by country size beyond the economic optimum: China and the Ottoman empire seem rather obvious examples consistent with this implication. But even for an absolutist monarchy like France, size might have been a problem. Perhaps this country was "too big" from an economic point of view, because the fiscal pressure on kings to maximize rents and military power led to excessive expansion. As Braudel (1992, p. 325) emphasizes "[France's] territorial expansion [was] ... beneficial ... in several ways to the monarchial state ... [but] seriously hampered it's economic development." A distance problem interfered with the development of a truly national market; France in the sixteenth and seventeenth centuries looks more like an agglomerate of self-sufficient regions, than a truly national market. Active markets were limited to areas near big cities. Size interfered with the functioning of the political administration: "bringing together a national assembly in a country as large as France was a difficult... undertaking."[25] As we noted in chapter 3, the American founding fathers also noted how time to reach the capital to participate in national government activities was the constraint for a country at that time.

The issue of "excessive" expansion was not merely a French problem. In general "the maxim that says one should chop off provinces from states, like branches from a tree, in order to strengthen them, is likely to remain in books for a long time before it is listened to in the councils of Princes."[26] Perhaps the fact that England was an island helped preventing excessive annexation of provinces, given the natural sea borders, even though the issue of excessive size may later apply to the British empire, if not to Britain itself. Kennedy (1987) provides a sweeping historical exploration of how excessive expansion of dictatorial empires often leads to their decline.

As for trade, while the small city-states thrived on international transactions, the large absolutist regimes sought national self-sufficiency and domestic trade in domestic markets. As Wilson (1967) notes "by the second half of the sixteenth century [primitive ideas about trade] had already given rise to a corpus of legislation ... aimed at national self sufficiency and the nourishment of national production." Similarly English trade policies turned very protectionist in the early seventeenth century. In this period England introduced legislation geared toward "reducing the need for import and the drain of treasure by developing manufacturers" (from an official document cited by Wilson 1967, p. 533).

In summary, from the small, open, and democratic city-states, with their light and cheap governments, the world evolved into large countries, with larger domestic markets pursuing self-sufficiency, and run by Leviathans always in search of new forms of revenues to support lavish consumption of the elites and wars.

11.4   The Modern National State

From around the end of the eighteenth century, one can start talking about the birth of a political institution, the "nation-state," in forms that are quite similar to the current ones. In Europe we observe the transformation of existing states, such as England, France, and Spain, and the creation of new ones, like Germany and Italy. In North America, the United States and, a few decades later, Canada, became federal states, developing from a loose federation of independent provinces and territories. Nationalism and liberalism were two political forces closely tied together: both demanded more open and liberal societies in economic and political terms. Liberal ideas also brought about a phase of European free trade. Interestingly, the smaller countries—the Netherlands, Denmark, Portugal, Switzerland, and to some extent Sweden and Belgium—were the first to adopt a free trade stand; England and France followed later (Bairoch 1989).

As the liberal theorists of the time knew well, nation-states are not necessary in a totally free market economy. The world could be organized as a single free market area, a world market of free trading individuals. Nation-states were viewed as the second best, given the heterogeneity of individuals with different races, cultures, and ideologies. According to liberal philosophy, a nation-state had to be of sufficient size to form a viable unit of development but not more. In other words, since a world of complete free trade was unattainable, countries had to reach a certain size in order for the national economy to be viable. For example, the *Dictionaire Politique* of Garnier-Pagès, in 1843, described as "ridiculous" that Belgium and Portugal should be independent nations because their markets were too small.[27] Giuseppe Mazzini, one of the architects of Italian unification, thought that the optimal number of nation states in Europe was 12, given economic considerations (i.e., market size) and the ethnic composition of Europe. For instance, he did not take seriously the nationalistic aspirations of Sicilians, Bretons, Welsh, and even the Irish, because he considered their economies to be too small.[28] While for absolute monarchs the size of states mattered almost exclusively for military and taxing purposes, in the liberal world of Adam Smith size of countries mattered because of markets. The "national question," as the Mazzini had well understood, could not be analyzed without an eye on economic feasibility and market size.

The ethnic composition of Europe allowed the carving of reasonably sized geographical units. However, Tilly and Tilly (1973, p. 44) note that "almost all European governments took steps which homogenized their populations: the adoption of state religion, expulsion of minorities, institution of a national language, eventually the organization of mass public instruction." This is interesting because it suggests that cultural fractionalization may in fact be an endogenous variable such as we modeled it in chapter 5. In a sense, all ideas of nationalism imply the necessity and the virtue of homogeneous nation-states.

The unification of Germany certainly has a strong economic motivation related to market size. The German nation started in 1834 as a customs union (the *Zollverein*) and thus ensured low barriers to trade among its members. Participation in the customs union was viewed as an economic necessity for small- and medium-sized states whose markets were too small to prosper without more free trade. Before the *Zollverein*, "German merchants and manufacturers began to object to the discouraging complexity of custom tariffs that created a series of costly hurdles ... many businessmen demanded an end to these unnatural impediments, faced by neither British nor French rivals."[29] With the unification Prussia collapsed all preexisting currencies into one and banned restrictions on faster mobility. In one word, Prussia created a single market.[30] Thus one of the prime motivations for German unification was the construction of an economically more viable entity, that is, a search for an optimal economic size of the country. A second motivation that sealed the German unification in 1870 was the external threat of a conflict with France. Riker (1964, p. 35) notes that "the Federation of 1871 originated under circumstances of great foreign hostility and was therefore aimed at improving the military-diplomatic position of the German states."[31] Similar arguments about foreign threats underlie the consolidation of the Austria-Hungary under Emperor Franz Joseph. Interestingly, increasing pressure from ethnic minorities led to a compromise with the stronger minority (the Magyars) in order to control the rest. In our analysis' terminology, the Hapsburg dual monarchy could be read as a leviathan's response to a change in the no insurrection constraint.[32]

According to Riker (1964) external threats, and the need to create a viable defense, underlie the creation of a US constitution that led to the replacement of a loose federation of independent states by a system of "centralized federalism." In Riker's "military interpretation of the constitution," the basic force that brought about the consolidation of the United States was the fact that European threats were a clear and imminent danger for the United States. The English were threatening in the northwest and the Spanish in the southwest. Building a viable army and a navy was one of the first tasks initiated by the first two presidents, George Washington and John Adams, who were particularly obsessed by the need for a strong navy.

External defense was also an important issue in the *Federalist Papers*. Interestingly, in the third paper John Jay makes an argument related to our discussion of chapter 7 about the likelihood of occurrence of conflict if a large country breaks down into many small ones. Jay writes that "it is of high importance to the peace of America that she observes the laws of nations [Portugal, Spain, Britain] and to me it appears evident that this will be more perfectly and punctually done by one national government than it could be by . . . thirteen separate states." In other words, it is more likely that a conflict will occur when more independent nations interact with each other, a point discussed in detail in chapter 7.

However, external threat was not the only motivation that lead to the Union. A second one was the economies of scale in fiscal policy. In the *Federalist Paper* 13, Hamilton makes this very clear. He writes: "When the dimensions of a state attain a certain magnitude, it requires the same energy of government and the same form of administration which are requisite in one of much greater extent." Thus, for Hamilton, as size increases, the per capita costs of running a government decrease. Madison strongly argues against the objections toward the Union based on government expenses. It is precisely because of the economies of scale argument that "the thirteen states will be able to support a national government better than one half or one third or any number rules than the whole." In fact, in Jay's view, "if the states are united under one government, there will be but one national civil list to support; if they are divided into several confederacies, there will be as many different national civil lists to be provided for." In Federalist paper 12, he further argues that the tax system would be more efficient in the Union.

The establishment of a common market was a third force underlying the Union. As Moore (1967) puts it, the capitalist northerners "wanted to be able to do business without bothering about state and regional frontiers." In his celebrated economic interpretation of the American Constitution, Beard (1913) notes that the trade benefits of size also mattered because a large country can be more powerful in commercial disputes in a world that is far from free trade. This is essentially the argument of Hamilton in Federalist paper 43: "The trader . . . will acknowledge that the aggregate balance of commerce of the United States would bid far to be much more favorable than that of thirteen states without union or with partial union." In Federalist paper 3 Madison had written that in commercial disputes a larger country would be more likely to be offered satisfaction even without the use of force precisely because a large country is stronger. John Jay in the Federalist paper 5 went on to say that commercial treaties between thirteen separate countries would be less favorable and more complex to handle than the commercial treaty of a single nation. The bottom line is that the founding fathers viewed size as beneficial in pursuing trade in a largely protectionist world.

The heterogeneity of views within the Union, however, threatened its survival throughout its first few decades. As the Civil War made clear all the benefits of the union—security, economies of scale in government and market size—bring about high costs of heterogeneity. The Civil War was the result of conflicts of preferences about economic policy (especially trade policy) between the industrial north and the agricultural south, and heterogeneity of preferences about slavery. One cannot sum up the causes of the Civil War more eloquently than Moore (1967, p. 123), as he writes, "it is impossible to speak of purely economic factors as the main causes behind the [civil] war, just as it is impossible to speak of the war as mainly a consequence of moral differences. Slavery was the moral issue that aroused much of the passion on both sides. Without the direct conflict of ideas over slavery the events leading up to the war and the war itself are totally incomprehensible. At the same time it is plain as the light of the sun that economic factors created a slave economy in the south just as economic factors created different social structures with contrasting ideals in other parts of the country."

An interesting question is whether such a costly and devastating war was worth the benefit of keeping the nation together. Of course, any normative (i.e., ethical) welfare analysis that takes into account the utility of every person involved should count as a major social gain the end of the horrible institution of slavery. This said, one may ask, from a positive perspective—that is, as a way to analyze actual political forces at work—whether such costly war was worth the benefits of unification to the (white) decision-makers in the two parts of the country—or couldn't they just go their own way and simply trade with each other? Historians of the American south have often raised this question, which, in the terminology of our model, we can rephrase as follows: Were the benefits of scale, defense, and elimination of barriers to trade in the United States sufficient to justify fighting the war rather than acknowledging heterogeneity of preferences and breaking apart? Richard Shryock (1933) writes that if secession had not been fought by the northern states, "it is obvious that each of the suggested republics would have been smaller and less powerful than the present one, but it hardly follows that they would have been less prosperous or happy." In other words, why could not north and south go their separate ways maintaining free trade with each other? Why did the north choose to fight the secession so aggressively? The answer to this question is, of course, extremely difficult, both in an ex ante and in an ex post sense. Ex ante, the answer is probably a combination of fear of loosing security against foreign threats, nationalistic pride, and commercial interest. A *Boston Herald* article in 1860—cited by Stampp (1991, p. 31)—notes that if the south gained independence, its "first move . . . would be to impose a heavy tax upon the manufacturers of the North, and an export tax upon the cotton used by Northern manufacturers." Whether or not this expectation was justified, it does suggest that the fear of protectionism contributed to a sense of necessity of keeping the country together.

It is obviously impossible to do justice to a complex phenomenon like the American Civil War in a few paragraphs. Our point is that the forces that played a role were a combination of ideological and cultural differences, conflicts about domestic and external trade, and security considerations that were broadly consistent with the theoretical ideas discussed in the previous chapters. Or, to put it more modestly, the theoretical framework that we sketched out above seems to provide some useful lenses for looking at this monumental and complex historical event.

In summary, in the period of the so-called birth of the national state, the trade-off between economic size and heterogeneity was a critical determinant of the political and ideological movements underlying nation building. The consolidation of loose federations of states, into more centralized federations like in Germany and the United States, was dictated by the need of defense from foreign aggression, and by the desire to create large free trade areas.

11.5   Colonial Empires

In the two decades that followed the 1848 unrest in Europe there was a spectacular increase in trade and the diffusion of capitalism. The last three decades of the century were, instead, characterized by a much slower growth, and in particular, the period 1873 to 1879 became known as the Great Depression until the 1930s.

Between 1800 and 1870 the share of international trade quadrupled, from 2 percent to 8 percent of GDP (see Estevodoreal and Taylor 2002). From 1870 to the First World War total trade continued to increase but at a much lower rate. This was because most of trade was within colonial empires. Data on world trade in this period do not separate out the trade of colonizers with their colonies.

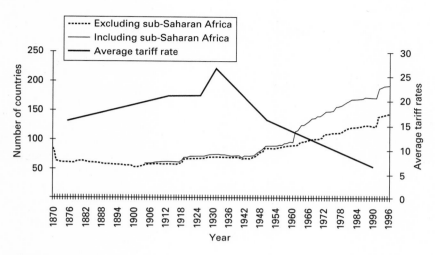

Figure 11.1
Average tariff rate and the number of countries (unweighted country average rate for Austria, Belgium, France, Sweden and the United States. Reproduced from Alesina, Spolaore, and Wacziarg (2001).

Whether or not one can consider the period 1870 and 1913 one of trade expansion and liberalization or just the opposite is a matter of contention between historians, for several reasons, as documented by Estevodoreal, Frontz, and Taylor (2002) who also present an excellent review of the literature. To begin with the data are imperfect. Second, this period witnessed a spectacular fall in transportation costs, so one could observe at the same time increasing protectionism and increasing trade.[33]

Figure 11.1 shows that average tariff rates for countries with available data increased between 1870 and 1915. Starting in 1873, the trade policy of Germany turned sharply protectionist (Craig 1978), and when Germany in 1879 introduced a new large tariff, free trade was "dead," as Bairoch (1989) writes. According to him, this event "marks the end of the period [of free trade] and the return of protectionism on the continent."[34]

This view is somewhat extreme among historians. Free trade between colonizers did not disappear, but certainly 1870 marks a turn toward a more protectionist stand. Without the fall in transportation costs and the gold standard with facilitated trade, the protectionist move of the major powers would have created much larger effects on trade.[35] To put it differently, the sharp increase in tariffs and other protectionist policies and the large reduction in costs of transportation and communication obfuscated the normal effect of protectionist measures on trade and financial flows. While the intention of the policy makers was to implement inward-looking policies, their effect on trade flows was mitigated by the extraordinary fall in transportation costs.

From 1880 to the First World War European powers expanded their control over much of the globe. The manufacturing boom of the previous decades, coupled with stagnant domestic markets, "wetted the appetite of merchants seeking new markets and manufacturers seeking new sources of raw materials."[36] At the same time, ethnic problems and separatist movements increasingly became a major factor in domestic and international politics.

Increasing protectionism and the need for bigger markets to absorb a newly developed mass production required large markets. The answer to these tensions was the building of colonial empires. Colonialism was a way of expanding markets and secure sources of raw materials, and flag waving became useful in unifying heterogeneous citizens against outsiders.

Colonial powers imposed trade restrictions so that trade routes from the colonies of one European power to those of another were closed. Hirschman (1945, p. 79) notes that "a decrease of trade due to restrictionism increases the probability of national jealousies and desires for territorial expansion." The connection between the increase in trade protection and the need for larger colonial empires, seemed clear even to contemporary observers. "If you were not such persistent protectionists," the British premier told the French ambassador in 1897, "you would not find us so keen to annex territories."[37]

To be sure, the British were just as protectionist as the French, as Hobsbawn (1987, p. 135) writes, "Britain was in a position to develop its international trade to an abnormal extent ... simply because of relations with the underdeveloped overseas world; ... her industry expanded into an international vacuum ... cleared by the activities of the British navy."[38] In some places like Africa, the British and the French ceded their territories directly to private companies, making the connection between economic interests and territorial expansion even tighter.[39] Landes (1998, p. 426) notes that "the merchants ... sought trade not territory as such ... but they did not want to be robbed or bullied by native dealers or officials ... so when Europeans ran into trouble, they called on their home government for help."

Similar considerations apply to American expansion at the end of the nineteenth century. The acquisition of Alaska, Hawaii, Samoa, Cuba, and the Philippines (among other territories) between 1865 and 1898 was justified in the United States on the basis of the necessity to expand American markets and supply routes. At the same time the US trade policy took a sharply protectionist turn: the average tariff rate increased, starting in the 1860s, from 20 to about 47 percent.[40] British and French hegemony over much of the world put a limit on the US access to many markets, justifying in the eyes of American advocates of expansion an overseas pursuit of their Manifest Destiny. In the colonial era, when political control limited the potential for economic interactions with large portions of the world, building an empire was the only way to secure markets and supply routes.

The Spanish and Portuguese empires were also motivated by trade flows and market size. These two countries were largely dependent on trade with their colonies and imposed a trading monopoly and monopsony on them. In particular, since the Spanish economy was heavily dependent on its trade with overseas colonies, it greatly suffered when the empire collapsed at the beginning of the nineteenth century. For national movements in Latin America, political independence was viewed as necessary to break "the external trade monopoly ... and have a chance to raise capital on the international market."[41] All of the newly independent countries in Latin America in the midnineteenth century adopted an outward looking strategy, reduced trade barriers and embraced a strategy of export-led growth: "By mid-century a consensus had emerged throughout the countries of Latin America in favor of export-led growth."[42]

Clearly, the trade of colonial countries with their colonies was not "fair," in that this involved monopoly and monopsony rents as well as pure exploitation of raw materials and labor. The colonies were too poor to represent large markets for the colonizers, but they did represent important sources of raw materials. Nevertheless, one of the motivations for expanding colonial empires was the expectation of market expansion, in the context of an increasingly protectionist world.

Colonial empires represented a brilliant solution, for the colonizers, to the question of the trade-off between size and heterogeneity. The size of the empire guaranteed economic and military benefits; the unequal, unfair and marginalized treatment of colonies reduced the costs of heterogeneity of the citizens of the empires.

11.6   Borders after the First World War

Figure 11.2 shows the countries created and eliminated in five-year periods from 1870 until today. It excludes sub-Saharan Africa, for which the identification of countries in the nineteenth century was somewhat problematic. African tribes did not share the European obsession with borders. As Herbst (2000, p. 35) argues, "precolonial Africa was a world where the extension ... of power meant something very different from the broadcasting of power in Europe." Power in precolonial Africa did not coincide with the control of land.

The German unification, which eighteen encompassed independent states, explains the dip at the beginning of this figure. However, very few new countries were created from 1875 until the Treaty of Versailles, and some countries were absorbed by other countries. Whereas there were 64 independent countries (besides sub-Saharan African) in 1871, this number declined to 59 in 1914. The Treaty of Versailles, in the aftermath of the First World War, vastly redesigned European borders, and created several new countries. Figure 11.4 identifies this by the peak occurring in 1919.

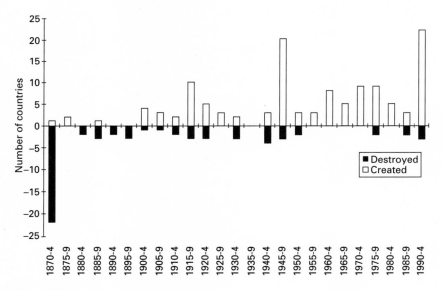

Figure 11.2
Countries created and destroyed over five-year periods from 1870 to 1990, excluding sub-Saharan Africa. Reproduced from Alesina, Spolaore, and Wacziarg (2001).

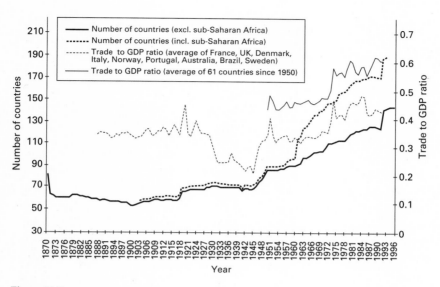

Figure 11.3
Trade openness and number of countries. Reproduced from Alesina, Spolaore, and
Wacziarg (2001).

The guiding principle of the Treaty of Versailles was homogeneity, and
urged by the American president Woodrow Wilson as the identification
of one country, one people. However, this principle would not be applied to the colonies as the European world leaders failed to address the
question of the rights and aspirations of people living outside of Europe.

The Treaty of Versailles vastly mishandled the redrawing of borders,
leaving behind a host of unfulfilled nationalistic sentiments and tensions
within Europe. Nevertheless, international borders hardly changed at
all in the interwar period, until the late 1930s, with the unfolding of
the Second World War. Interestingly, as figure 11.3 shows, in the interwar period very few new countries appeared. Among the new countries,
Egypt (independent in 1922) was merely an issue of classification largely
independent from Britain, whereby its status switched from a protec-
torate to a semi-independent country. Leaving aside Vatican City, the
only other countries to gain autonomy between 1920 and the Second
World War were Ireland (1921), Mongolia (1921), Iraq (1932), and Saudi
Arabia (1932).

The interwar period was characterized by a collapse of free trade,
the emergence of dictatorships, and by belligerence in international relationships. The Great Depression completed the gloomy picture. All

the factors that, according to our analysis, should *not* be associated with the creation of country borders, were fulfilled by nationalistic aspirations. In addition colonial powers held onto their empires and repressed independent movements. They all were adamant in refusing self-determination to their colonies.

The connection between a bellicose and protectionist word and the maintenance of a colonial empire was well understood by Winston Churchill. Jenkins (2001) reprints a letter that essentially defines Churchill's views about colonialism in the interwar period. The letter is addressed to the marquess of Linlithgow who had advocated Indian independence or, at least, autonomy. Churchill spells out in the clearest way his views on why England should hold on to her empire. The long citation from Churchill's letter in May 1932 (Jenkins 2001, p. 457) is particularly enlightening:

the mild and vague liberalism of the early years of the twentieth century... have already been superseded by a violent reaction against Parliamentary and electioneering procedures and by the establishment of dictatorships real or veiled in almost every country. Moreover the loss of our external connections the shrinkage of our foreign trade and shipping brings the surplus population of Britain within measurable distance from utter ruin. It is unsound reasoning therefore to suppose that England... will be willing to part with her control over a great dependency like India. The Dutch will not do it; the French will not do it; the Italians will not do it. As for the Japanese they are conquering a new Empire.... In my view England is now beginning a new period of struggle and fighting for life and the crux of it will be not only the retention of India but a much stronger assertion of commercial rights.

Churchill observes that colonial empires cannot be given up in a bellicose period in a world ruled mostly by protectionist dictators. He goes so far as to pronounce the marquess' views, which were optimistic in regarding the world as prosperous and peaceful, and thus conducive to supporting India's independence as "twenty years behind the times." Once again, Churchill was right: it would take about twenty years of relative peace, democracy, and trade liberalization before the colonial empires could break apart.

The case of eastern Europe is also interesting. The collapse of the Russian monarchy was accompanied by a host of nationalist revolutions, within Russia, in Ukraine, in the Baltic States, and in Central Asia. The vast territorial entity of the former Russian empire did not disintegrate as Lenin offered autonomy to various regions as a bribe to preserve the Soviet Union.[43] Later on, as the Soviet Union became increasingly centralized, external threats, internal needs of economic self-sufficiency, and the benefits of size in a bellicose world helped keep the Soviet federation together.

To recapitulate a bit for a better perspective, our claim is that the Treaty of Versailles left many peoples dissatisfied with existing borders, in Europe as well as in the developing world. The pressures for historic recognition of borders and nationalist movements could not materialize and break apart empires because of the protectionist stance of dictatorial regimes. This configuration of events following the end of the First World War stands in sharp contrast with the aftermath of the Second World War, which saw the restoration of democracies, progressive trade liberalization, and relative peaceful international relations (at least in comparison with the interwar period). The outcome of the Second World War, however, served to empower the Soviet dictatorship, which would become ever more bellicose. The post–Second World War conflict therefore became organized around a US–USSR cold war.

11.7   Borders after the Second World War

11.7.1   Secessions

In the fifty years that followed the Second World War, the number of independent countries increased dramatically. There were 74 countries in 1948, 89 in 1950, and 193 in 2001. As a consequence of this increase in the number of independent political units, the world now comprises a large number of relatively small countries: in 1995, 87 of the countries in the world had a population of less than 5 million, 58 had a population of less than 2.5 million, and 35 less than 500 thousands. Over these fifty years, the share of international trade in world GDP increased dramatically. The volume of imports and exports in a sample of about 60 countries rose by about 40 percent.

However, the increase in international trade in the last half-century should not be misread as a simple result of counting countries. Theoretically, if two countries split, their resulting trade to GDP ratios would automatically increase, as a formerly domestic trade becomes international as shown in figure 11.5 for a set of countries *whose borders did not change since 1870*. Also in figure 11.3 we used average tariffs on foreign trade for a selection of countries with available data, a more direct reflection of trade policy, to display a similar historical pattern.

The correlation between the number of countries and trade liberalization is captured by figure 11.4 in which we plot the detrended number of independent countries against the detrended trade over GDP ratio,

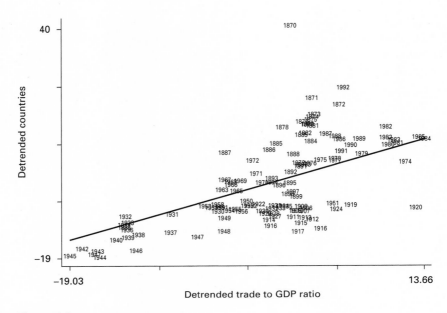

Figure 11.4
Scatter plot of detrended number of countries against detrended trade to GDP ratio, excluding sub-Saharan Africa, 1870 to 1992.

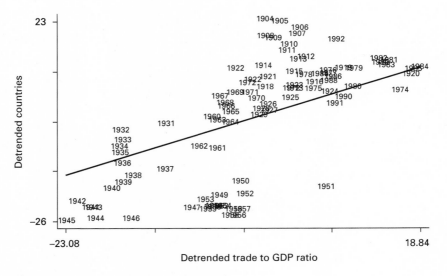

Figure 11.5
Scatter plot of detrended number of countries against detrended trade to GDP ratio, including sub-Saharan Africa, 1903 to 1992.

including sub-Saharan Africa from 1905 onward, and without it from 1870 onward.[44] As both figures show, the correlation is very strong. Since both variables are detrended, this positive correlation is not simply due to the fact that both variables increase over time. Unlike in figure 11.3, where there was a sharp drop in the number of countries between 1870 and 1871, due to the unification of Germany, 1871 is on the regression line and 1870 is well above it. This suggests that too many countries existed before German unification relative to the level of openness. As we argued earlier, especially in chapter 6, two forces are at work simultaneously: smaller countries benefit from open trade regimes, so as small countries emerge, it is in their interest to press for more open trade regimes.[45]

The third worldwide trend, beyond trade liberalization and the increase in the number of countries, is progressive democratization. In 1972 out of 143 countries, 43 could be considered politically free and democratic, 33 partly free, and 67 non-free. By 2001, out of 192 countries, 85 could be classified as free, 58 partially free and 49 non-free. Free countries rose from less than 30 percent to about 45 percent. The ratio of non-free fell from 47 to 20 percent.[46] As we showed in our model, democratization accompanied the breakdown of large countries into smaller ones, and there was more decentralization in countries that do not break apart.

Two phenomena vastly contributed to the increase in the number of countries: (1) decolonization of the developing world; (2) the collapse of the Soviet Union.[47] However, several new countries (e.g., Singapore) were created independent of these two events.

The aftermaths of the First and Second World Wars offer an interesting contrast. While World War I was followed by a collapse of trade, frozen borders, and the retrenchment of democracy, World War II was followed by opposite tendencies. The pattern of what went together after the two world wars is consistent with our theory.

Now, since the former colonies often left behind, especially in Africa, borders that had little to do with ethnic, religious, and cultural homogeneity, they contributed to the profound political instability of many regions. African borders were designed relatively peacefully by the European colonizers in the Berlin conference of 1884 to 1885. As Herbst (2000) notes, the Europeans used arbitrary lines based on latitude and longitude to map out Africa. About 44 percent of African boundaries are straight lines and correspond to astrological measurements or and some others are parallel to some other set of lines. At the time of these colonies' independence in the 1960s, African leaders made a conscious decision not to meddle with the borders inherited from the colonizers, despite their arbitrariness. In addition the new African rulers, in order to preserve personal power, completely embraced the idea of a European style "state" and rejected pre-colonial styles of political organization.

Students of contemporary Africa have suggested that there are too many small countries on this continent (Gottman 1973; Stock 1993). The ethnic fractionalization of the continent has led to too many countries from the point of view of "economic efficiency" (Stock 1993). Technically this point is questionable. With free trade even small political units should prosper. Large countries would imply greater fractionalization within a country with potentially disastrous consequences. Easterly and Levine (1997) and Alesina et al. (2003) attribute the very poor economic performance of this region to the ethnic heterogeneity present in many countries. As a consequences any attempts at solving African politicoeconomic problem by creating large and more heterogeneous states would be counterproductive.

In figure 11.4 the "spike" in the early 1990s reflects the increase in the number of counties after the collapse of the Soviet Union. The breakup of the Soviet Union is a clear example of new countries' democratization as dictatorial reins of a regime loosen.

Trade liberalization has helped in the process. Many of the countries that re-emerged from the Soviet block are quite small. For instance, Latvia has a population of less than 3 million, Estonia about 1.5 million, and the Kirgiz Republic less than 5 million. Even the breakup of Czechoslovakia led to the creation of two relatively small political units of about 10 and 5 million citizens. Czechoslovakia is a case where differences in the level of development and different histories lead to a breakup. Trade between the two countries dropped by one-third after separation, and the Czech Republic immediately started a process of integration with the European Community.

As we saw in the previous chapters, small countries can prosper only in a world of free trade and if they adopt open policies. Therefore it would have been much more difficult, if not impossible, for many former Soviet Republics to break away, had they expected to be economically isolated in a protectionist world, like the world of the Thirties. If today's world were as protectionist and isolationist as in that of the 1930s, the newly created small states emerging (or remerging) from a collapsed Soviet republic would have had a much harder time surviving, making secession from the Soviet Union less attractive (at least economically speaking). Instead, many of the newly independent countries in Eastern Europe, and in the former Soviet Union, are aggressively pursuing their economic links with the West, and are pushing to gain entry in the European Community. The point is that democratization of the Soviet Union created the basis for the breakup of the country and entry into the free trade regime compared to the protectionism of the 1930s which has made the secession economically much less costly.

11.7.2   Decentralization without Separation
The fact that many more countries that gained independence were formed ex novo over the last decade is only one of the manifestation of the effect of political separatism. The tendency toward smaller political unit is indeed broader for two reasons. One is that certain regions may extract various favors from national governments in order not to break away. So even if secessions were not observed, the possibility of their occurrence would influence the politico-economic landscape. The second is that even where regions do not press for secession, they demand, and often obtain, more independence from the national governments.

In Spain, after the collapse of the Franco dictatorship in the mid-1970s, the regional governments obtained more autonomy. Two regions have been particularly vocal. In the Basque region the motivation is mostly cultural and linguistic, but in Catalonia there is further an economic argument, that the region in being the wealthiest of Spain is a net loser in the system of interregional transfers. Income and cultural differences also underlay recently revamped federalist movements in Italy. Northern regions consider their transfer to the south excessive, and different historical developments, well analyzed by Putnam (1993), have led to a sharp cultural divide between the north and south. Progressive devolution of power to the regions has been one of the most important political developments in Italy since the 1970s. The United Kingdom has recently granted more autonomy to Scotland and Wales.

Quebec presents an especially interesting case. The desire for independence in Quebec was revamped by the implementation of the North American Free Trade Agreement (NAFTA). With freer trade in North America, technically it would be easy for a relatively small country like Quebec to prosper. As we saw above, at least for Canada, national borders still matter, so trade among Canadian provinces is much easier than trade between Canadian provinces and US states. Two distant Canadian provinces trade much more with each other than with US states and Canadian provinces bordering each other, even though distance is a strong determinant of trade flows. This implies that there might be a cost for Quebec in trade flows if it were to become independent, and such an argument was made in 1996 by opponents of the self-determination referendum. As the perceived economic costs of succession fall with greater North American economic integration, the likelihood of Quebec gaining independence can be expected to increase. In fact the development of a true free trade area in North America might reduce these costs and make Quebec separatism more attractive. Note that an independent Quebec would leave the rest of Canada geographically disjoint. This may be one reason why Quebec has been able to extract several concessions from the central government that dissuade the breakup.

As for the developing world, decentralization is increasingly viewed as a response to the problems induced by ethnic fractionalization (World Bank 1998), although local governments in many poor developing countries do not have the capacity to carry through the task. As we noted in chapter 9, often decentralization has led to increasing fiscal problems transferred from localities to the central government. Latin America provides an especially clear example in its two large federal states, Argentina and Brazil. Colombia has a similar problem. In Columbia, after the major constitutional reform of 1991 which vastly increased the prerogative of local governments, large budget deficits soon appeared, in contrast to a tradition of relative fiscal balance. In Africa, since the independence of colonies, central governments have been in constant struggle with local chiefs for control of land and power.

11.7.3   Unifications

The 1990s were a time of two important unifications in Europe: the reunification of Germany and the European Union. The German reunification does not pose a real "problem" for our theory. The breakdown of Germany was a somewhat "artificial" response at the end the Second World War. The reunification simply moved the clock backward, ending a war induced separation. Interestingly in Germany the different levels of income achieved in west and east led to significant stress in the politico-economic transfers between the two regions. Fifty years of two philosophically opposing regimes created costly differences in reunification. The European Union is, potentially, a much larger issue. It reflects the exact opposite occurrence in this period of globalization. However, many observers believe that Europe will never be a federal state in the usual sense. Instead, several countries in Europe will form a loose confederation of independent states, joined in a common currency area, with coordinated policies to support this common currency, in addition to a free-trade area supplemented by a harmonization of regulations and standards.

As economic integration is progressing at the European level, regional separatism is more vocal in several member countries of the Union, such as the United Kingdom, Spain, Belgium, Italy, and even France.[48] There are indications, as many have argued, that Europe will (and perhaps should) become a collection of regions (Brittany, the Basque region, Scotland, Catalonia, Wales, Bavaria, etc.) loosely connected within a European confederation of independent regions.[49] Such a development then would be consistent with our argument: if linguistic, ethnic, and cultural minorities feel that they are economically viable in a truly European common market, they can safely separate from their home countries. This argument is often mentioned in the European press.

One may argue that the nation-state in Europe is threatened from above because of the necessity of developing supranational juridical institutions, and from below because of rampant regional movements. These movements feel they do not really need Madrid, Rome, or Paris, when they can be loosely associated to the Europe of regions politically, and fully integrated in the Union economically. Newhouse (1997) puts it rather starkly: "[In Europe], the nation-state is too big to run everyday life and too small to manage international affairs."

We devote the entire next chapter to develop and discuss these arguments in detail.

12   The European Union

12.1   Introduction

Fifteen European countries have created supranational institutions—including a parliament, a court system, a commission, and a council of ministers—to which they have delegated substantial policy prerogatives. How does the European Union fit in our model? The trade-off between economies of scale and heterogeneity of preferences that underlies our analysis offers a useful insight into the process of European integration.

European integration started in the 1950s when security considerations were an important factor. The idea was that deepening economic cooperation, especially in the strategically important areas of coal and steel, was a way of preventing devastating intra-European conflicts. In subsequent decades, with the increase in economic integration, trade barriers were removed. In 1992 a second phase of integration was started by the creation of a single European market. A significant step in the 1990s was the introduction of a single currency now adopted in twelve of the fifteen countries.

For a decade now, European integration seems to have gone beyond its goal of enforcing peace and security and a common market. European institutions have obtained, in many aspects of public life, attributions that usually are the domain of national governments. Table 12.1, from Alesina and Wacziarg (1999) shows that these European institutions are involved in many policy areas, although at different levels in these areas. In order to carry out all of these tasks, Europe has set up some novel institutions. Europe has a parliament that is much less powerful than a national parliament but can, in principle, become the center of legislative production for all its member states. Europe has a council of ministers that is both the executive arm of the Union and a deliberative body.

Table 12.1
Policy responsibilities of the EU and their extent

	Extensive	Shared	Limited
Economic and social areas			
Competition		X	
Cultural policy			X
Regional policy		X	
Employment and social policy		X	
Enterprise policy		X	
Equal opportunities		X	
Industrial policy		X	
Public health			X
Solidarity and welfare			X
Consumer policy		X	
Monetary policy	X		
Education, training and youth			X
Environment		X	
Internal market	X		
Research and technology		X	
Trans-European networks and mobility			X
Sectoral policies			
Agriculture	X		
Fisheries	X		
Transportation		X	
Information and telecommunications		X	
Audiovisual policy			X
Energy		X	
External policies			
Common foreign and security policy			X
Development policy		X	
Humanitarian aid		X	
Common trade policy	X		
Justice and home affairs			
Asylum, external borders, immigration		X	
Judicial and police cooperation		X	
Drugs		X	
Trade in human beings			

Sources: Nugent (1994, ch. 10), and Europa Web site (official Web site of the EU). Reprinted from Alesina and Wacziarg (1999).

The European Commission is becoming more like a central government. The recent extension of majority voting, as opposed to unanimity, in the council of ministers has increased the legislative role of this institution. Finally, the European court has been active in interpreting and enforcing European legislation.

How do we interpret this process? First, let us be clear that Europe is not a "state" (not even a federal state) in the way we have defined it, following Max Weber: the European Union does not have the monopoly of legitimate coercion over its citizens, and it is extremely unlikely that the member states (especially in an enlarged Europe) will ever relinquish it. Then the question is, What is the European Union if not a state? To some extent the Europe is a union of states that serves the purpose of taking advantage of economies of scale, and creating a level of government with limited prerogatives were benefits of scale are large and heterogeneity of preferences low. The principle of subsidiarity that should be the basis of European integration is consistent with this interpretation, and also consistent with our analysis. This principle states the following: "In areas which do not fall within its exclusive competence, the Community shall take action, in accordance with the principle of subsidiaries, only if and in so far as the objectives of the proposed action cannot be sufficiently achieved by the Member States and can therefore, by reason of the scale or effects of the proposed action, be better achieved by the Community" (Article 3b, *Treaty Establishing the European Community*, Maastricht, 1991).

In spirit, by this principle European-level institutions should only operate in areas where economies of scale and externalities make it inefficient for national government to operate independently. Areas like defense against foreign aggression, free trade, the environment, and antitrust are natural policy areas where economies of scale and externalities call for supranational institutions. The trade-off between economies of scale and heterogeneity of preferences that underlies our model offers a suitable interpretation of European integration, if the latter is viewed as an application of this principle of subsidiarity. The subsidiarity principle is, at least on paper, consistent with our model of the trade-off between economies of scale and heterogeneity of preferences.

However, as emphasized by many observers, and especially by Alesina, Angeloni, and Schuknecht (2001), European-level institutions are involved in areas where economies of scale are far from obvious and heterogeneity of preferences among European citizens are high. Thus the principle of subsidiarity cannot be applied consistently. Indeed, as

Europe has moved toward integration, the process has been stalled by British reluctance, repeated Danish rejections of European treaties, a recent Irish rejection of the Treaty of Nice, and a general feeling that European citizens are less enthusiastic than their leaders about further coordination and uniformities of policies.

At the moment the European Union is engaged in a "constitutional phase" that is expected to produce a constitutional chart for Europe in order to clarify these unsettled issues. Our analysis suggests that the European Constitution should strictly and rigorously follow the principle of subsidiarity: European institutions should restrict their involvement to a limited set of areas that guarantee security and free markets.

If Europe has deviated somewhat from this principle, how do we explain it? Our model hints at an explanation that is related to the oft-mentioned democratic deficit of European institutions. A vast European bureaucracy has developed, relatively distant and isolated from the voters, that has appropriated many prerogatives and now leads to an excessive centralization. In fact European citizens have views about what the EU should do that are consistent with the spirit of our model: they feel that Europe should focus on a few prerogatives with high economies of scale.

12.2   What Should Europe Do?

We begin by asking the question: What does our model suggest that the EU do? In broad terms the answer is simple: European institutions should centralize prerogatives for which economies of scale and externalities are important, and for which heterogeneity of preferences among European citizens and member countries is low.

Having said that, the question of how to measure economies of scale, externalities, and heterogeneity of preferences is not easy. For instance, it would be hard to deny that policies that promote free trade within Europe have high economies of scale and internalization of externalities and low heterogeneity of preferences. Every country would benefit from larger and more open intra-European market.

In general, in specific policies, how to evaluate this trade-off is not a priori indisputable. The prolonged debate that accompanied the introduction of a common currency and the unification of monetary policy is an example. The debate was essentially about whether or not the European Union is an optimal currency area, a discussion that can be reinterpreted well in the framework of the trade-off between economies of scale and heterogeneity.[1] A common currency reduces transaction costs in trade; the larger the common currency area, the larger are the benefits of scale (reductions of transaction costs).[2] Money is like a common language: the more people use, the larger the benefits of easier communication. In addition a common currency makes the price system in Europe more transparent market in terms of competition. So we can regard a common currency as an important element of free trade and a common marketplace, which is particularly important for the European countries that heavily trade with each other. A commitment to a common currency also avoids the negative externalities of competitive devaluations and promotes price stability within the Union. For the Union, price stability has of course a public good character.

A country joining the monetary union, however, relinquishes facilitating its own monetary policy, and a country cannot use its monetary policy to stabilize idiosyncratic shocks to their economies. Uncorrelated idiosyncratic economic shocks of various economies, and differences in preferences over the relative weights to be assigned to different goals of monetary policy, generate the heterogeneity costs of joining a monetary union. Different countries might prefer different monetary policies at different points in time, but they cannot have an independent monetary policy if they join a currency union. The extensive economic debate about the pros and cons of the European monetary union can be interpreted completely within this scheme of the trade-off between heterogeneity and benefits of scale and internalization of externalities. Those economists who opposed the monetary union emphasized the degree to which domestic monetary policy can and should target idiosyncratic shocks. Those who favored the union downplayed the size of the heterogeneity of shocks and/or the possibility of a domestic response and emphasized the scale and externality benefits.

Another interesting example is defense and foreign policy. Economies of scale in defense spending are obvious, even though Europe has been a free-rider in this area with respect to the United States. A unified Europe clearly can achieve larger benefits than several small countries acting alone at the international bargaining table. Although peace and security were two of the motivating factors that started the process of European integration, European countries traditionally have had different views and interests in foreign policy. This is not surprising since many of these countries have fought each other for centuries. Recent events in the Balkans, Afghanistan, and Iraq have mirrored the differences of views and sharp disagreement within Europe. The United

Kingdom is typically much closer to the United States than continental
European countries, especially France. Germany has a stronger interest
in eastern Europe then most of the other European countries. Defense
and foreign policy would seem one of the most obvious candidates for
a European-level centralization, but the strength of heterogeneity of
preferences has created serious impediments.

In fiscal policy and taxation, regulation of markets, education, and
social protection and welfare, a heterogeneity of preferences exists relative to supranational economies of scale and other externalities. These
policy domains are best left in the hands of national governments. In
some cases certain domestic policies indirectly interfere with free trade
where regulations have been introduced to protect domestic markets.
Thus such internalization of externalities would call for a European
involvement. However, this argument has a certain limit, for it could
justify the centralizing of any policy prerogative at the European level.
Unfortunately, some observers use this argument to call for a heavy dose
of fiscal coordination in Europe.

The more critical issue is that of redistributive policies across member
countries. However, a policy that moves resources from wealthier to
poorer members of the union can be implemented only if it is centralized
at the union level. Heterogeneity of preferences is likely to be very acute
on this point. This is the reason why richer countries are less typically
enthusiastic than poorer ones about fiscal centralization.[3]

The size of the European Union therefore is in a state of flux. Some
member countries have not adopted all the common policies, such as
the common currency and border control policies while others have.
There are member countries that have applied for admission, mostly to
reap the benefits of the large western European common market. The
size of the Union and what it does are intrinsically connected issues.
One could even think of two types of unions. A relatively a small Union,
formed by very homogeneous countries might choose to centralize certain policy prerogatives. Clearly, when heterogeneity is low, countries
are in a position to take full advantage of economies of scale in policy
areas. A different type of union is a large one composed by several relatively heterogeneous countries. In this configuration the union central-
izes only a very limited amount of functions where economies of scale
are very large. In many other policy areas heterogeneity of preferences
would be a binding constraint. In effect, centralization and size cannot
be increased without admitting more heterogeneous members. This is
one of the unresolved tensions of the current European Union, which

appears be looking both into expanding its size and its degree of centralization. According to our analysis, these two goals are incompatible.[4]

All these are ideas discussed more formally by Alesina, Angeloni, and Etro (2001a, b) as a bias of centralization. To see how this might arise, let us suppose that a union is formed based on certain expectations that relatively few policy prerogatives will be centralized. If these expectations are credible, countries with relatively heterogeneous preferences relative to the core might join. However, ex post, a number of core members close to the median preferences of the Union may choose to centralize policies, contrary to the plan in the formation of the Union. If after the Union is formed, certain regions or countries at some distance from the center are at a disadvantage, potential members may opt out, reducing the benefits of economies of scale. The result, if the Union is too small and too centralized, would resemble that which we discussed in chapter 4 where we observed the (lack of) credibility of transfer programs within national borders. Institutional solutions to this problem require that the Union clearly specify ex ante which prerogatives belong to the Union and which to the member state. In a sense this is what the principle of subsidiarity implies.

12.3   What Does the European Union Do?

How does the distribution of prerogatives between an EU institution and national governments coincide with the normative criteria sketched above? We will explore this issue by closely following the analysis provided by Alesina, Angeloni, and Schuknecht (2001), whose objective was to study the legislative production of the EU in a systematic and quantitative fashion.[5]

These authors break down the legislative production of the EU into nine broad categories: *international trade*, which includes both external provisions and the policies aimed at the establishment of the common internal market; *common market*, which includes a variety of provisions promoting the free internal movement of goods, services, capital and people; *money and finance*, which includes monetary and exchange rate policy, payments systems, and financial market regulation and legislation, bank supervision, fiscal and tax policies, and so on; *education, research, and culture*, which includes youth policies, research, technology, and so on; *environment*, which includes legislation geared toward preserving the environment; *business relations (sectorial)*, which includes all policy designed to affect the behavior and performance of various economic sectors as well as the agricultural policy; *business relations (nonsectorial)*, which encompasses undertaking laws, market competition, and state subsidies; *international relations*, which includes foreign policy, defense, and foreign aid, and finally, *citizen and social protection*, which includes home affairs, justice, consumer protection, civil rights, health, and labor relations as well as structural and regional redistributive funds.

The critical question is how to evaluate these broad categories along the trade-off of economies of scale and externalities versus the heterogeneity of preferences. International trade, common market, international relations, and environment are quite high in the externalities or economies of scale end of the trade-off. Even within these areas we should make important distinctions. For instance, while in the area of defense, economies of scale may be especially important, in foreign aid such efficiencies are nonexistent since European countries have different preferences about how to allocate foreign aid.[6]

The areas of education, research, and culture as well as citizen and social protection should show very high levels of heterogeneity of preferences. Economies of scale are more limited in these areas. The difference in views of the United Kingdom in social welfare policies in fact accounts for the limited system of social protection and labor regulation there compared with continental European countries.

The rational for heavy union involvement in sectorial business relations, especially in agriculture, has often been questioned. Some of these policies have created obstacles to market integration. However, in areas like communication and transportation, there promise to be significant economies of scale.

The nonsectorial business relations is an area where Union involvement may be reasonably based on an externality argument. Antitrust intervention has important crossborder dimensions. In subsidies and state aid, the logic of EU involvement is similar because such government policies could undermine the level playing field in the common market.

Finally, we are left with the vast array of policies in the money and finance domain. Most critical is, of course, the common currency.

Another large area concerns budget balances. The European Union has a fairly elaborate rules that prescribe limits on budget deficits.[7] Whether or not such external rules can be justified is still debated in Europe. In the United States, in contrast, many states have voluntarily adopted various forms of balanced budget rules, but there is no federal mandate on this issue.[8] A priori, there is no strong argument in favor of Union involvement in budget policies. The argument often used is cast in terms of convergence toward a single currency: nonuniform budget policies are viewed by some as an impediment to inflation control and monetary unification. Also fiscal constraints were considered at a time when several member countries had difficulty implementing budget policies.

Regarding taxation, there should be, in principle, high heterogeneity of preferences among member countries. Indeed, large differences exist in the composition of sources of revenues of these countries. Arguments in favor of tax coordination view the benefits of such international transactions. Baldwin and Krugman (2000), however, show that the argument in favor of tax coordination is weak. Beyond monetary unification any further coordination of monetary and financial policy would be undesirable. Table 12.2 shows how the policy domains line up in the economies of scale and heterogeneity of references trade-off.[9]

From survey evidence, most European citizens think that money and finance, environment, and international relations are areas in which Union involvement is welcome. Education and culture, agriculture, and most areas of citizen and social protection are viewed as national.

Table 12.2
Classification of policy domains

	Policy domains	Externalities	Preference assymmetry	Devolution
One	International trade	High	Low	EU/global
Two	Common market	High	Low	EU
Three	Money and finance	Medium/high	?	National/EU
Four	Education, research, and culture	Low	High	Local/national
Five	Environment	Medium/high	High	National/EU/global
Six	Business relations (sectoral)	Low	High	National
Seven	Business relations (nonsectoral)	High	?	EU/global
Eight	International relations	Medium/high	Low	National/EU
Nine	Citizen and social protection	Low	High	Local/national

Source: Reprinted from Alesina, Angeloni, and Schuknecht (2001).

Migration and crime prevention are viewed as areas of mixed Union and national involvement.

Finally, let us turn to redistributive policies. Redistributive policies that cross national borders can be achieved only at the Union level, and some of the union level policies indirectly imply redistributive flows. In addition the European Union has a (small) budget that is used explicitly for redistributive purposes. Views on whether or not the Union should engage in redistributive policies are closely connected with per capita income. Poorer countries, of course, favor Union level intervention in this area; richer countries oppose it.

The question is whether the current attribution of responsibilities between European institutions and national government is consistent with our earlier discussion. It appears rather that Europe has gone too far in some high heterogeneity/low economies of scale policy areas and not far enough in other policy areas with the opposite characteristics (see Alesina and Wacziarg 1999). Alesina, Angeloni, and Schuknecht (2001) examine European institutions in terms of legislative, executive, and judicial growth and arrive at a number of conclusions:

1. The volume of EU legislation increased dramatically in the period 1971 to 2000. The number of legislative sets and court decisions increased by 700 percent in these three decades. The rate of growth has slowed in recent years.

2. Despite all the legislation, the EU share of GDP has remained very low compared to national budgets. EU expenditures rose from 0.4 percent of GDP in 1975 to 1.1 percent in 2000.

3. The involvement of the EU in the international trade and common markets remains high.

4. On issues of monetary policy, EU involvement has persisted, but in fiscal policy it is not so determined to set policy goals.

5. EU involvement in nonsectorial business policy, particularly antitrust has been on the rise. This is consistent with arguments about the appropriate economic role of the Union.

6. Involvement in education and research has been limited, but since the preferences in this area range widely, it is not clear why the Union should have a presence at all.

7. In citizen and social protection the EU has effected an increasing presence. As argued above, wide-ranging preferences in this area suggest rather that the EU involvement should be very small, if at all.

8. The largest area in volume of legislation is agriculture, which is treated as a sectorial business area. In volume over 40 percent of current secondary legislative acts (and 50 percent of EU budget) concerns agriculture, although agriculture constitutes only about 2 percent of GDP of the European economy. Clearly, this level of legislative production is extraordinary and cannot be in any way justified.[10]

9. The EU devotes relatively little attention in its legislative output to the environment.

10. The EU's involvement in international relations and defense is small.

Unfortunately, the integration of Europe has lead to relatively uncontrolled bureaucracies that make day to day decisions. In some instances their decisions have deviated from the defined principles and have been the result of political bargains. As we showed extensively in our own model of democratic control, in Europe it is precisely a democratic deficit that has lead to an excessive emphasis on centralization. No doubt, the European Union is involved in areas where the heterogeneity of preferences is high and the benefits in terms of economies of scale are not obvious. These areas include citizen and social protection and sectorial business policies, in particular, agriculture. In other areas it is unclear why there should be any intervention at all, like education and foreign aid. There are yet areas where the Union may be not be going far enough in preserving competition and free trade and internalizing the economies of scale in defense.

12.4   Union, Countries, and Regions

In institutional design European governments have relinquished their responsibilities both to the European Union and to regional and local governments. The local governments have become if anything even more vocal in their demands as a result of the European Union. For example, Catalonia is a region that may not "need" Spain if it were to become a member of the European Union. To put it differently, once a region is a member of a large common market, including even a common currency area, and can enjoy free trade, the incentives for the region to seek independence or autonomy increases. The national government is much less important for the economy of the region. In fact, in the United Kingdom, Spain, Italy, France, and Belgium the demands of regions for more independence from their national government have gone hand in hand with European integration.

Many observers, for instance, Drèze (1995), have suggested that Europe should develop toward a union of regions, that is, a loose federation of independent regions like Catalonia, Wales, Brittany, and Northern Italy. This is because European national governments have become too small for certain policy prerogatives and to big for others. So their existence is being threatened both from above—the European Union—and from below—regional governments.

It is certainly premature to announce the end of national states in Europe. We have to agree with Keohane and Nye (2000, p. 12) that "contrary to some prophetic views, the nation state is not about to be replaced as the primary instrument of domestic and global governance." Nevertheless, the increasing regional demands for autonomy are consistent with our analysis that, as we have emphasized many times, the cost of being politically small is decreasing with economic integration. In the Europe we see that many regions can afford to be independent if they enjoy the benefits of the European common market.

12.5   Conclusion

It is often said that today Europe, in its free trade and deep economic integration, is a type of federation, like the United States. The ambiguity between these two institutional paths is confusing for Europe the integration process, especially as more heterogeneous countries are admitted to reap the benefits of the large common market area. There are thus two visions of Europe that could be said to bear resemblance to the conflict between Republicans, and Federalists, of Jefferson and Hamilton, in eighteenth-century America. A Jeffersonian vision of Europe would be consistent with the arguments developed in this book. European integration can better capture the benefits of free trade in a global economy. Some supranational institutions like a European central bank, a European court, and antitrust policies would be necessary to ensure a proper functioning of a common European market.

The vision of Europe as a federal state is much less consistent with the arguments of this book, according to which large political unions are unnecessary in a world of free trade and common markets. Indeed, for Europe to become federal state, it would have to create a European government with the monopoly of coercion over its citizens. This is not within the realm of reality in today's Europe, which may soon gain twenty-five more members. Quite simply, it is not possible for Europe to became a federal state.

The distribution of responsibilities between European level institutions and national governments will be a critical building block of a European constitution. It will be interesting to observe its evolution, since any such constitution should be very clear and unequivocal about these roles, it would need to be based on an evaluation of the trade-offs between the heterogeneities of preferences and the benefits of centralization in order for externalities and economies of scale to be internalized.

13   Conclusions

13.1   What Have We Accomplished?

We think of a nation-state as the result of trade-offs between the benefits of economies of scale (broadly defined) in the provisions of public goods and policies versus the costs of heterogeneity of preferences in the population over the same public goods and policies. Certain policy prerogatives can be delegated to subnational levels of governments, and some international organizations and unions of countries have assumed certain policy domains where international spillovers and international economies of scale are important. However, what defines a nation-state remains the monopoly of coercion and the legal use of force within its boundaries.

The nature of trade-off between the benefits of scale and the costs of heterogeneity depends on several economic and institutional forces. First, there is the political regime. Dictators prefer large states so that they can extract more rents from their citizens: repressing regional movements and ethnic, religious, or linguistic minorities has almost always been a focus of every successful dictator, from the absolute monarchs of the seventeenth century, to the colonial empires of the nineteenth and twentieth century, to the Soviet dictators, and to present-day dictators. Contrary to the centralization tendencies of dictatorships, separatism and decentralization have often been characteristic of democratization. In Spain regional autonomy flourished after the collapse of the dictatorship in the 1980s. Czechoslovakia broke apart after becoming democratic. The democratization of the developing world has also been a process of decentralization in order to strengthen democratic institutions. More generally, in the post Second World War, and especially in the last quarter of the twentieth century democratic movements became the major reason for the increase in the number of independent countries.

We have explored in this book whether a free and democratic world generates the "optimal" number of countries. This is the number of countries that optimizes the trade-off between economies of scale and heterogeneity of preferences. We found that this was not necessarily the case. Taking full advantage of economies of scale requires the use of transfers between regions because differences in preferences concerning central policies may result in uneven distributions of benefits among regions of one country. For instance, Quebec has received a favorable treatment from the rest of Canada because of its separatist threat. Lacking a system of politically feasible transfers, certain regions, distant in preferences or geographically from the center of government may choose to break away, even at the cost of losing significant economies of scale. The matter is further complicated if interregional redistribution must occur because of income differences across regions. For example, in Italy and Spain large income flows move from the richer to the poorer regions. Whether or not in a democracy appropriate transfer schemes can be politically supported to the point of enforcing the "optimal" size of the nation is not certain. We discussed how commitment problems may make these transfers difficult to implement.

A more peaceful world can be organized in smaller and more numerous states. Being large helps when much has to be spent on defense, a sector where economies of scale are important. Small countries might organize themselves into coalitions, but it is only safe to be small in a peaceful world. Not surprisingly, then, the end of the cold war coincided with an explosion of political separatism. The reduction in the probability of a global confrontation has been associated with the creation of numerous new states.

However, with large numbers of independent states not organized tightly around two blocs, the probably of small and localized conflicts increases. This also explains why the "peace dividend" which one could have expected from the end of the cold war may turn out to be quite small. The distant chance of a nuclear confrontation between two superpowers has been replaced by the higher probability of localized conflicts.

Openness to trade, and more generally, international economic integration, is related to the size of countries. In a world of trade barriers, the size of a country determines the size of its market. However, with completely free trade and economic integration, market size and country size are not correlated: for every country the size of the market is the world. Therefore small countries can prosper in a world of free trade but cannot in a world where economies have to be self-sufficient. One implication is that small countries will enthusiastically support free trade. The second is that as the world economy becomes more integrated, the trade-off between heterogeneity of preferences and economy of scale "tilts" in favor of small size, as in a world of free trade even small countries can prosper. Thus, as trade becomes more liberalized, small regions are able to seek independence at lower cost. A consequence is that the phenomenon of economic integration is intricately connected with political separatism.

The trend toward economic integration and political separatism over the last fifty years has resulted in the number of independent countries almost tripling. In contrast, in the interwar period, a collapse of trade and a surge of trade barriers was accompanied by the consolidation of colonial empires, and no breakdown or separation of countries occurred, despite the nationalistic sentiments undermined by the Treaty of Versailles. More distant history also shows that small countries can do well if they can trade, while large ones prosper in a hostile "closed" world. The city-states of Italy and Northern Europe prospered because of sea trade. Large colonial empires at the end of the nineteenth century grew in part because of the need to create larger markets in a world that was becoming more protectionist.

However, does country size matter for economic success? As economists are fond of saying, it depends. In theory, with complete free trade and economic integration, political borders should not affect the market size or any economic interaction of citizens of small or large countries. Indeed, very small countries like Singapore have done extremely well, precisely because through free trade they have accessed the world economy. Technically, then, as the world economy becomes more integrated, the size of countries should matter less for economic success.

However, evidence shows that in today's world borders do matter. The border between Canada and the United States is one of the most open in the world. Nevertheless, two distant Canadian provinces trade with each other more than any US state with a nearby Canadian province. Why this is the case is not fully understood by economists. A complex web of information costs, differences in legislation, standards, and currencies may explain it, but the relative importance of all these factors is uncertain. The point is that if the American–Canadian border is so "thick," other borders will be even more so. Even without any explicit trade barriers and free and open markets, political borders appear to matter for economic exchange more than would be expected in theory.

As the world becomes more populated by small and integrated economies, there will be increasing need for supranational institutions to preserve markets and coordinate policies. So far the United Nations, the World Trade Organization, and various regional trade agreements and common currency areas are the primary examples. For small and open economies currency unions have reduced trading costs and created larger markets. The heterogeneity cost in sharing a currency is that a small country adopting another country's currency must give up its independent monetary policy and follow the one chosen by the anchor country. Sometimes it is beneficial to give up the independence of a policy instrument, money, to gain the economies of scale of large and open markets.

The economic theory of optimal currency areas implies that as the number of countries increases and their average size decreases, the number of currencies should decrease as the degree of economic integration increases. This appears to be an actual trend as twelve countries in Europe, Ecuador, and El Salvador, several countries in Africa, and even in the Middle-East are discussing the adoption of a common currency. Unilateral adoptions of the Euro in central and eastern Europe are almost certain as well as more cases of dollarization.

Many states have delegated more functions to subnational levels of governments. The theory of fiscal federalism suggests that polices should be handled by the smallest jurisdictions that can exploit economies of scale and internalize the externalities of the policy. The motivation of decentralization is that the heterogeneity of preferences can be better handled if the central government delegates policy prerogatives to localities. In practice, not all cases of decentralization have been successful; many have lead to the emergence of large fiscal imbalances and policy inefficiencies, especially in developing countries. The main reason is that the fiscal relationships between the central and local governments can easily be mishandled and lead to overspending and deficits at the local level. Thus, while, in theory, decentralization may optimize the trade-off of the economies of scale of a large country reducing the costs of heterogeneity of preferences of different regions, in practice, decentralization has often created more problems that it has solved.

In a world where separatism and decentralization are on the rise, several countries in Europe have intensified a process of economic and political integration. The European Union has entered a constitutional phase. These countries are drafting a constitution that will create a political jurisdiction just short of a federal state but will imply considerably more integration than a trade agreement combined with a currency union. Does this contradict our approach, and more important, is this a mistake for Europe? We think not in both instances. Europe will likely remain a union of tightly integrated economies but with independent political units. We can see the European Union as another example of the supranational organization required as markets become more integrated with very large economies of scale and pervasive externalities. In such areas Europe could, and should, do better. While the tendency toward excessive centralization in areas with *low* economies of scale and *high* heterogeneity costs may be due to a democratic deficit, it could be fixed by more democratic accountability.

Nevertheless, in Europe, regional separatism has not faded away. Some regions of Europe may not need their national capitals if they can depend on a European common market, a European currency, and a Central Bank. This is the way political separatism easily becomes a consequence of economic integration, and some observers do speak of a future Europe composed of a union of regions, that is to say, a union of independent Scotland, Brittany, Northern Italy, Catalonia, and the like.

13.2   What Is Missing?

As we mentioned in the introduction, we raise more questions in this book than we have answers. This is because we are exploring a vastly uncharted area of research, at least in economics. It is only natural that several questions remain unanswered. Here are a few.

First, we treated openness and economic integration as exogenous, that is, we did not try to explain these features. While we readily recognize that country size and openness affect each other, we have argued that as market becomes more open, and trade easier, it is less costly for regions to seek independence. We could have considered models that generate two equilibria, one with large countries and high trade barriers, and the other with small countries and low barriers.

A second point concerns the endogeneity of the degree of conflict. We discussed different potential conflicts and the pressures exerted by belligerent regions on a desired country size. We have not explored fully how a configuration of countries might affect the level of conflict and military technology. At a deeper level, military spending might be viewed as endogenous to the country size and not as an exogenous factor. Likewise we have not explicitly analyzed issues of civil wars in the dynamics of separatism and secessions.

Third, more could be done about discrete changes in country size. In many chapters we discussed the size of countries as if it could change continually in response to small changes in certain variables, like openness. Obviously we are not attempting to be fully realistic. In reality borders are adjusted discretely; that is, large changes occur only at certain historical junctures. Large fixed costs to border changes are an important component in these dynamics.

Fourth, and related to the previous point, is the more general issue of dynamics. We aimed in our analyses to relate the size of countries to certain parameters, such as the degree of openness, and then see how the size of countries would change for different values of these parameters. The question of dynamic adjustments was therefore not fully explored.

Fifth, we could generalize many of the analytical simplifications, but we feel that the mathematical extensions would just add complexity to a basic story. No doubt, an extension could include a second dimension in our unidimensional world, or describe the world as a circle rather than as a line. Potentially more interesting might be to raise the analysis to a nonuniform distribution of individuals as would account for different levels of population density in the world. A further extension might take into account population mobility within and across borders.

Sixth is the interesting possibility of an extension that would allow for an imperfect correlation between geographical and ideological distance. That would account more formally for minority groups being isolated. Many good insights might come from such a complex and realistic framework.

Seventh, there is the question of military alliances. In this area there exist important works by many political scientists but few economists. Our chapters on wars may seem to beg for this extension. Similarly we could treat in our analysis the issue of trade blocs.

Eighth, we could do much more with empirical evidence. For instance, we could provide more accurate measurements of economies of scale, as well as of government in terms of taxation per capita and country size in chapter 10. In general, our aim was to provide a large number of testable implications that are open to a more systematic and thorough confrontation with the empirical evidence.

Finally, it goes without saying that our sweeping historical analysis of chapter 11 just scratched the surface. As mere amateurs, we took the ride, but more professional historians could do more and better.

13.3   So What Next?

Making predictions is a mine field. Nevertheless, we are bold enough to ask: If our analyses are on the right track, what might we expect of the future?

First, to the extent that market integration and relatively free trade can be maintained, the tendency toward separatism and decentralization will persist. The benefits of size diminish in a more integrated world, and regions and groups that do not share common views on national policies will find it economically less attractive to be part of large countries. In a world of free trade one needs to ask whether a region that breaks away negatively affects the country's trade. That is to say, what is the loss to the rest of the country in freely accepting the newly independent neighboring country as a trading partner? How much Canada might lose if Quebec became independent? From a purely economic point of view the answer is very little.

Excessive insistence on keeping heterogeneous countries together has implied sizable costs in religious, ethnic, racial, and cultural animosities among peoples as recent events in the Balkan states amply testify.

In sub-Saharan Africa the number and shape of states is still a pressing issue. There is a sense that the African borders cut across racial, religious, and tribal cleavages in ways that destabilize the continent and impede economic development. The question is not whether there are too many or too few countries in Africa, but rather, whether political borders cut across racial and religious cleavages.

In a more democratic world borders need to satisfy citizens' aspirations. Democratic governments can respond to demands of local autonomy by decentralizing, but there is a limit as to how much a central government can delegate to regions. To the extent that democratization will continue to expand, so will separatist movements.

A peaceful and economically integrated world of small countries will depend on the supranational institutions that enforce free trade and the functioning of markets. The traditional national state may need the apparatus of multinational organizations, including trade organizations, monetary unions, and supranational courts. It is becoming fashionable to discuss a new financial architecture, that is to say, as a way of thinking about institutions protecting free and well-functioning financial markets in a highly integrated world. We feel that while a certain amount of supranational public goods and institutions can guarantee free trade and well-functioning markets, this is not an area to necessarily enlarge. Heavy government intervention in national economies does not improve the functioning of markets, and the same applies to supernational institutions. In a more integrated world there will be a need for supranational institutions, financial and legal, but not for large federations of countries.

What has changed in the last fifty years is not only the map of the world but the nature of states. From a system where central governments had most of the policy prerogatives a complex web of interaction has developed involving different levels of government, from worldwide to local organizations. Decentralization is currently a popular trend.

This trend will likely continue. However, every time functions are redistributed among bureaucracies, there is a tendency for duplication, inefficiency, and conflict as institutions attempt to hold as much as possible as their own. A second problem concerns the so-called democratic deficit. In a multinational world of highly integrated democracies only a few political institutions can "control" the provision of supranational public goods. Supranational institutions typically do not have the same political legitimacy of national parliaments. As a result any functions they delegate may raise complex issues of legitimacy for democratic theory.

So, to return to where we started, we argue that the organization of governments should move away from an all-encompassing state to a much more complex system of political jurisdictions, even though nation-states will remain at the core of this system. The highly integrated, free, and relatively democratic world of today is in search of such a flexible system of political jurisdictions where choices exist over the fundamental trade-offs between the benefits of size and the costs of heterogeneity.

Notes

Chapter 1

1. Unless otherwise specified, we measure a country's size by its *population* (total inhabitants). As we consider the size of a country's economy, we do this as is usual, measured by the total income of its nationals (gross national product, GNP) and by the total income produced within the country's borders (gross domestic product, GDP).

2. As of January 2002 the United Nations had 189 members. In March 2002 Switzerland voted to become the 190th member state. In May 2002 East Timor became independent, and that now brings the total members to 191. The Vatican City has chosen to remain outside the United Nations. Therefore the current number of internationally recognized states is 192. That does not include Taiwan, which is no longer a member, having been replaced by mainland China in 1971, and is not recognized as an independent state by most other governments though it retains de facto independence. If Taiwan is included, the total number of existing countries would be 193 as we write (July 2002). The number of countries would be even higher if one were to include territories, such as Bermuda and Hong Kong, that are not fully independent but have separate government institutions and issue their own currency.

3. Laws, in the *Dialogues of Plato,* cited in Dahl and Tufte (1973).

4. Recent important contributions include, for example, Henderson (1983) and Tilly (1990).

5. As noted by Findlay (1996): "Insofar as they are considered at all in economics, the boundaries of a given economic system . . . are generally considered as given."

6. For instance, see Sachs and Werner (1995), Gallup, Sachs, and Mellinger (1998), and Sachs, Mellinger, and Gallup (2001).

7. Max Weber (1958, originally written in 1918) gave a classical definition of the modern state as "a human community that (successfully) claims the monopoly of the legitimate use of physical force within a given territory." Tilly (1990) defines "states" as "coercion-wielding organizations that are distinct from households and kinship groups and exercise clear priority in some respect over all other organizations within substantial territories," while he defines "national states" as "states governing multiple contiguous regions and their cities by means of centralized, differentiated, and autonomous structures." For an historical perspective on the emergence of the modern "sovereign state" amongst alternative systems see Spruyt (1994).

8. For example, see Connor (1978).

9. For example, see Plano and Olton (1969) cited in Connor (1978).

10. In an article originally published in *The Wall Street Journal*, Robert Barro (1991) succintly captures this trade-off: "We can think of a country's optimal size as emerging from a trade off: a large country can spread the cost of public goods, . . . over many taxpayers, but a large country is also likely to have a diverse population that is difficult for the central government to satisfy."

11. This is true, by definition, for "pure" public goods. The standard economic definition of a public good is that its use by one agent does not prevent other agents from using it. For example, see Samuelson (1954) and Laffont (1988, ch. 2).

12. We document this fact empirically in chapter 10. See also Alesina and Wacziarg (1998).

13. This evidence and explanation is discussed in Easterly and Rebelo (1993).

14. For a survey of the empirical literature on defense, see Sadler and Hartley (1995).

15. We document this effect in chapter 10. See also Alesina, Spolaore, and Wacziarg (2000).

16. See Sachs and Sala-i-Martin (1992).

17. However, as we will see in chapter 4, the existence of redistributive transfers may sometime lead even *poorer* regions to opt for secession. See also Bolton and Roland (1997).

18. Easterly and Levine (1997) have documented convincingly how ethnic heterogeneity often interferes with the implementation of growth-enhancing policies. Mauro (1995), La Porta et al. (1999), and Alesina et al. (2003) show that various measures of quality of governments in a cross section of countries are generally inversely related to the degree of ethnic fragmentation. Alesina, Baqir, and Easterly (1997), Alesina and La Ferrara (2000, 2002), and Alesina, Baqir, and Hoxby (2000) document various aspects of the costs of heterogeneity in American localities.

19. The *Spirit of the Laws*, vol. 1, bk. 8, cited in Dahl and Tufte (1973), our italics. However, Montesquieu recognized that small states are at a disadvantage in the provision of key public goods, such as defense. He wrote: "if a republic is small, it is destroyed by an outside force, if it is large, it is destroyed by an internal vice." (*The Spirit of the Laws*, vol. 1, bk. 9).

20. For example, Hamilton in Federalist 9 wrote: "[T]he opponents of the plan proposed have, with great assiduity, cited and circulated the observation of Montesquieu on the necessity of a contracted territory for republican government."

21. Over the long run the heterogeneity of preferences may also depend on the configuration of political borders and on the actions of governments. While we will not develop a fully fledged theory of endogenous heterogeneity, we will touch upon this issue in chapter 5.

22. An essentially efficiency-driven explanation of institutional change in the long run was provided by North and Thomas (1973). However, later North (1981) abandoned the efficiency view of institutions. For an in-depth discussion of these issues, see North (1990).

23. Technically, if every potential loser could be compensated, the switch to an efficient configuration of borders would be a Pareto improvement. If full compensations were available at no cost, the optimal configuration of borders would be the only Pareto efficient

solution—it is the only allocation that cannot be changed through Pareto improvements. However, as we argue in this book, in general, compensation schemes are difficult or impossible to implement through political institutions.

24. "Leviathan" is a biblical word that originally meant "sea-monster." Since the classical book by Hobbes (1651), "leviathan" has come to mean "autocratic ruler." In the contemporary economic literature, "leviathan" is often used to denote any government that maximizes its own revenues as its main objective (e.g., see Buchanan 1975; Brennan and Buchanan 1980).

25. The Middle East is another region where inefficient and arbitrary borders—drawn by colonial powers after the collapse of the Ottoman empire—have become a source of political and economic trouble. For a discussion, see Cleveland (1994).

26. This quotation from Pareto is reported by Powell (1999, ch. 1) in his excellent account of formal modeling in international relations. On models as simplifying metaphors, see also Krugman (1995).

27. However, national governments (except in very small countries) do not usually assume responsibility for all public policies and provide all public goods. A certain number of functions are delegated to subnational level of governments, and vary from country to country. The question of decentralization and its relationship to the size of countries and the configuration of national borders is addressed more specifically in chapter 9.

Chapter 2

1. To be sure, there is also ample disagreement about how much a government should tax, but we do not address this point here.

2. Leaving aside countries formed by island chains, the United States (including Alaska) is one of few examples of territorial noncontinuity.

3. A very incomplete list includes Epple and Romer (1991), Cutler and Glaeser (1997), and Alesina, Baqir, and Hoxby (2000).

4. See Alesina, Angeloni, and Etro (2001a) for a discussion of how externalities across jurisdictions may lead to the formation of multinational unions.

5. A related point was made, in a different context, by Dahl and Tufte (1973, p. 141), who considered the theoretical possibility of different and changing jurisdictions—depending on the "problem at hand"—but concluded that "just as a central nervous system would quickly become overloaded by a proliferation of specialized organs constantly changing in size and shape, so the costs of communication and information, and therefore of control, would become overwhelming if citizens were confronted with an indefinite number of changing units. In fact, in complex political systems these costs already appear to be so high as drastically to impair citizen effectiveness."

6. Coercion is especially important in this context, since individuals might choose to free ride and not to pay for public goods in the absence of some coercive power by the public good provider (i.e., the state).

7. We could also consider a circle, with no substantive changes in the results.

8. A recent excellent book that includes insightful unidimensional analyses of spatial issues is Fujita and Thisse (2002).

9. See Tam (1999) for an interesting attempt to extend this type of model to two dimensions.

10. The parameter g (which measures the maximum utility from public goods for an individual who enjoys all of his most favored types) can be set equal to zero without loss of generality. We will do so in the rest of this analysis.

11. This point will be further discussed in chapter 9.

12. For simplicity, we will abstract from the constraint that the numbers of jurisdictions must be integers. As in proposition 2.1, the analysis can be reformulated to take such a constraint into account.

13. In this proposition, for simplicity, we again abstract from integer constraints.

14. The condition is necessary for the optimality of providing M public goods by unified governments. It is sufficient if we rule out the possibility that economies of scope may also arise when a government jointly provides a number of public goods larger than 1 but *smaller than M*. The analysis can be easily extended to such general cases. The details are available from the authors on request.

15. While economies of scope mean that doing different things at the same time is cheaper, organizational and transactional costs mean that doing different things separately is more expensive. Obviously the two ideas are closely related, and organizational and transaction costs associated within specialized and overlapping jurisdictions could be formally modeled as economies of scope within centralized jurisdictions.

Chapter 3

1. This is an implication of the Coase theorem, named (or, some say, misnamed) after Coase (1960). The textbook version of the Coase theorem essentially states that in the absence of transactions and bargaining costs, people should be expected to agree on efficient allocations. In chapter 4 we will have more on the Coase theorem and its relevance for our analysis.

2. More specifically, we assume that the parameter values that underlie the result of proposition 2.1 hold.

3. Other things being equal, more homogeneous regions of the world would be partitioned in large countries, while more heterogeneous regions would be partitioned in small countries.

4. In chapter 4 we will extend the analysis to the case where transfers and taxes depend on the location of individuals. In chapter 4 we will also look at income differences among individuals within countries.

5. See Black (1948) for the original formulation of the median voter theorem.

6. The result that the public good located at the median is very general. The fact that the median coincides with the middle of the country follows from the assumption of a uniform distribution of the population. The median would coincide with the middle for any symmetric distribution, a uniform distribution being one of them. With more general distributions of the population, the public good would still be at the median, but the latter would not necessarily be in the middle.

7. Analogous but less clear-cut was the move of the Brazilian capital from Rio de Janeiro to Brasilia in 1960. Brasilia is closer to the geographical center of Brazil but not located at

the center of the country's population distribution. The Brazilian government at the time might have expected Brasilia to become closer to the center of population distribution through the development of the uninhabited Brazilian heartland. Whether the creation of Brasilia was an example of efficient capital relocation or—as many think—a major economic blunder remains hotly debated among Brasilians to this day.

8. By contrast, the maximization of average utility can be ethically rationalized by the famous veil-of-ignorance argument of expected utility first proposed by Harsanyi (1953, 1955). Technical details on these issues are provided in section 3.4.

9. Technically, a change in which everybody gains is called a "Pareto improvement."

10. This is an application of the Coase theorem.

11. However, as we will see in chapter 4, even if the system can be designed, it might not be credible. If changing borders is costly, people far from the center may well expect (rationally) that once borders are determined, transfers would not be implemented in equilibrium.

12. This section can be skipped by the nontechnical reader, but the example provided is quite simple and can illustrate well the intuition.

13. Here k is the density of taxes paid by an individual. Since the mass of individuals is normalized to 1, total taxes will pay for the total cost of the public good, which is indeed k.

14. Note that the condition ensures 50 percent in favor of breakup not only in the old unified country counted as a whole, but also in each of the two newly formed countries.

15. This section heavily draws from Alesina and Spolaore (1997).

16. We ignore the integer problem, assuming that $\sqrt{a/4k}$ is an integer. Otherwise, the efficient number of countries N^* is given by either the largest integer smaller than $\sqrt{a/4k}$ or the smallest integer larger than $\sqrt{a/4k}$.

17. We will consider a relaxation of this hypothesis in chapter 4.

18. We know that this assumption is not verified in the real world. People who live along the borders of countries are usually not allowed to choose which country to join (although local referenda do take place occasionally). In this chapter we are studying the ideal case where political borders are determined freely by individuals, rather than by negotiations or conflicts between central governments. We will consider realistic forms of border determination in chapter 5. The role of conflict will be explored in chapters 7 and 8.

19. This technical assumption is made to make the problem analytically tractable and obtain closed form solutions.

20. In the appendix to this chapter we show that the same results hold if we use a different rule B, namely require that a change of borders be admissible if a majority of voters of the new countries created by the change of borders are in favor of it.

21. Technically a move from voting equilibrium to efficient equilibrium would not be a Pareto improvement. In that respect the voting equilibrium is Pareto efficient.

22. This is true by the law of large numbers. More generally, see Judd (1985).

23. However, see Diamond (1967) and Sen (1970).

24. Suppose that the utility of the worst-off individual were maximized by a configuration of countries of *different* size. By making the largest country smaller, one could increase the utility of the worst-off individual, which gives us a contradiction.

25. For additional discussion on the role of alternative secession rules, see Bordignon and Brasco (2001).

26. The other solution is $s_i \cdot s_{i+1} = 2k/ag$; this is the unstable solution of rule A discussed in the appendix.

27. Details of the derivation can be found in the appendix to Alesina and Spolaore (1997).

28. We assume that when there is indifference, the individual will opt for the status quo (no secession).

Chapter 4

1. In fact $\frac{1}{8}$ is the midpoint between 0 and $\frac{1}{4}$, and $\frac{3}{8}$ is the midpoint between $\frac{1}{4}$ and $\frac{1}{2}$.

2. The Coase theorem is based on a classical article by Ronald Coase (1960), in which he challenged the economists' conventional wisdom on externalities and taxes. Coase developed his arguments through examples and never stated any formal theorems. Therefore there exist various interpretations of Coase's results that are known as the Coase theorem. Overall, the standard textbook version of the theorem boils down to the proposition that in the absence of transactions and bargaining costs, individuals will agree on an allocation of resources that maximizes the total size of the pie—that is, they will agree on an efficient allocation. Sometimes the Coase theorem is also meant to include Coase's results for the more realistic case of positive transaction costs (e.g., see Glaeser, Johnson, and Shleifer 2001). For an introduction to the Coase theorem, see Mueller (1989, ch. 2). A critical discussion of the applicability of the Coaseian approach to politics is provided in Olson (2000, ch. 3). Formal analyses of collective action in which Coaseian efficiency fails to be achieved in equilibrium are provided by Dixit and Olson (1998) and Ray and Vohra (1999, 2001).

3. A branch of economic theory, mechanism design, tries to develop systems of incentives to make individuals reveal their true preferences about public goods; for example, see Laffont (1987).

4. For more discussion on this credibility problem in federations, see Alesina, Angeloni, and Etro (2001a).

5. See Alesina and Perotti (1997), Perotti (2000), and Persson and Tabellini (1999, 2000) for a discussion.

6. This assumption will be relaxed in the next section.

7. Of course, for individuals who are very distant from the government (high l_i), t_i and/or r_i may be negative.

8. It is worth stressing that we are limiting our analysis to the range of parameter values between no compensation ($q = 0$), and full compensation ($q = a$), defined, as we will see below, as everyone having the same utility. One could think of transfer schemes that redistribute so much away from the center to the borders, that individuals at the center are worse off than individuals at the periphery (overcompensation). This is a rather unrealistic case where $q < 0$. We rule it out for analytical simplicity, since it would introduce analytical

complications in our analysis (e.g., preferences over the location of the government may cease to be single-peaked). We focus here on the case where preferences are single-peaked.

9. Of course, such an individual is different from the median voter among the government types. For example, if there exists only one country in the segment $[0, 1]$, the median voter over government types is located at $\frac{1}{2}$, but the median voters over compensation schemes are located at $\frac{1}{4}$ and $\frac{3}{4}$.

10. See, for instance, Alesina et al. (1999).

11. This is the case studied by Haimakno, LeBreton, and Weber (2000).

12. We return to this issue in chapter 9, but see also Oates (1999) for a survey of this literature.

13. Equation (4.25) is analogous to equation (12) in Bolton and Roland (1997, p. 1064). However, our equation differs from the Bolton-Roland equation in that we assume economies of scale in public good provision. Bolton and Roland assume that separation reduces everyone's income proportionally. As we will see in chapter 6, separation does lower pre-tax income in a world of barriers to international trade. In this section we abstract from those costs, while we maintain our assumption of economies of scale. Our alternative specification allows us to derive an exact closed-form decomposition of the three effects.

14. This effect is similar to the efficiency effect described by Bolton and Roland (1997): unification, all other things equal, increases the size of the pie.

Chapter 5

1. As we mentioned in chapter 1, Buchanan and coauthors were influential in popularizing the use of the term "Leviathan" as equivalent to "rent-maximizing government" in the economic literature.

2. More generally, Leviathans may need to obtain the consensus of at least part of the population in order to remain in power and pursue their rent-maximizing objectives. On this point, see the work by Grossman (1991) and Acemoglu and Robinson (2000).

3. The result would be appropriately modified if average income is a function of the supply of public goods. We abstract from this point in the analysis. For recent discussions, see McGuire and Olson (1996) and Olson (2000).

4. See Kennedy (1991) for a popular discussion of the collapse of over extended empires.

5. In the real world each Leviathan would also have to face any constraints due to the existence of other Leviathans who desire to rule large countries. Following an important paper by Friedman (1977), our focus will be on an equilibrium where Leviathans maximize their aggregate net rents. Friedman argues that such outcome should emerge even in a world in which Leviathans war over territory. Here we ignore the explicit use of force by Leviathans either against their population or against other Leviathans. We will discuss issues of conflict and war in chapters 7 and 8.

6. An alternative way for a Leviathan to maintain a large state when faced with higher demands from a heterogeneous population is to decentralize and allow some form of limited autonomy to the vocal minorities. We return to this issue in chapter 9.

7. An interesting topic that we do not develop here is whether Leviathans would use compensation schemes, if available.

8. More precisely, the solution is N_δ if it is a positive integer. Otherwise, it is given by the positive integer closest to N_δ.

9. We will also assume that $m < a_0/a_1$.

10. It is immediate to check that, when $a_1 = 0$, the elasticity $(dN_\delta/d\delta)(\delta/N_\delta)$ reduces to $\frac{1}{2}$, as implied by equation (5.5).

Chapter 6

1. For general treatments of the field, see Barro and Sala-i-Martin (1995) and Aghion and Howitt (1998).

2. Rivera-Batiz and Romer (1991) provide a model of international trade in which the marginal contribution of trade to growth over the long term comes entirely from international spillovers of knowledge. In their survey of the literature on trade and growth. Grossman and Helpman (1991) stress the crucial role that the extent of knowledge spillovers across national borders play in determining the long-term relationship between trade, growth, and welfare.

3. In these types of models, various proxies are used for distance, including both geographical and political measures, such as sharing language, currency, and legal origins.

4. Obstfeld and Rogoff (2001) draw the consequences of these border effects on issues of portfolio allocation in international markets.

5. Haas (1975) later repudiated his own neofunctionalist theory. For a recent review of the literature in international relations, see Gilpin (2001, ch. 13).

6. More generally, knowledge spillovers across international borders may be neither absent nor complete. The empirical literature has found that international knowledge spillovers exist (Coe and Helpman 1994; Irwin and Klenow 1993; Bernstein and Mohnene 1994) but are not internationally complete and instantaneous (Lichtenberg 1992). Eaton and Kortum (1994) find that the diffusion of technological knowledge is more rapid within political borders than across borders. In fact, the size of crossborder spillovers will depend on the degree of international economic integration.

7. We are ruling out preferential agreements and other asymmetries as far as international exchanges are concerned.

8. If $\sqrt{[a - 4(1 - \omega)h]/4k}$ is not a positive integer, then the efficient number of countries N^* is given by the maximum of one and the integer closest to $\sqrt{[a - 4(1 - \omega)h]/4k}$.

9. If $\sqrt{[a - 2(1 - \omega)h]/2k}$ is not a positive integer, then the equilibrium number of countries is given by the maximum of one and the integer closest to $\sqrt{[a - 2(1 - \omega)h]/2k}$.

10. The model builds on Alesina, Spolaore, and Wacziarg (2000) and Spolaore and Wacziarg (2002).

11. As usual, the results generalize to any standard CRRA utility function $(C_{it}^{1-\sigma} - 1)/(1 - \sigma)$ with $\sigma > 0$.

12. For a derivation of this Euler equation, see, for example, Blanchard and Fischer (1989, ch. 2) or Barro and Sala-i-Matin (1995, ch. 2). Remember that we are assuming a log-utility function in (6.1), and therefore the elasticity of intertemporal substitution is equal to one. Moreover we are implicitly assuming that all taxes are lump sum.

13. For a derivation of this result, see Barro and Sala-i-Martin (1995, ch. 2).

14. Spolaore (1995) provided an explicit model of multiple equilibria in the number of countries and endogenous openness.

Chapter 7

1. If disputes were resolved by impartial supranational institutions, the nationality of each party would be irrelevant to the resolution of the dispute. However, this would mean that there would exist some supranational jurisdiction providing a supranational public good (unbiased enforcement of international law). In this chapter we depart from international law and assume that international exchanges take place across political borders in an anarchic world where only a country's power matters. We will return to the issue of the enforcement of international law in chapter 8.

2. For some early discussion on the relationship between size and military spending, see Dahl and Tufte (1973). For an overview, see Hartley and Sandler (1995).

3. In chapter 6 resources depend endogenously on production and trade, but there is no conflict.

4. The function $d_i/(d_i + d_j)$ specifies a conflict resolution technology and is a special case of a contest success function $\phi(d_i, d_{i'})$, as is extensively used in the formal literature on conflict; for example, see Tullock (1980), Hirshleifer (1989, 1991, 1995a, b), Grossman (1991), Skaperdas (1992), and Powell (1999). $\phi(d_i, d_{i'})$ is sometime interpreted as country i's probability of winning. In that were our case, the share that goes to individual i would be interpreted as the expected value. Since we assume linear preferences (risk neutrality), this alternative interpretation would make no difference.

5. As we discussed above, empirically this relationship is affected by the presence of international alliances and free-riding within them.

6. As usual, we disregard the fact that $\widetilde{N}$ must be an integer.

7. For example, see Levy (1989), Bueno de Mesquita and Lalman (1992), Maoz and Russet (1993), and Bueno de Mesquita et al. (1999).

8. An exception in the political science literature is Dahl and Tufte (1973).

9. For a discussion of country unions that share the emphasis of this book, see Alesina, Angeloni, and Etro (2001a).

Chapter 8

1. This following discussion is based on Spolaore (2001).

2. For a dissenting view, see Barbieri (1996).

3. For an extensive discussion, see Powell (1999).

4. However, Gartzke (1999) has criticized the second mechanism as a plausible explanation of rational wars in the absence of uncertainty and asymmetric information. While we
have not explicitly extended our model to allow for asymmetric information, we expect
such extensions to strengthen our results.

5. For simplicity, we rule out the option of surrender without a fight.

6. When the costs associated with open conflict are asymmetric, countries that are weak in
terms of military strength but face low war costs may obtain more at the bargaining table
than countries with bigger muscles but also larger war costs. Specifically, for $c_j \neq c_{j'}$, we
have

$$\alpha_j^* = \frac{d_j}{d_j + d_{j'}} + \frac{c_{j'} - c_j}{2R},$$

provided that both countries obtain through bargaining at least as much as they would
through open conflict.

7. On these issues a classical discussion is by Shelling (1966). See also Fearon (1995) and
Van Evera (1998).

8. When $\max\{E_j, E_{j'}\} \leq c$, (fight, fight) is *not* an equilibrium in weakly dominated
strategies as long as $e_j > 0$ and $e_{j'} > 0$.

9. Therefore, as we mentioned before, wars occur in equilibrium because of the standard
commitment problem that arises in a Prisoner's Dilemma. For a discussion of commitment
problems in international relations, see Powell (1999).

10. Note that for $\max\{E_j, E_{j'}\} \leq c$, our game is a general case of the Stag Hunt Game cited
in Harsanyi and Selten (1988) and Farrell (1988), and discussed in Aumann (1990). See
also Fudenberg and Tirole (1991, pp. 20–21). For an application to international relations
in a different but related context, see Jervis (1978).

11. The definition of coalition-proof Nash equilibrium proceeds by induction on the size
of all possible coalitions of players. As in the standard definition of Nash equilibrium,
the definition requires that no one-player coalition can improve its situation by deviating.
Then the definition requires that no two-player coalition can improve the situation of its
members by deviating, but the only joint deviations that are allowed are those from which
no member of the deviating coalition has an incentive to deviate individually. In other words,
all two-player deviations must be Nash equilibria of the two-player game induced by
holding the strategies of all the other players fixed. Then, for games with more than two
players, three-player coalitions are considered, and so on, all the way to the grand coalition of all players. For every two-player game, the set of coalition-proof Nash equilibria
coincides with the set of Nash equilibria that are not Pareto dominated by any other Nash
equilibrium. For a formal definition of coalition-proof Nash equilibrium, see Bernheim,
Peleg, and Winston (1987).

12. In principle, tight supranational alliances could therefore be classified as countries in
our framework insofar as they satisfy our definition. In practice, states that join actual
military alliances tend to retain sovereignty on most matters.

13. By assuming one individual in each region (or, more generally, M individuals with
identical preferences, as studied in appendix B), we can disregard issues of preference
aggregation within regions. In particular, any voting rule would deliver the same decision
within each region. Therefore we will refer to a region as an individual player in the rest
of the analysis.

14. For simplicity, we assume that the constraint $d_j \leq \sum_{i \in S_j} y_i$ is never binding in equilibrium.

15. We do not model those factors explicitly. In a different framework, Hess and Orphanides (1995, 1997) explore a government's incentives to start an avoidable war as a function of economic and political conditions.

16. As we already mentioned, to keep the analysis simple, we implicitly assume that geography and/or technology prevent third parties from getting involved in these bilateral conflicts. In other words, we rule out the possibility of transfer and/or commitment technologies that could allow a third country to promise outside help to a country in conflict in exchange for a share of the spoils.

17. Without loss of generality, we assume that the "surprise loss" is the same across countries.

18. It is important to note that the concept of "coalition," in this context, should not be confused with the concepts of "region," "country," or "government." Here coalition will be used consistently with the technical definition of coalition-proof equilibria, namely as *any subset of players*. Therefore we refer to "coalitions of governments" in stage two and three, and "coalitions of regions" in stage one, simply as subsets of players that may jointly deviate from any proposed equilibrium. In particular, note that a coalition of regions is just a *subset of players*, while a country formed by one or two regions is the *outcome of a strategy profile*.

19. While we have chosen to focus on coalition-proof equilibria, we are ready to entertain the possibility that in some contexts a broader notion of equilibrium can be usefully employed. For instance, in some historical circumstances communications between governments in conflict could be extremely difficult, and/or mutual trust could be low. See Aumann (1990) for a critical view of the notion that preplay communication is sufficient to ensure the self-enforceability of any agreement to play the Pareto-dominant equilibrium. In our game each player has an incentive to convince the other to bargain no matter whether he himself plans to bargain or fight. Now, consider a mistrustful player who would play the Pareto-dominated but risk-dominant strategy "fight" in the absence of communication. He may see no reason to change his mind if informed that the other player requests to bargain. Therefore preplay communication between governments may not be enough: some minimum amount of international trust is needed in order to sustain "bargain" as an equilibrium. In those cases countries deciding over unification or independence may reasonably have pessimistic expectations over the outcome of conflict and, for instance, expect conflict to be resolved through fight, no matter whether E is larger or smaller than c. Pessimistic expectations over the ability of governments in conflict to coordinate on the goods bargaining outcome may sustain an alternative equilibrium, that is, a subgame perfect but *not* coalition-proof equilibrium characterized as follows. For all $0 < h_w \leq h_e$, $\pi \geq 0$, $c \geq 0$ and $0 \leq \rho \leq 1$, there exists a "pessimistic" subgame perfect equilibrium (which is not coalition-proof) such that:

- *Four independent regions* ($N = 4$) *for*

$$\frac{\pi}{4} \left(\frac{R}{4} + c \right) \leq h_w.$$

- *A unified west and two independent countries in the east* ($N = 3$) *if and only if*

$$h_w < \frac{\pi}{4} \left(\frac{R}{4} + c \right) \leq h_e.$$

• *A unified west and a unified east* ($N = 2$) *if and only if*

$$\frac{\pi}{4}\left(\frac{R}{4}+c\right) > h_e.$$

In other words, pessimistic beliefs over conflict resolution may induce the formation of large countries (i.e., a size distribution of countries that would be consistent with coalition-proof equilibria only if $\rho = 1$). Optimistically, we see our equilibrium selection based on the expectation of coordination as more realistic in the modern world. However, we do not rule out a priori that alternative "pessimistic" equilibria may have been observed historically.

20. A similar corollary can be derived when the number of countries goes from 2 to 3, or from 3 to 4.

21. For Granger causality tests of the trade-conflict and conflict-trade relationships, see Gasiorowski and Polachek (1982).

22. A direct application of this alternative model of conflict to our game of endogenous country formation would require a detailed specification of how different preferences over specific issues are distributed across regions and aggregated by unified governments. While this may represent an interesting extension, we leave it for future research.

23. See Bernheim, Peleg, and Winston (1987, p. 8).

Chapter 9

1. See, however, Tanzi (2000) for an important dissenting opinion.

2. For an excellent survey of the field, we refer the reader to Oates (1999). See also Inman and Rubinfeld (1997) and Hooge and Marks (2001b).

3. This problem is related to the analysis of pork barrel politics in Shepsle et al. (1981).

4. For an excellent overview of the literature on transition economies, see Roland (2000); chapter 11 of that volume discusses the relationship between federalism and transition and contrasts in the former Soviet Union and China.

5. As for the case of established market economies, even in transition economies the exact nature of the fiscal relationship between localities and the central government is critical for the functioning of the system, as shown by Zhurouskaya (1999) and Shleifer and Treisman (2000).

6. As in chapter 2, for simplicity and without loss of generality, in the rest of the analysis we will set $g = 0$.

7. This example of overlapping jurisdictions is the same as that illustrated of chapter 2 (figure 2.2) if we substitute j' with A and j'' with B.

8. In proposition 9.2 we assume that all jurisdictions of type A are of equal size. The proposition would be slightly modified, without much gain of insight, if we were to allow for jurisdictions of unequal size. Part 1 implies that all individuals who belong to the same B-jurisdictions must also belong to the same A-jurisdiction, and that for all jurisdictions of the same type and of equal size, the ratio of B-jurisdictions to A-jurisdictions must be an integer. Part 2 follows directly from the definition of a maximum.

9. To simplify the analysis, we assume that the location of public good B, once the borders of a decentralized jurisdiction are established, will not be within the power of the leviathan but will be located at the middle of the jurisdiction. This way we are implicitly assuming that decisions within the decentralized jurisdictions will be driven by the median voter. If the leviathan could also control the location of B, he would choose to locate it closer to the center of the country because that would reduce the costs.

10. Below we briefly discuss an alternative specification where the leviathan could also influence the location of the local public good within each separate jurisdiction.

11. Total welfare (i.e., the sum of everybody's utilities) with only one jurisdiction providing both A and B is

$$W_1 = sy - s2a \left(\frac{s}{4} \right) - k_A - k_B,$$

while total welfare with one jurisdiction to provide A but two to provide B is

$$W_2 = sy - sa \left(\frac{s}{4} \right) - sa \left(\frac{s}{8} \right) - k_A - 2k_B.$$

Hence W_1 is larger than W_2 if and only if equation (9.4) holds. Similarly we could show that two B-jurisdictions are better than three jurisdictions if and only if $k_B \geq as^2/24$.

12. The equation is a direct implication of the no insurrection constraint. In general, when both goods are provided centrally (i.e., they are located at the middle of the country), each individual at a distance i from the government will obtain utility $u_i = y - t - 2al_i$. Since the leviathan must provide utility higher or equal to u_0 to at least a fraction δ of the population u_i, he will provide exactly u_0 to the individual at a distance $l_i = \delta s/2$. Hence this individual's utility will be $u_0 = y - t - a\delta s$, which can be rewritten as (9.5).

13. This equation derives from the geometry of utilities when public good A is located at the middle of the country (i.e., at a distance $s/2$ from the left border) while two public goods B are located, respectively, at distances $s/4$ and $3s/4$ from the left border (call these points b_1 and b_2). Clearly, since individuals are uniformly distributed, half of the population is located between b_1 and b_2. For each individual located between b_1 and b_2 the sum of the distances from the two public goods (i.e., the distance from A plus the distance from the nearest B) is equal to $s/4$. Hence a leviathan who has to provide utility at least as large as u_0 to at least $\delta \leq \frac{1}{2}$ of the population will need to set taxes such that $u_0 = y - t - 2a(s/4) = y - t - as/2$, which can be rewritten as equation (9.7). These results are illustrated in figure 9.1.

Chapter 10

1. On the first issue, see Tanzi and Schuknecht (2000) and the references cited therein. On the determinants of economic growth, see Barro and Sala-i-Martin (1995) and Barro (1997). An informal discussion of the growth literature is provided by Easterly (2001).

2. For more discussions of defense spending in relation to economic variables, see Hartley and Sandler (1995).

3. See Alesina, Baqir, and Hoxby (2000) for a much more detailed discussion of the role of density as a determinant of the size of government based on data of US localities.

4. Results for different specifications and different time periods are available on request.

5. On this point, see also Persson and Tabellini (2003).

6. In this system the coefficients on the same variables are constrained to equality across equations, and crossequation correlations of the disturbances are explicitly taken into account. Since disturbances are allowed to vary across equations, our approach corresponds to a flexible random effects estimator. Efficiency can be expected to improve because of this and because the number of observations is multiplied by six compared to OLS. Finally, the standard errors on the coefficient estimates are robust to heteroskedasticity through the use of a White correction applied to the SUR framework.

7. Various statistical tests conducted by Alesina, Spolaore, and Wacziarg (2000) confirm the validity of the choice of instruments.

8. School districts are local governments that have jurisdiction on education. Municipalities are cities and towns. Special districts are jurisdictions that offer certain specific public goods by joining the reserves of more than one municipality.

9. Interestingly a vast literature argues that there are too many small localities in the United States. For instance, see Rusk (1999) and Calabrese et al. (2000) and the references cited therein. Such observations provide some indirect support for the result of too many jurisdictions in a democracy derived in chapter 3 with regard to national borders.

10. For excellent examples of this line of research, see Epple and Romer (1991) and Calabrese et al. (2002).

Chapter 11

1. Braudel (1992, p. 120). On the extent of Venetian wealth, see also McNeill (1974).

2. Braudel (1992, p. 177).

3. See Israel (1995) for a detailed discussion.

4. Braudel (1992, p. 180). They included Holland, Iceland, Utrech, Gelderland, Overijssel, Friesland, and Groningen.

5. Cipolla (1995).

6. Braudel (1992, p. 206).

7. Braudel (1992, p. 133).

8. Merriman, (1996, p. 53).

9. From Lane (1966, p. 535), cited by Putnam (1993, p. 125).

10. Davies, (1996), p. 519.

11. Tilly (1990), p. 76.

12. Jones (1981, p. 130).

13. Tilly (1990, p. 79).

14. Tilly (1990, p. 63).

15. This classification is taken from Eartman (1997).

16. See Eartman (1997) and the references cited therein for an explanation of different evolutions of early bureaucratic organizations. He argues that timing was very important in the formation of states, for influencing the nature of the regime.

17. Eartman (1997).

18. See, for instance, Kennedy (1987, pp. 80–81).

19. McKenney (1993, p. 72).

20. Faroghi et al. (1994, p. 546).

21. Hourani (1991, pp. 208–11).

22. Faroghi et al. (1994, p. 546).

23. Jones (1981).

24. Jones (1981, p. 198).

25. Eartman (1997, p. 91).

26. Braudel, (1992, p. 323).

27. This citation appears in Hobsbawn (1990).

28. See Hobsbawn (1990) and Davies (1996).

29. Merriman (1996, p. 629).

30. Hallerberg (1996) provides a useful analogy on the creation of a simple market in Germany in the 1870s and the current process of economic integration in Europe.

31. Some of these foreign hostilities were the Austria-Prussian war of 1866 and the Franco-Prussian war of 1870. See also Craig (1978, ch. 1) for an extensive discussion of this point.

32. The failed Polish insurrection and the victorious Italian one represent two cases of liberal-nationalistic movements. The success of the Italian case had less to do with the utopian ideals of Mazzini, and more to do with the expansionary instincts of the King of Sardinia.

33. See Bairoch (1989) for a discussion of the effect of transportation cost declines on trade in this period.

34. For a broad discussion of trade and growth in this period, see O'Rourke and Williamson (2001).

35. See Estevadoreal, Frontz, and Taylor (2002) and the references cited therein.

36. Merriman (1996, p. 960).

37. Hobsbawn (1987, p. 67).

38. Hirschman (1945) provides a lucid discussion of the relationship between political power and patterns of trade.

39. One might wonder whether the colonization of Africa was overall "good business" for the Europeans. Perhaps nationalistic pride led Europeans to overcolonize. See Herbst (2000) for more discussion. More generally, as Landes (1998) emphasizes, the later cases of colonization, which included the division of Africa, had less to do with expanding markets and more with militaristic goal.

40. Moore (1967, p. 150).

41. Bulmer-Thomas (1994).

42. Bulmer-Thomas (1994). However, the reliance on import duties as a source of fiscal revenue implied a lower bound on trade taxes, particularly because political instability and border disputes in the region had important fiscal consequences.

43. Riker (1964, p. 39).

44. These figures are take from Alesina, Spolaore, and Wacziarg (2000).

45. One implication is on the timing of increasing openness and secessions. Some steps toward more openness may precede, and other may follow, the progressive increase in the number of independent countries.

46. Freedom house classified countries in terms of political freedom on a scale of 1 to 7. Countries with an index from 1 to 2.5 are classified as free, between 3 and 5.5 partially free, and between 5.5 and 7 non-free.

47. One could argue that the Soviet Union was also a colonial empire.

48. For a recent discussion of rising regionalism in Europe, see Newhouse (1997).

49. See Drèze (1991).

Chapter 12

1. For the classic work on optimal currency areas, see Mundell (1961); for recent developments, see Alesina and Barro (2002), and Alesina, Barro, and Tenreyro (2003).

2. Recent results by Rose (2000) and Frankel and Rose (2002) suggest that these effects can be quite large. See Alesina, Barro, and Tenreyro (2003) for discussion of the literature.

3. One can think of an analogy with US localities. The proliferation of US local governments can be interpreted as a way for wealthy suburbs to escape redistributive taxation favoring inner critics.

4. For a detailed discussion of this issue with explicit reference to the recent Treaty of Nice, see Baldwin et al. (2001).

5. See, however, that paper for references to the related literature.

6. See Alesina and Dollar (2000).

7. These rules originated in the Maastrich Treaty and were tightened by a so-called stability and growth section.

8. For a discussion of the effect of these rules on US state budget policies, see Poterba (1994).

9. This is a public opinion survey conducted every half-year of citizens in all member countries of the European Union. Unfortunately, because of the small sample size (1,000 individuals for each member state), the survey questions relate to what the European Union should do, vis-à-vis the national governments.

10. This value of 40 percent is a bit inflated by the fact that many pieces of agriculture legislation are small in their coverage; that is, they may establish very specific regulations.

References

Acemoglu, D., and J. Robinson. 2000. Why did the west extend the franchise? Democracy, inequality, and growth in historical perspective. *Quarterly Journal of Economics* 115: 1167–99.

Ades, A., and E. L. Glaeser. 1995. Trade and circuses: Explaining urban giants. *Quarterly Journal of Economics* 110(2): 195–227.

Ades, A., and E. L. Glaeser. 1999. Evidence on growth, increasing returns, and the extent of the market. *Quarterly Journal of Economics* 114(3): 1025–45.

Aghion, P., and P. Howitt. 1998. *Endogeneous Growth Theory*. Cambridge: MIT Press.

Alcola, F., and A. Ciccone. 2001. Trade and productivity. Unpublished manuscript.

Alesina, A., I. Angeloni, and F. Etro. 2001a. The political economy of unions. NBER Working Paper, Cambridge, MA.

Alesina, A., I. Angeloni, and F. Etro. 2001b. Institutional rules for federations. NBER Working Paper, Cambridge, MA.

Alesina, A., I. Angeloni, and L. Schuknecht. 2001. What does the European Union do? NBER Working Paper, Cambridge, MA.

Alesina, A., R. Baqir, and W. Easterly. 1999. Public goods and ethnic divisions. *Quarterly Journal of Economics* 114: 1243–84.

Alesina, A., R. Baqir, and C. Hoxby. 2000. Political jurisdictions in heterogeneous communities. NBER Working Paper 7859, Cambridge, MA.

Alesina, A., and R. Barro. 2002. Currency unions. *Quarterly Journal of Economics* 117: 409–30.

Alesina, A., R. Barro, and S. Tenreyro. 2003. Optimal currency areas. *NBER Macroeconomic Annual*. Cambridge: MIT Press, forthcoming.

Alesina, A., A. Devleeschauwer, W. Easterly, S. Kurlat, and R. Wacziarg. 2003. Fractionalization. *Journal of Economic Growth*, forthcoming.

Alesina, A., and D. Dollar. 2000. Who gives foreign aid to whom and why? *Journal of Economic Growth* 5: 33–64.

Alesina, A., and E. La Ferrara. 2000. Participation in heterogenous communities. *Quarterly Journal of Economics* 115(3): 847–904.

Alesina, A., and E. La Ferrara. 2002. Who trusts others? *Journal of Public Economics* 85: 207–34.

Alesina, A., and R. Perotti. 1997. The welfare state and competitiveness. *American Economic Review* 87: 921–39.

Alesina, A., and R. Perotti. 1998. Economic risk and political risk in fiscal unions. *Economic Journal* 108: 989–1009.

Alesina, A., and E. Spolaore. 1997. On the number and size of nations. *Quarterly Journal of Economics* 112: 1027–56.

Alesina, A., and E. Spolaore. 2000. Conflict, defense spending, and the number of nations. Mimeo. Harvard University and Brown University.

Alesina, A., E. Spolaore, and R. Wacziarg. 2001. Economic integration and political disintegration. *American Economic Review* 90: 1276–96.

Alesina, A., and R. Wacziarg. 1999. Is Europe going too far? *Carnegie–Rochester Conference Series* 51: 1–42.

Alesina, A., and R. Wacziarg. 1998. Openness, country size and the government. *Journal of Public Economics* 69: 305–22.

Anderson, B. 1991. *Imagined Communities: Reflections on the Origin and Spread of Nationalism.* London: Verso.

Anderson, J. L., and E. von Wincoop. 2001. Gravity with gravitas: A solution to the border puzzle. NBER Working Paper 8079, Cambridge, MA.

Arzaghi, M., and V. Henderson. 2002. Why countries are fiscally decentralizing? Brown University.

Aumann, R. J. 1990. Nash equilibria are not self-enforcing. In *Economic Decision-Making: Games, Econometrics and Optimisation,* edited by J. J. Gabsewicz, J.-F. Richard, and L. A. Wolsey. New York: Elsevier Science Publishers.

Bairoch, P. 1989. The paradoxes of economic history—Economic laws and history. *European Economic Review* 33: 225–49.

Baldwin, R., E. Berglöf, F. Giavazzi, and M. Widgren. 2001. Nice try: Should the Treaty of Nice be ratified? CEPR, London.

Baldwin, R., and P. Krugman. 2000. Agglomeration integration and tax harmonization. CEPR Working Paper 2630, London.

Barbieri, K. 1996. Economic interdependence: A path to peace or a source of international conflict? *Journal of Peace Research* 33: 29–49.

Barro, R. 1991. Small is beautiful. *The Wall Street Journal,* October 11.

Barro, R. 1997. *Determinants of Economic Growth: A Cross Country Empirical Study.* Cambridge: MIT Press.

Barro, R., and X. Sala-i-Martin. 1995. *Economic Growth.* New York: McGraw-Hill.

Barzel, Y. 2002. *A Theory of the State.* New York: Cambridge University Press.

Bean, R. 1973. War and the birth of the nation state. *Journal of Economic History* 33: 203–21.

Beard, C. 1913. An economic interpretation of the Constitution of the United States. New York: Macmillan.

Bernheim, B. D., B. Peleg, and M. D. Whinston. 1987. Coalition-proof Nash equilibria: Concepts. *Journal of Economic Theory* 42(1): 1–12, June.

Berstein and Mohnene. 1994. International R&D spillovers between US and Japanese R&D intensive sectors. Working Paper 9420, New York University, C. V. Starr Center.

Besley, T., and S. Coate. 1999. Centralized versus decentralized provision of public goods: A political economy analysis. NBER Working Paper 7084, Cambridge, MA.

Bhagwati, J. 1993. Regionalism and multilateralism: An overview. In *New Dimensions in Regional Integration*, edited by J. De Melo and A. Panagariya, Cambridge: Cambridge University Press.

Black, D. 1948. On the rationale of group decision making. *Journal of Political Economy* 90: 988–1002.

Blanchard, O., and S. Fisher. 1989. *Lectures on Macroeconomics*. Cambridge: MIT Press.

Bolton, P., and G. Roland. 1997. The breakup of nations: A political economy analysis. *Quarterly Journal of Economics* 112(4): 1057–80.

Bolton, P., G. Roland, and E. Spolaore. 1996. Economic theories of the break-up and integration of nations. *European Economic Review* 40: 697–705.

Bookman, M. 1993. *The Economics of Secession*. New York: St. Martin Press.

Bordignon, M., and S. Brusco. 2001. Optimal secession rules. *European Economic Review* 45: 1811–34.

Boulding, K. E. 1962. *Conflict and Defense: A General Theory*. New York: Harper.

Bowling, K. 1991. *The Creation of Washington DC: The Value and Location of the American Capital*. Fairfax, VA.

Braudel, F. 1992. Perspectives of the World. *Civilization and Capitalism: 15th–18th Century*, vol. 3. Berkeley: University of California Press.

Brennan, G., and J. Buchanan. 1980. *The Power to Tax: Analytical Foundations of Fiscal Constitutions*. Cambridge: Cambridge University Press.

Brito, D. L., and M. D. Intriligator. 1995. Arms Races and Proliferation. In Hartley and Sandler (1995).

Breton, A., and A. Scott. 1978. *The Economic Constitution of Federal States*. Toronto: University of Toronto Press.

Buchanan, J. M. 1965. An economic theory of clubs. *Economica, 32*: 1–14.

Buchanan, J. M. 1975. *The Limits of Liberty: Between Anarchy and Leviathan*. Chicago: University of Chicago Press.

Buchanan, J. M., and R. L. Faith. 1987. Secessions and the limits of taxation: Towards a theory of internal exit. *American Economic Review* 77: 1023–31.

Buchheit, L. 1978. *Secession: The Legitimacy of Self-Determination*. New Haven: Yale University Press.

Bueno de Mesquita, B., and D. Lalman. 1992. *War and Reason: Domestic and International Imperatives*. New Haven: Yale University Press.

Bueno de Mesquita, B., J. D. Morrow, R. M. Siverson, and A. Smith. 1999. An institutional explanation of the democratic peace. *American Political Science Review* 93: 791–807.

Bulmer-Thomas, V. 1999. *The Economic History of Latin America since Independence*. Cambridge: Cambridge University Press.

Casella, A., and J. Feinstein. 2003. Public goods in trade: On the formation of markets and jurisdictions. *International Economic Review*, forthcoming.

Cipolla, C. 1995. *Storia facile dell'economia italiana dal Medioevo a oggi*. Rome: Mondadori.

Coase, R. 1960. The problem of social cost. *Journal of Law and Economics* 3: 1–44.

Coe, D. T., E. Helpman, and A. W. Hoffmaister. 1994. North–south R&D spillovers. International Monetary Fund Working Paper 94144. Washington, DC.

Connor, W. 1978. A nation is a nation, is a state, is an ethnic group, is a. . . . *Ethnic and Racial Studies* 1(4): 377–400.

Cremer, H., A. M. DeKerchove, and J.-F. Thisse. 1985. An economic theory of public facilities in space. *Mathematical Social Sciences* 9: 249–62.

Cutler, D., and E. Glaeser. 1997. Are ghettos good or bad? *Quarterly Journal of Economics* 112: 1055–90.

Dahl, R. A., and E. R. Tufte. 1973. *Size and Democracy*. Stanford: Stanford University Press.

Davis, L., and R. Huttenback. 1986. *Mammon and the Pursuit of Empire*. New York: Cambridge University Press.

Davies, N. 1996. *Europe*. New York: Oxford University Press.

DeLong, B., and A. Shleifer. 1993. Prices and merchants: European city growth before the industrial revolution. *Journal of Law and Economics* 35: 671–702.

Deutsch, K. 1969. *Nationalism and Its Alternatives*. New York: Knopf.

Diamond, P. 1967. Cardinal welfare, individualistic ethics, and interpersonal comparison of utility: A comment. *Journal of Political Economy* 75(9): 765–66.

Dixit, A., and M. Olson. 1998. Does voluntary participation undermine the Coase theorem? *Economics Letters* 61: 3–11.

Downing, B. M. 1992. *The Military Revolution and Political Change: Origins of Democracy and Autocracy in Early Modern Europe*. Princeton: Princeton University Press.

Drèze, J. H. 1991. Regions of Europe: A feasible status, to be discussed. *Economic Policy* 17: 206–307.

Dudley, L. 1992. Punishment, reward and the fortunes of states. *Public Choice* 74: 293–315.

Eartman, T. 1997. *Birth of the Leviathan*. Cambridge: Cambridge University Press.

Easterly, W. 2001. *The Elusive Quest for Growth: Economists' Adventures and Misadventures in the Tropics*. Cambridge: MIT Press.

Easterly, W., and R. Levine. 1997. Africa's growth tragedy: Policies and ethnic divisions. *Quarterly Journal of Economics* 112: 1203–50.

Easterly, W., and S. Rebelo. 1993. Fiscal policy and economic growth: An empirical investigation. *Journal of Monetary Economics* 32(3): 417–58.

Eaton, J., and S. Kortum. 1994. International patenting and technology diffusion. *Board of Governors of the Federal Reserve System Finance and Economics Discussion Series* (November).

Elazar, D. J., ed. 1984. *Federalism and Political Integration*. Lanham, MD: University Press of America.

Ellis, J. 2000. *The Founding Brothers*. New York: Knopf.

Engel, C., and J. Rogers. 1996. How wide is the border? *American Economic Review* 86: 1112–25.

Epple, D., and T. Romer. 1991. Mobility and redistribution. *Journal of Political Economy* 99: 828–58.

Estavodoreal, A., and A. Taylor. 2002. A century of missing trade. *American Economic Review* 32(1): 383–93.

Faroghi, S., B. McGowan, D. Quataret, and S. Pamuk. 1994. *An Economic and Social History of the Ottoman Empire*. Cambridge: Cambridge University Press.

Fearon, J. D. 1995. Rationalist explanations for war. *International Organization* 49: 379–414.

Findlay, R. 1996. Towards a model of territorial expansion and the limits of empire. In *The Political Economy of Conflict and Appropriation*, edited by Michelle R. Garfinkel and Stergios Skaperdas. Cambridge: Cambridge University Press.

Frankel, J., E. Stein, and S. Wei. 1997. Continental trading blocs: Are they natural or supernatural? In *The Regionalization of the World Economy*, edited by J. Frankel. Chicago: University of Chicago Press.

Frankel, J., and A. Rose. 2002. An estimate of the effect of common currencies on trade and income. *Quarterly Journal of Economics* 117: 437–66.

Frankel, J., and D. Romer. 1999. Does trade cause growth? *American Economic Review* 89: 379–99.

Friedman, D. 1977. A theory of the size and shape of nations. *Journal of Political Economy* 85(1): 59–77.

Frey, B., and R. Eichenberger. 1999. *The New Democratic Federalism for Europe*. London: Edward Elger.

Fudenberg, D., and J. Tirole. 1991. *Game Theory*. Cambridge: MIT Press.

Fujita, M., and J.-F. Thisse. 2002. *Economics of Agglomeration: Cities, Industrial Location, and Regional Growth*. Cambridge: Cambridge University Press.

Gallup, J. L., J. Sachs, and A. D. Mellinger. 1998. Geography and economic development. Presented at the Annual Bank Conference on Development Economics, World Bank, Washington, DC, April.

Garner, P. 2001. The role of international rivalry in long-run growth. Unpublished manuscript. Brown University.

Gartzke, E. 1999. War is in the error term. *International Organization* 53(3): 567–87.

Gasiorowski, M., and S. Polachek. 1982. Conflict and interdependence: East–west trade and linkages in the era of detente. *Journal of Conflict Resolution* 26: 709–29.

Glaeser, E., S. Johnson, and A. Shleifer. 2001. Coase versus the Coasians. *Quarterly Journal of Economics* 116(3): 853–99.

Gilpin, 2001. *Global Political Economy. Understanding the International Economic Order.* Princeton: Princeton University Press.

Gottman, J. 1973. The significance of territory. Charlottesville: University Press of Virginia.

Grossman, G., and H. Elpman. 1991. *Innovation and Growth in the Global Economy,* Cambridge: MIT Press.

Grossman, H. I. 1991. A general equilibrium model of insurrections. *American Economic Review* 81(4): 912–21.

Grossman, H. I. 2000. The state: Agent or proprietor? *Economics of Governance* 1(1): 3–11.

Grossman, H. I. 2002. Constitution or conflict? NBER Working Paper 8733, Cambridge, MA.

Grossman, H. I., and M. Kim. 1995. Swords or plowshares? A theory of the security of claims to property. *Journal of Political Economy* 103(6): 1275–88.

Haas, E. 1958a. *The Uniting of Europe: Political, Social and Economic Forces.* Stanford: Stanford University Press.

Haas, E. 1958b. The challenge of regionalism. *International Organization* 12: 444–58.

Haas, E. 1964. *Beyond the Nation-State.* Stanford: Stanford University Press.

Haas, E. 1975. The obsolesence of regional integration theory. Research Series 25. Institute of International Studies, Berkeley.

Haimanko, O., M. LeBreton, and S. Weber. 2000. Transfers and polarization. Unpublished manuscript. CORE, Catholic University of Louvain.

Hall, R., and C. Jones. 1999. Why do some countries produce more output per worker than others? *Quarterly Journal of Economics* 114: 83–116.

Hallerberg, M. 1996. Tax competition in Wilhelmine, Germany, and its implications for the European Union. *World Politics* 40: 324–57.

Hamilton, A., ed. 1787. *The Federalist Papers.* Reprinted 1987. New York: Penguin.

Hartley, K., and T. Sandler, eds. 1995. *Handbook of Defense Economics.* Amsterdam: North-Holland.

Harsanyi, J. C. 1953. Cardinal utility in welfare economics and in the theory of risk taking. *Journal of Political Economy* 61: 434–35.

Harsanyi, J. C. 1955. Cardinal welfare, individualistic ethics, and interpersonal comparison of utility. *Journal of Political Economy* 63: 309–21.

Harsanyi, J. C., and R. Selten. 1988. *A General Theory of Equilibrium Selection in Games.* Cambridge: MIT Press.

Hartley, K., and T. Sandler. 1995. *The Economics of Defense.* Cambridge: Cambridge University Press.

Hayek, F. 1959. *The Constitution of Liberty*. Chicago: University of Chicago Press.

Helliwell, J. 1998. *How Much Do National Borders Matter?* Washington, DC: Brookings Institution.

Henderson, J. V. 1983. Industrial bases and city sizes. *American Economic Review* 73(2): 164–68.

Herbst, J. 2000. *States and Power in Africa*. Princeton: Princeton University Press.

Hess, G. D., and A. Orphanides. 1995. War politics: An economic, rational-voter framework. *American Economic Review* 85(4): 828–46.

Hess, G. D., and A. Orphanides. War and democracy. *Journal of Political Economy* 109(4): 776–810.

Hirschman, A. 1945. *National Power and the Structure of Foreign Trade*. Berkeley: University of California Press.

Hirshleifer, J. 1989. Conflict and rent-seeking success functions: Ratio versus difference models of relative success. *Public Choice* 46: 247–58.

Hirshleifer, J. 1991. The technology of conflict as an economic activity. *American Economic Review* 81(2): 130–34.

Hirshleifer, J. 1995a. Theorizing about conflict. In Hartley and Sandler (1995).

Hirshleifer, J. 1995b. Anarchy and its breakdown. *Journal of Political Economy* 103: 26–52.

Hobbes, T. 1651. *Leviathan*. Reprinted 1982. New York: Penguin.

Hobsbawn, E. J. 1987. *The Age of Empires*. New York: Vintage Books.

Hobsbawn, E. J. 1990. *Nations and Nationalism since 1870*. Cambridge: Cambridge University Press.

Hobsbawn, E. J. 1996. *The Age of Extremes: A History of the World, 1914–1991*. New York: Vintage Books.

Hochman, O., D. Pines, and J.-F. Thisse. 1995. On the optimal structure of local governments. *American Economic Review* 85(5): 1224–40.

Hooghe, L., and G. Marks. 2000. Optimality and authority: A critique of neo-classical theory. *Journal of Common Market Studies* 38(5): 795–816.

Hooghe, L., and G. Marks. 2001a. *Multi-level Governance and European Integration*. Boulder, CO: Rowman and Littlefield.

Hooghe, L., and G. Marks. 2001b. Types of multi-level governance. European Integration online Papers (EIoP), vol. 5, 11. *http://eiop.or.at/eiop/texte/2001-011a.htm*.

Hotelling, H. 1929. Stability in Competition. *Economic Journal* 39: 41–57.

Hourani, A. 1991. *A History of the Arabs People*. Cambridge: Harvard University Press.

Huntington, S. 1993. The clash of civilizations? *Foreign Affairs* 72(3): 22–28.

Inman, R. P., and D. L. Rubinfeld. 1997. The political economy of federalism. In *Perspectives on Public Choice*, edited by D. C. Mueller. Cambridge: Cambridge University Press, ch. 4.

Irwin and Klenow. 1994. Learning-by-doing spillovers in the semiconductor industry. *Journal of Political Economy* 102(6): 1200–27.

Isard, W. 1988. *Arms Races, Arms Control, and Conflict Analysis.* New York: Cambridge University Press.

Israel, J. 1995. *The Dutch Republic.* Oxford: Oxford Unviersity Press.

Jacob, P. E., and J. V. Toscano, eds. 1964. *The Integration of Political Communities.* Philadelphia: Lippincott.

Jenkins, R. 2001. *Churchill.* New York: Plume.

Jones, E. L. 1981. *The European Miracle: Environments, Economies, and Geopolitics in the History of Europe and Asia.* Cambridge: Cambridge University Press.

Judd, K. L. 1985. The law of large numbers with a continuum of IID random variables. *Journal of Economic Theory* 35(1): 19–25.

Keohane, R. O., and J. S. Nye. 2000. *Power and Interdependence.* Pearson Education.

Kennedy, P. 1987. *The Rise and Fall of the Great Powers: Economic Change and Military Conflict from 1500 to 2000.* New York: Random House.

Keynes, J. M. 1920. *The Economic Consequences of the Peace.* New York: Harcourt.

Krugman, P. 1991. *Geography and Trade.* Cambridge: MIT Press.

Krugman, P. 1995. *Development, Geography, and Economic Theory.* Cambridge: MIT Press.

Laffont, J. J. 1988. *Fundamentals of Public Economics,* rev. English ed. Trans. by John P. Bonin and Helene Bonin. Cambridge: MIT Press.

Landes, D. 1998. *The Wealth and Poverty of Nations.* New York: Norton.

Lane, F. C. 1958. Economic consequences of organized violence. Reprinted in *Profits from Power: Readings in Protection Rent and Violence Controlling Enterprises.* Albany: State University of New York Press.

Lane, F. C. 1966. *Venice and History.* Baltimore: Johns Hopkins University Press.

La Porta, R., F. Lopez-De-Silanes, A. Shleifer, and R. Vishny. 1999. The quality of government. *Journal of Law, Economics, and Organization* 15(1): 222–79.

LeBreton, M., and S. Weber. 2001. The art of making everybody happy: How to prevent a secession. Unpublished manuscript.

Levy, J. S. 1989. The causes of war: A review of theories and evidence. In *Behavior, Society, and National War,* edited by P. E. Tetlocket. Oxford: Oxford University Press.

Lichtenberg, F. R. 1992. R&D Investment and international productivity differences. NBER Working Paper 4161, Cambridge, MA.

Lucas, R. 1988. On the mechanics of economic development. *Journal of Monetary Economics* 22(1): 3–42.

Madison, J. 1787. Federalist Paper No. 10. Reprinted in *Federalist Papers,* 1987. New York: Penguin.

Mansfield, E. D., and H. V. Milner, eds. 1997. *The Political Economy of Regionalism.* New York: Columbia University Press.

Maoz, Z., and B. Russet. 1993. Normative and structural causes of the democratic peace, 1946–1986. *American Political Science Review* 87(3): 624–38.

Mauro, P. 1995. Corruption and growth. *Quarterly Journal of Economics* 110(3): 681–712.

McCallum, J. 1995. National borders matter: Canada–U.S. regional trade patterns. *American Economic Review* 85(3): 615–23.

Mack Smith, D. 1989. *Italy and Its Monarchy*. New Haven: Yale University Press.

McKenny, R. 1993. *Sixteen Century Europe*. New York: St. Martin Press.

McGuire, M. C., and M. Olson. 1996. The economics of autocracy and majority rule: The invisible hand and the use of force. *Journal of Economic Literature* 34(1): 72–96.

McNeil, W. H. 1974. *Venice: The Hinge of Europe, 1081–1797*. Chicago: University of Chicago Press.

Merriman, J. 1996. *A History of Modern Europe*. New York: Norton.

Meltzer, A., and S. Richard. 1981. A rational theory of the size of government. *Journal of Political Economy* 89: 914–27.

Milesi-Ferretti, G. M., R. Perotti, and M. Rostagno. 2002. Electoral systems and public spending. *Quarterly Journal of Economics* 117(2): 609–57.

Montesquieu. 1748. *The Spirit of the Laws*. Cambridge: Cambridge University Press, 1989.

Mundell, R. 1961. A theory of optimum currency areas. *American Economic Review* 51: 509–17.

Murdoch, J. C. 1995. Military alliances: Theory and empirics. In Hartley and Sandler (1995).

Murphy, K. M., A. Shleifer, and R. W. Vishny. 1989. Industrialization and the big push. *Journal of Political Economy* 97(5): 1003–26.

Mitrany, D. 1966. *A Working Peace System*. Chicago: Quadrangle.

Moore, B. 1967. *Social Origins of Dictatorships and Democracy*. Boston: Beacon Press.

Mueller, D. 1989. *Public Choice II*. New York: Cambridge University Press.

Musgrave, R. 1959. *The Theory of Public Finance*. New York: McGraw-Hill.

Musgrave, R. A. 1971. Economics of fiscal federalism. *Nebraska Journal of Economics and Business*. Reprinted in Musgrave (1986), ch. 3, pp. 33–42.

Musgrave, R. A. 1986. *Public Finance in a Democratic Society*. New York: New York University Press.

Musgrave, R. A. 1998. *Approaches to a Fiscal Theory of Political Federalism*. Elgar Reference Collection, vol. 88. Cheltenham, UK: International Library of Critical Writings in Economics.

Newhouse, J. 1997. Europe's rising regionalism. *Foreign Affairs* 76(January–February): 67–84.

North, D. 1981. *Structure and Change in Economic History*. New York: Norton.

North, D. 1990. *Institutions, Institutional Change and Economic Performance*. Cambridge: Cambridge University Press.

North, D., and R. P. Thomas. 1973. *The Rise of the Western World: A New Economic History*. Cambridge: Cambridge University Press.

Oates, W. E., and J. J. Wallace. 1988. Decentralization in the public sector: An empirical study of local governments. In *Fiscal Decentralization: Quantitative Studies*, edited by H. S. Rosen. Chicago: University of Chicago Press.

Oates, W. 1972. *Fiscal Federalism*. New York: Harcourt Brace.

Oates, W. 1999. An essay on fiscal federalism. *Journal of Economic Literature* 37: 1120–49.

Olson, M. 1982. *The Rise and Decline of Nations*. New Haven: Yale University Press.

Olson, M. 2000. *Power an Prosperity: Outgrowing Communist and Capitalist Dictatorships*. New York: Basic Books.

Olson, M., and R. Zeckhauser. 1966. An economic theory of alliances. *Review of Economics and Statistics* 48: 266–79.

O'Rourke, K., and J. Williamson. 2001. *Globalization and History: The Evolution of a Nineteenth-Century Atlantic Economy*. Cambridge: MIT Press.

Panizza, U. 1999. On the determinants of fiscal centralization: Theory and evidence. *Journal of Public Economics* 74: 97–139.

Pareto, V. 1935. *The Mind and Society*, Vol. 1, Hartcourt, Brace, New York.

Perotti, R. 2000. Fiscal policy in good times and bad. *Quarterly Journal of Economics* 114(4): 1399–1436.

Persson, T., and G. Tabellini. 1996a. Federal fiscal constitutions: Risk sharing and redistribution. *Journal of Political Economy* 104: 979–1009.

Persson, T., and G. Tabellini. 1996b. Federal fiscal constitutions: Risk sharing and moral hazard. *Econometrica* 64: 623–46.

Persson, T., and G. Tabellini. 1999. The size and scope of government: Comparative politics with rational politicians. *European Economic Review* 43: 699–735.

Persson, T., and G. Tabellini. 2000. *Political Economics: Explaining Economic Policy*. Cambridge: MIT Press.

Persson, T., and G. Tabellini. 2003. *The Economic Effects of Constitutions*. Cambridge: MIT Press, forthcoming.

Pirenne, H. 1968. *Mohammed and Charlemagne*, trans. by B. Miall. New York: Barnes and Noble.

Plano, J. C., and R. Olton. 1969. *The International Relations Dictionary*. New York: Holt, Rinehart and Winston.

Polachek, S. 1980. Conflict and trade. *Journal of Conflict Resolution* 24: 55–78.

Polachek, S. 1992. Conflict and trade: An economic approach to political international interactions. In *Economics of Arms Reduction and the Peace Process*, edited by W. Isard and C. H. Anderton, Amsterdam: North-Holland, ch 4.

Polachek, S. W. 1992. Conflict and trade: An economics approach to political international interactions. Amsterdam: North-Holland.

Portes, R., and H. Rey. 2000. The determinants of cross-border equity flows. GEP Discussion Papers 446, London School of Economics.

Poterba, J. 1994. State responses to fiscal crises: The effects of budgetary institutions on fiscal policy. *Journal of Political Economics* 102: 165–87.

Powell, R. 1999. *In the Shadow of Power: States and Strategies in International Politics.* Princeton: Princeton University Press.

Putnam, R. 1993. *Making Democracy Work.* Princeton: Princeton University Press.

Qian, Y., and G. Roland. 1998. Federalism and the soft budget constraint. *American Economic Review* 88: 1143–62.

Rawls, J. 1971. *A Theory of Justice.* Cambridge: Harvard University Press.

Ray, D., and R. Vohra. 1999. A theory of endogenous coalition structures. *Games and Economic Behavior* 26(2): 286–336.

Ray, D., and R. Vohra. 2001. Coalitional power and public goods. *Journal of Political Economy* 109: 1355–84.

Riker, W. 1964. *Federalism.* New York: Little Brown.

Rivera-Batiz, L. A., and P. M. Romer. 1991. Economic integration and endogenous growth. *Quarterly Journal of Economics* 106: 531–55.

Rodriguez, F., and D. Rodrik. 1999. Trade policy and economic growth: A skeptic's guide to the cross national evidence. *NBER Macroeconomic Annual.* Cambridge: MIT Press.

Rodrik, D. 1998. Why do more open economics have bigger governments? *Journal of Political Economy* 106(October): 997–1032.

Roland, G. 2000. *Transition and Economics.* Cambridge: MIT Press.

Romer, P. 1986. Increasing returns and long run growth. *Journal of Political Economics* 94: 1002–37.

Romer, T. 1977. Majority voting on tax parameters: Some further results. *Journal of Public Economics* 7(1): 127–33.

Rose, A. 2000. One money, one market: Estimating the effects of common currencies on trade. *Economic Policy* 30: 9–48.

Rusk, D. 1999. *Inside Game/Outside Game.* Washington, DC: Brookings Institution.

Sachs, J., A. D. Mellinger, and J. L. Gallup. 2001. The geography of poverty and wealth. *Scientific American* 284: 70–74.

Sachs, J., and X. Sala-i-Martin. 1992. Fiscal federalism and optimum currency areas: Evidence for Europe from the United States. In *Establishing a Central Bank: Issues in Europe and Lessons from the US,* edited by M. Canzoneri, P. Mausson, and V. Grilli, Cambridge: Cambridge University Press.

Sachs, J., and A. Warner. 1995. Economic reform and the process of economic integration. *Brookings Papers on Economic Activity* 1: 1–117.

Samuelson, P. 1954. The pure theory of public expenditure. *Review of Economic and Statistics* 36: 387–89.

Schelling, T. C. 1960. *The Strategy of Conflict.* Cambridge: Harvard University Press.

Sen, A. 1979. *Collective Choice and Social Welfare.* Amsterdam: North-Holland.

Skaperdas, S. 1992. Cooperation, conflict and power in the absence of property rights. *American Economic Review* 82(4): 720–39.

Shleifer, A., and D. Treisman. 2000. *Without a Map: Political Tactics and Economic Reform in Russia.* Cambridge: MIT Press.

Skaperdas, S., and C. Syropoulos. 1996. Competitive trade with conflict. In *The Political Economy of Conflict and Appropriation,* edited by Michelle R. Garfinkel and Stergios Skaperdas, Cambridge: Cambridge University Press.

Smith, A. 1976. *The Wealth of Nations.* Chicago: University of Chicago Press.

Smith, R. 1995. The demand for military expenditure. In Hartley and Sandler (1995).

Spolaore, E. 1995. Economic integration, political borders and productivity. Prepared for the CEPR/Tel Aviv Conference on Regional Integration and Economic Growth, December.

Spolaore, E. 2001. Conflict, trade and political borders. Brown University.

Spolaore, E., and R. Wacziarg. 2002. Borders and growth. NBER Working Paper 9223, Cambridge, MA: Mimeo.

Spolaore, E., and A. Alesina. 2000. War, peace and the size of countries. Mimeo. Brown University and Harvard University.

Spruyt, H. 1994. *The Sovereign State and Its Competitors: An Analysis of Systems Change.* Princeton: Princeton University Press.

Stampp, K. M. 1991. *The Causes of the Civil War.* Cambridge: Cambridge University Press.

Stein, E. 2000. *Czecho/Slovakia.* Ann Arbor: University of Michigan Press.

Stock, R. 1993. Africa south of the sphere: A geographical interpretation. New York: Guillard Press.

Tam, H. 1999. *Taxation, Appropriation and State.* PhD dissertation. Harvard University.

Tanzi, V. 2000. *Policies, Institutions and the Dark Side of Economics.* Cheltenham, UK: Edward Elgar Publishing.

Tanzi, V., and L. Schuknecht. 2000. *Public Spending in the Twentieth Century: A Global Perspective.* Cambridge: Cambridge University Press.

Tenreyro, S. 2001. The causes and consequenes of currency unions. Unpublished manuscript.

Thomson, E. A. 1974. Taxation and national defense. *Journal of Political Economy.*

Tiebout, C. 1956. A pure theory of local expenditures. *Journal of Political Economy* 64: 416–24.

Tilly, C. 1990. *Coercion, Capital and European States, AD 990–1990.* Cambridge, MA: Blackwell.

Tilly, C., and L. Tilly. 1973. *The Rebellious Century, 1830–1930.* Cambridge: Harvard University Press.

Tullock, G. 1974. *The Social Dilemma: The Economics of War and Revolution.* Blacksburg, VA: University Pub.

Tullock, G. 1980. Efficient rent seeking. In *Toward a Theory of the Rent-Seeking Society,* edited by J. M. Buchanan, R. D. Tollison, and G. Tullock. College Station: Texas A&M University Press.

Vamvakidis, 1997. How important is a large market for economic growth? Mimeo. International Monetary Fund and Harvard University.

Van Evera, S. 1998. Offense, defense, and the causes of war. *International Security* 22: 5–43.

Weber, M. 1958. *From Max Weber: Essays in Sociology.* Oxford: Oxford University Press.

Wacziarg. 1998. Measuring the dynamic gains from trade. World Bank Policy Research Paper, 2001. Washington, DC.

Weingast, B. R. 1995. The economic role of political institutions: Market-preserving federalism and economic development. *Journal of Law, Economics, and Organization* 11: 1–31.

Weingast, B. R., K. A. Shepsle, and C. Johnsen. 1981. The political economy of benefits and costs: A neoclassical approach to distributive politics. *Journal of Political Economy* 89: 642–64.

Wilson, C. H. 1967. Trade society and state. *Cambridge Economic History of Europe* 4: 487–576.

Wittman, D. 1991. Nations and states: Mergers and acquisitions; dissolutions and divorce. *American Economic Review Papers and Proceedings* 81(2): 126–28.

Wittman, D. 2000. The size and wealth of nations. *Journal of Conflict Resolution*: 868–84.

Yarborough, B., and R. Yarborough. 1998. Unification and secession: Group size and escape from lock-in. *Kyklos* 61: 171–95.

Young, R. 1994. The political economy of secession: The case of Quebec. *Constitutional Political Economy* 5: 221–45.

Young, R. 1995. *The Secession of Quebec and the Future of Canada.* Montreal: McGill-Queen University Press.

Zhuravskaya, E. 1999. Incentives to provide local public goods: Fiscal federalism, Russian style. Unpublished manuscript.

Index